SOUTHEAST ASIAN PLAYS

EDS. CHERYL ROBSON & AUBREY MELLOR

AURORA METRO BOOKS

With thanks to all who helped with this book including:

Ricardo G. Abad, Layne Alera, Joachim Emilio Antonio, Joem Antonio, Tuyen Boal, Stephanie Charamnac, Chong Tze Chien, Jose Christomo, Giles Croft, Joe Dalisay, LeQuy Duong, Kelly Falconer, Arthur Foo, Anna Furse, Karlo Antonio Galay-David, Barbara Hatley, Ivan Heng, Tan Tarn How, Shaza Ishak, Koes Juliadi, Irfan Kasban, Jo Kukathas, Ann Lee, Leow Puay Tin, Melissa Lim, Suchen Christine Lim, Robin Loon, Helen Mangham, Faiza Marzoeki, Pawit Mahasarinand, Glen Sevilla Mas, Kumiko Mendl, Raymond Miranda, Amir Muhammad, Helen Musa, BaoChan Nguyen, Yang-Mai Ooi, Ridzwan Othman, Andrea Pasion-Flores, William Phuan, Ruth Pongstaphone, Venka Purushothaman, Charlene Delia Jeyamani Rajendran, Nerida Rand, Kathy Rowland, Frances Rudgard, Hj. Yudiaryani, Haresh Sharma, Arun Subramanian, Huzir Sulaiman, Alvin Tan, Mark Teh, Pham Tir Thanh, Maung Maung Thein, Nyein Way, Sokhorn Yon and Ovidia Yu.

CONTENTS

INTRODUCTION

This volume is but a taste of the rich variety of performance work that in many cases is only beginning to be written down. Though now in English, there is little in common in these eight plays from seven very different nations in a region connected mainly by geography. Until the founding of ASEAN, in 1967, Southeast Asia (SEA) was known to the world as the East Indies. Covering 11 nations and 626 million inhabitants, over more than 4.4 million square kilometres, the southeast of the continent plunges into the sea, diversifying into many thousands of islands and languages as it reaches into the Pacific. One of the largest and fastest-growing economies of the world, with a combined annual turnover of 2.8 trillion US dollars, it contains arguably the richest variety of arts, customs, cuisines and landscapes – and distinctively defined peoples. However, this part of the world is under-represented, especially in theatre and dramatic writing, and its vivid diversity deserves to be known beyond its splendid beaches and tourist spots. In collecting a first volume of Southeast Asian playscripts we prioritised material that other countries (including SEA) might be interested in performing, with an aim to introduce not only the writers but also the cultures that produced them.

Theatre across Asia remains close to its oral traditions and to its prime expression in dance and music. Every country has its impressive, skilful, colourful performance traditions, with the wealth of styles and forms having even more numerous regional variations. It is well known that Brecht was influenced by the arts of Chinese *Xiqu* (erroneously known as 'opera') but few know the influence of Balinese performance upon Artaud and Grotowsky.

Asia's love of performance remains tangible and can be seen at village level as well as in its large arts centres; so it is not surprising that with its economic developments Asia is drawing performance influences from anywhere that excites. In some cases this has left regional variants of traditional performance styles endangered, but in others, fascinating experiments are drawing from their heritage and mixing concepts with the best from Europe and the Americas.

Southeast Asia is also a region at considerable peace with – and interested in – its neighbours: companies commonly mix performers of several countries on their stages, and collaborations, often long-term, result in unique theatre that shows considerable leadership – not only in theatrical innovation but also in cultural, racial and religious tolerance and respect. English-language theatre is common in Singapore, but so are plays in Chinese and modern Japanese plays are often seen in many of these countries. However, in Southeast Asia it is still easier to buy a British playscript than one by a Thai or Vietnamese. More and more, English is the language used when Asian companies and artists communicate, and though interest in these works will be global, their first foreign productions are most likely to be seen in this region.

Fascinating as traditional Asian theatre remains, its roots in vastly different worlds mean that traditional performance can seem very foreign, often alienating. I have experienced the touring of both traditional and contemporary works and emphatically believe that it is the contemporary that brings us together: within spoken drama we more easily relate to characters and their problems, however different their living conditions might be. The contemporary plays in this volume radically depart from SEA traditional theatre and several reveal their authors' cosmopolitan influences and their globalised and highly networked lives. All plays are internationally accessible, their language and form familiar, and the acting style generally naturalistic. This collection does not include any musicals or music theatre, though both are extremely popular, and it does not cover the most experimental work of writers and theatre-makers consciously exploring intercultural and interdisciplinary combinations. A prime example is the region's best-known international director, Ong Keng Sen, who pioneered extraordinary combinations of styles, forms and genres and through Theatrework's 'Flying Circus Project' develops cross-nation performances with a range of companies such as Myanma's Theatre of the Disturbed. We have, however, selected plays with direct appeal to Western audiences and are confident they will find directors and actors to inhabit their characters.

Storytellers and leading performers always had the respect of their community, but most countries in this region still retain a collaborative approach to theatre-making and new work can often be yet another re-telling of a section of a larger work, as Southeast Asia is home to many huge oral epics that continue to inspire – *The Ramayana* being common to many. Along with Western-style theatre buildings, Western forms of drama arrived with the colonisers; but wider assimilation is post-colonial, and quick to explore local and contemporary themes. Modern drama was in many cases crucial in the struggle for independence, and is still playing a role in nation-building. Content, especially topicality, rarely the focus in traditional arts, is a prime feature of SEA's contemporary dramatic literature, as revealed in this collection.

Alfian Sa'at's *Nadirah* is highly topical as it addresses the theme of mixed marriages; in asking if mother and daughter can worship different gods, Sa'at welcomes the new developments in Singapore's multi-racial and multi-faithed society. In *Plunge,* ex-economist Jean Tay shines satirical light on the Asian Economic Crisis, and with considerable boldness and innovation reveals Singapore's sophistication on the global market (she has since followed with a related play called *Boom*). Malaysian writer, Ann Lee, brings a female journalist face to face with a gruesome murderer, only to question if he has been falsely imprisoned since he was a boy. *Tarap Man* articulates the region's growing interest in truth and justice.

Refreshing evidence of liberal thinking comes from Vietnam's Đăng Chương, with *Dark Race*, a satirical look at personal integrity in business and political leaders; and Floy Quintos considers the misrule that has held many Asian countries back in *An Evening At The Opera*. This is a behind-the-scenes portrayal of elite and sinister power, echoing a Philippines that is hopefully gone. In Tew Bunnag's *Night of the Minotaur*, from Thailand, power is confined to a cave and treated like a beast. The powerless are given voice in the plays from Indonesia and Cambodia, respectively in Joned Suryatmoko's *Piknik* and Chhon Sina's *Frangipani*, reminding us that poverty can easily lead to abuse and exploitation.

Publication is not a necessary goal in the performing arts, and theatre scripts are merely blueprints for productions, especially in this region. As elsewhere, second productions and revivals are rare, so publication becomes important to preserving some of this ephemeral art form and to allowing play texts to find a wider international readership. Though some of these works were written and performed in English, a play's origins are of course defined by language, e.g. a Vietnamese play is written in Vietnamese etc. Consequently the huge majority of new dramatic literature in this flourishing region remains unknown outside of language borders; even within countries plays are not readily circulated, as they are not commonly published in their original (often local) language, and are further neglected in translation. The development of skilled literary translators in the region is happening slowly, but the focus is primarily on poetry and fiction.

Japan is the only country I know where its government spends considerably on translations of plays into English; but, sadly, despite efforts of collections such as this, an English-speaking repertoire still doesn't include either classic or contemporary Asian plays. The authors in this collection are bi- or multi-lingual, and most works are newly translated, with some playwrights having their first play published. We have not included bi-lingual plays, but in Malaysia and Singapore three languages in the one play are quite common.

Unlike India, China and Japan with their vast recorded heritage of dramatic literature, the smaller countries have only recently been able to focus on the importance of contemporary literature. Poetry often came first, though usually by the internationally educated, and it often flourished, as it could always evade censorship. Novels followed, at first unusual but soon enjoyed and acclaimed, even internationally, such as Tan Twan Eng's *The Garden of Evening Mists* and Suchen Christine Lim's *The River's Song*, and many are now on schools' study lists. Reading them will give excellent context for the plays.

With some exceptions, playwriting with an individual voice is relatively new, despite some deceased giants in the past, such as Indonesia's W.S. Rendra and Singapore's Kuo Pao Kun, whose work is published and internationally performed. New writing has long been supported by visionary directors in every country, such as Krishen Jit, Rolando Tinio, Alvin Tan; and dedicated centres, like Jo Kukathas' pioneering Instant Cafe in Kuala Lumpur, are now being established – for example, Manila's Sipat Lawin and Singapore's

Centre 42. Script collaboration is common, and often the actors make considerable contributions, especially in Indonesia. The dramaturge role is still new, though more common in dance works and company-produced works rather than as personal support for an individual playwright, and feedback to writers must be sensitively handled, as not only is 'face' involved, but writers are not used to having an advisor or editor, and though often they work with a trusted director, such is usually towards the end of the writing process, not during.

Traditional theatre always had a place for satirical inserts and social comment, but entirely new playscripts, especially when written to argue new ideas, were first seen as a Western concept. The proscenium arch was innovative, and European touring productions not uncommon, Shakespeare impacted widely, though mostly in India, whilst foreign residents enjoyed dressing up to dabble in amateur theatre. However, following independence, the reaction against expatriates' theatre saw an explosion of new forms, embracing new ideas from almost anywhere, including influences such as Brecht, the Absurdists and The Living Theatre and using them to tell local stories of relevance. Dance and physical storytelling have remained strong, and in Indonesia, Cambodia, Myanmar and Vietnam, governments have deliberately prioritized dance and crafts as the most endangered parts of their culture and have had remarkable success in rescuing and revitalising many regional variants. But 'The Word' is still considered more potent than the abstractions of music and dance, and censorship can still be found. However, in most governments in the region, there is an enlightened interest in what an artist can bring to a nation.

Some beautiful old theatre buildings have survived from colonial days – see the two splendid opera houses in Vietnam; but, until independence, these never belonged to the people, whose participation in performance was far less formal. But arts centres are now a sign of prestige and modernity; and though glass and concrete structures can be daunting for ordinary people, even in the West, they house a number of spaces that support exhibitions, performances and, importantly, meeting places for both community and creatives. Further signs of healthy arts scenes are found in the converted shopfronts and warehouses used as homes for small theatre groups and arts groups.

People in Southeast Asia fully embraced new technology several decades ago, and portable entertainment, both local and global, is greatly loved; as in the West, digital technology and social media is drawing audiences away, but new technology grows more evident in local performance. Unusual and site-specific locations – as well as audience involvement – often complement this, as practitioners work to meet every challenge. The film industries of most nations represented in this collection are more influential than their theatre, and in some cases writers manage to work in both, but the low status of playwriting is maintained by poor copyright laws, ensuring that even if a second production is achieved the author will often not receive any percentage of box office receipts from it. Though Singapore, Malaysia and the Philippines are ahead in their respect for playwriting and play publishing, elsewhere plays are produced through little more than a shared passion in a small group of people.

Though companies are numerous, large theatre companies are rare and any commissioning of plays needs government support or other patronage. Fortunately, universities have always had literary programs and in most countries have set up creative writing courses, drama departments, and drama schools, where international plays are studied and where new plays are supported and often produced – for example, in Thailand, Chulalongkorn University's most appropriate telling of the real Anna Leonowens story (Anna of *The King and I* fabrication – Chulalongkorn being then the Crown Prince whom she taught).

Drama festivals are plentiful, along with Writers' Festivals, such as in Ubud where it includes playreadings, and many were started by individuals such as Joned Suryatmoko, Director of the Indonesian Dramatic Reading Festival in Yogyakarta, and playwright/director Le Quy Duong's many Vietnam festivals, including Hue Drama Festival. In the Philippines, new writing has been enhanced by the annual Virgin Labfest held at the Cultural Center in Manila, and the annual Palanca Literary Awards that began in the 1950s. In 2015, Singapore ambitiously produced 50 Plays to celebrate its 50 years of independence, and Malaysia celebrated 30 years of its Five Arts

Centre with an impressive volume of its plays. Festivals abound in the region, often themed and with conferences included, creating meeting places and sharing and often featuring collaborative work. Thailand recently gave a Lifetime Achievement Award to its most prolific playwright, a woman, Daraka Wongsiri, and Singapore's Haresh Sharma, honoured with a cultural medallion, is one of the most published playwrights in all of Asia. Writing Prizes – such as the SEA Writers Award – are common and often prestigious, remunerative and encouraging. But, as any playwright will tell you, no prize is better than being accorded a fully mounted production.

Most plays in this collection have never been published, and some are chosen from a very small pool of available recent plays (Cambodia, Laos and Myanmar are taking early steps) but all plays are relatively new and one, *Frangipani*, is the writer's first play. These are not necessarily representative plays (rarely possible with a single work) but are by significant playwrights whose work can be further explored. Floy Quintos of the Philippines and Alfian Sa'at of Singapore are both prolific and nationally acclaimed and enjoy the benefits of a culture that is rich in publications, something shared with Malaysia, where Ann Lee is one of many important writers. But there are crucial differences, and each country deserves its own collection in English, such as Lontar's three volumes from Indonesia and the ASEAN series from the 1990s.

Theatre taste was not obviously influenced by colonisers, though I believe the British and the Spanish did much to share a love of written literature; and though the Philippines still performs zarzuelas and has a love of western musicals, every Asian country has its own ancient equivalent of musical theatre. Every country has a long history of telling its own stories and Southeast Asia is home to several huge ancient oral epics. In the Philippines, where the longest oral epic of all is still being collected, there is a focus on biographical plays – for examples I commend the many dramatisations of the life of their national hero, José Rizal. But some stories are still best told as fiction or as metaphor, and political leadership is explored this way in Quintos's *An Evening at the Opera* and in *The Night of the Minotaur* from Thailand's Tew Bunnag. The latter reveals something which is not uncommon: a familiarity with the myths and literature of the West.

Remarkably, Indonesia preserves dozens of regional forms of *Wayang*, or traditional performance, alongside a range of innovations; unique in Asia, its contemporary work manages to be very modern without showing any distinct Western influences. Protest literature is familiar not only in the Philippines, where it seems to grow stronger, but in all the countries included here; plays approaching once-taboo subjects, such as gay issues and feminism, have done much to help change perceptions and modernise societies. National identity is a common subject of newly independent countries, and plays about various legal and political decisions have all contributed to building the often difficult road to democracy.

At the geographic centre of SEA, Brunei has ancient roots but its modern theatre, growing from an active university, is finding relevance and innovation. Immense internal conflicts have made it difficult for Myanmar, Cambodia and Laos to build new literary or dramatic forms or even preserve old ones, but support groups such as the one around Chhon Sina in Cambodia are finding ways to develop writers' voices and build audiences. Vietnam and Indonesia have had remarkable success in retaining traditions whilst developing new ways, and though full-time writers are few, the wealth and diversity is impressive. The old French and Dutch colonisers left little love of literature, so credit must go to the people and their intent on modernizing and ensuring that vernacular, dialects and eloquent language is equally valued, along with ideas. Dang Chuong's *Dark Race* is refreshingly welcome, as it shows a progressive Vietnam that feels quite familiar, as does Joned Suryatmoko's *Piknik*: in portraying Javanese in Bali, it reflects the problems of foreign workers anywhere. These are all plays of ideas, selected for a work's ability to traverse national barriers and communicate out of context.

Thailand is actively building spoken drama, though its lack of translations still keeps its best qualities hidden. Unique in Asia as never having been colonized, Thailand has always valued performance, and its dance and dance dramas, *Lakhon* and *Khon* come readily to Westerners' minds; but the modern nation and its people are much more evident on its stages than traditional performance, which is sought mainly by the tourists. Interesting also is the growth of English-speaking theatre in Thailand; and that modern drama training can be found even in the provinces.

Though Indonesia, Malaysia and the Philippines share race and language origins, and cultural links are found everywhere in SEA, essential differences between the nations are numerous; but when it comes to the problems facing playwrights and new writing, there are many shared situations and dilemmas. Government funding of new work excels only in Singapore, and generally there are messy copyright laws and few incentives to encourage playwrights; and almost everywhere spoken drama is more interdisciplinary than pure: it is in transition to new expressions and is determined to strengthen. Political will is not always evident, and often in flux: a good example being Singapore, where priority was deliberately given to economy building, and only more recently are the arts valued as crucial to a robust society. But across the region, where security, employment and education are growing, so are the arts.

Many people have helped us find these works, and we know that this publication is only a glimpse into what is available. It is exciting to discover the other forms of play-making that exist in this region but we regret our inability to include, for example, the wonderful Indonesian work that is commonly improvised afresh with every performance. Similarly, we have not included works which rely upon the use of several languages, such as Koes Juliadi's *Clay Women of Kasongan*, or which are too locally-specific, or have specific performance styles or large musical or dance elements. But it is no accident that this collection includes many plays by women, and this is a sign of the equity that has emerged as a feature of these ancient-yet-young nations. Nations that are growing in pride, in industry, investment and in tourism, in innovation and in cultural originality.

Aubrey Mellor OAM

Lasalle College of the Arts, Singapore, 2016.

PLUNGE

JEAN TAY

First produced in 2001 by Action Theatre in Singapore.
Directed by Krishen Jit.

Characters

ISABEL – a young Singaporean woman in her mid-20s, newscaster
INA – a young Indonesian Chinese woman in her early 20s
CHORUS – made up of 3 men: Man A, Man B, and Man C

Setting

Asia.

Time

2 July 97 to June 98.
Headings marked with [ ] may optionally be projected on-screen.

ACT ONE: FUNDAMENTALS
SCENE 1: DESCENT

Gongs begin chiming in the darkness.

They continue to chime until they blend into the sound of the opening music coming on for the Seven O'Olock News.

Lights gradually come on during the news. We can see the shadow-lit silhouette of the newsreader. Projected behind her is a landscape of gleaming silver skyscrapers, the central business district. Everything about it speaks of progress and efficiency. The stage is full of modern, high-tech wide-screen television sets, on which we can also watch the news.

The music for the Seven O'Clock News *gradually fades away as the lights brighten on the newsreader and we can see her, wearing a pastel green Chanel suit. She has the clean, sculpted, impeccably made-up features and coiffured hair of your typical newsreader. Her voice is equally flawless, trans-atlantic, hint of an American/ British accent, crystal clear and emotionally disengaged. Her face is reflected in the many television sets around the room as she reports the news:*

ISABEL Good evening. Welcome to Channel 5.

This is Isabel Cheong, bringing you the *Seven O'Clock News* on the 2nd July 1997.

The Thai baht plunged to a record low against the dollar today, after the government floated the currency, ending uncertainty over Thailand's exchange rate policy. The flotation devalued the baht by fifteen to twenty percent while the Stock Exchange fell by seven-point-nine percent. It's the latest in a series of surprise measures by authorities trying to boost the economy, which is suffering its worst slump in over a decade.

She pauses. Lights dim on her, although she can still be seen. The spotlight brightens on Man A, who stands like a pillar through his following monologue. While he speaks, she adjusts her make-up, blouse, shuffles through her papers etc.

MAN A I had a dream last night.

I was waiting for a lift, when I heard the soft musical chime of approach.

The silver doors slid open and I stepped into a world of mirrored walls and marbled floor.

I press the button that says 'G' for ground, and it lights up, a warm orange.

The doors slide shut, and I am arching my neck upwards to see the orange light flee from one circle to the next.

Then I feel a terrifying lurch, and gravity yanks my heart from my body.

The solid floor gives way.

And the orange lights are flying, sparking over all the buttons.

I am in free fall.

And my body cannot catch up.

I ricochet off the walls of the elevator.

There is no floor, there is no ground.

I plunge straight into the centre of the earth.

Straight towards 'G' for gravity.

And when I finally think it is all over, when we hit 'G' and I think I can finally breathe again... It doesn't stop there.

I keep falling.

Lights fade on Man A, and brighten on Isabel.

ISABEL Indonesia succumbed to speculative attacks and floated the rupiah today. The rupiah dove on the news, plunging about four percent, while Indonesian stocks dropped to a thirteen week low.

Again she pauses as lights dim on her. Spotlight on Man B as he gives his monologue.

MAN B I had a dream last night.

I dreamt that I was standing on the edge of a suspension bridge.

A bridge between two separate lands, an umbilical cord of steel and asphalt, across a swelling river. Strong enough to carry eighty cars at a time, with waves cresting twenty feet below.

I stand at the edge, exhaust in my hair, my hand wrapped around the ropes of steel, my pocket full of change to pay the toll.

And as I look down, a crack snakes beneath my shoes.

Solid ground shatters like eggshell.

And I am in free fall.

Steel rivets and shards of asphalt splinter past my face, scratch my skin.

And when I feel I must finally stop, when my heel finally slaps hard surface.

It doesn't stop there.

I crash through the ragged face of the water, the weight of the coins in my pocket pulls me down.

Until I am completely wrapped in water, and all my orifices sealed.

But it doesn't stop there. I keep falling.

Lights fade on Man B, brighten on Isabel again.

ISABEL The South Korean won ended at a record low this afternoon, after the government declared that it would no longer defend the currency.

The won smashed through the psychologically significant one thousand dollar level in a single breath, while the stock index lost more than four percent.

MAN C I had a dream last night.

I dreamt that I was standing on top of a huge metal crane.

A lattice of bright silver with a hook of gold.

A machine that moved mountains, and I, borne aloft at its rearing head.

And as I watched, my feet booted and head helmeted.

The crane blurred, tarnished, and turned a coppery red.

Rust creeping up the edge of metal.

The scabs crumbling across my boots.

And beneath me, metal eaten as if by acid.

The teeth marks growing deeper by the moment.

The scarred, dissolving flesh of a leper.

This skeleton crumbles.

And I am in free fall.

And a dozen half-built office blocks rise to impale me. With their sharpened columns glinting in the sun.

And my body is shattered into a thousand separate pieces.

Flesh pulled from bone, severed from teeth.

But it doesn't stop there. I keep falling.

ISABEL And that's all that we have time for tonight. I'm Isabel Cheong, thank you for joining me. The next news bulletin will be at ten o'clock tonight. Have a pleasant evening.

Music blares on as the news bulletin comes to an end, and the lights dim on her. We see her silhouette, gathering her papers, shuffling them. The skyscrapers are bright behind her. She stands up, still looking through her papers.

Finally, she extracts a single sheet, and lights go out on her. But, the television set (or television sets) are still on, and she is still on air, speaking, although the sound is turned off. The men now hover around the television sets, gazing at her in worshipful adoration.

SCENE 2: ADORATION

MAN A Isabel darling, you were wonderful tonight.

MAN B Isabel, it was amazing.

MAN C Heaven, Isabel, heaven.

MAN A The way you raised your eyebrow, just then. Just like that.

MAN B You said controversy, just the way it should be said.

MAN C That divine brooch you wore.

MAN A You lifted the corners of your lips. A smile, just barely.

MAN B Con-TRAW-ver-sy. Not con-troh-VER-see.

MAN C And the suit. What an ensemble.

MAN A Very Mona Lisa. With Gauguin eyes.

MAN B I've never met someone who ennunciated the way you do.

MAN C That apple green is so you.

MAN A And that briefest bob of the head, when you said goodnight.

MAN B You hit Michel Camdessus. Ryutaro Hashimoto. Chavalit Yongchaiyudh. Bacharuddin Jusuf Habibie. Effortlessly.

MAN C Nothing less than Chanel, am I right?

MAN A Acknowledging, bringing us in, yet keeping that distance.

MAN B And the EDB, PIE, MOE, AYE, ERP, TDB, NWC. Not a stumble.

MAN C And the diamond-studded ears. Understated, yet classy.

MAN A You are the most amazing woman. Ever.

MAN B Your voice inspires me to new heights.

MAN C I would do anything for you, you know.

MAN A If you asked me to, I would set myself on fire.

MAN B Jump from the tallest building

MAN C Die for you.

MAN A I can't help it. I can't help falling.

Lights fade. A juke-box tune comes on, some tune along the lines of 'Can't Help Falling in Love'.

SCENE 3: NAME

Isabel has taken off her jacket. She is now Ina, in a simple tank top, hair tied into a limp ponytail, without make-up. Ina may be the same age as Isabel, or slightly younger. Lights fade up on Ina, who looks nervous and young, and clutches a single sheet of paper to her chest.

Ina speaks with a distinctly Indonesian accent, and we can almost hear her struggling at times with the language. Ina holds out a piece of paper, with two Chinese characters written on it. It is the same piece of paper that Isabel earlier extracted from the stack on her desk.

INA Hello. My name is Ina. I live in Jakarta and I study in the university. I would like to be a civil engineer. Not many girls study that, but I think it is very... powerful.

You see a rubbish heap or construction site, full of trash. Pieces of wood, buckets of concrete, broken glass and twisted wires. It's a mess. Disgusting. Dirty.

But then... but then you start to put the pieces all together, and slowly, it turns into something beautiful. Shining. All straight edges. Nothing crooked, or dirty or twisted any more. All you need is the knowledge. To put it together. Fit the jigsaw together. Every nail, every screw has its place.

That's power. I think. Putting together. (*Pauses*)

I have another name. But I don't use a lot.

It sounds like Ina too, but it looks different.

She takes out the piece of paper with the Chinese characters on it, and shows it to the audience.

This is my name. Ina. Ai nah.

Isn't it beautiful? Ai nah.

You see the strokes? Like the eyebrows of a beautiful woman.

Thick and strong. Tapered.

They arch from one end of the page to the other.

But if you take them apart, they are nothing more than ink stains on white paper.

A dirty piece of paper, that you crumple up and throw away.

But it's only when you put them together, the right way, then every speck has meaning.

Every flick of the brush tells you something.

You put them together, and that's me.

You see? Ina.

She pauses, as the men emerge, their shadows looming over her. Over Ina's following monologue, they murmur very softly the three official documents, or perhaps, it is projected over her.

INA My father doesn't like me to use my Chinese name.

He's a stern man, my father. Not the kind that hugs his children or kisses them.

And he doesn't like people speaking Chinese around the house.

I guess that's why he never taught me any.

I never learnt.

Can't write, can't read.

My grandmother wrote that for me. A long time ago.

I don't know what it means.

It's just a bunch of black marks.

Beat.

But not just.

[The Three Laws]

MAN A The 'Presidential Instruction on Chinese Religion, Beliefs and Traditions', states that manifestations of Chinese religion and belief can have an "undesirable psychological, mental and moral influence on Indonesian citizens as well as obstruct the process of assimilation." It bans celebration of Chinese religious festivals in public and states that religious practice of Chinese traditions must be kept indoors or within the household.

MAN B 'Instruction of the Ministry of Home Affairs No. X01/1977 on Implementing Instructions for Population Registration' authorises special codes to be put on identification cards indicating ethnic Chinese origin.

MAN C 'Circular of the Director General for Press and Graphics Guidance in the Ministry of Information on Banning the Publication and Printing of Writings and Advertisements in Chinese': restricts any use of Chinese to a single newspaper called Harian Indonesia, on the grounds that dissemination of materials in Chinese will obstruct the goal of national unity and the process of assimilation of ethnic Chinese.

As Ina finally stops talking, the chorus speak at their normal volume, almost tenderly.

MAN A I am protecting you from everything that makes you not me.

MAN B I am allowing you to assimilate, to ease the process of adjustment.

MAN C I am protecting you from things that may backfire.

MAN A From passions that may be incensed.

MAN B From glass that may cut.

MAN C From fires that may burn.

MAN A I am trying to protect you.

MAN B If I could have held you then, I would.

MAN C If I could have kept you safe, I would.

MAN A I would keep you from falling.

MAN B From burning.

MAN C From dying.

As they speak, the lights gradually fade on the men too, until it is completely dark.

SCENE 4: THEORY A (APPLE)

Lights come up on Man A, who has put on a pair of glasses to look professorly. There are all sorts of professional-looking charts and tables projected behind him. The music continues playing in the background as Man A speaks.

MAN A Ladies and Gentlemen.

I know. You all want to know why. Why?

And so, I will tell you why. I will explain to you exactly and precisely why the Asian economic crisis happened as it did. For this, I need a volunteer. Preferably one with some kind of fruit in hand. Preferably a fruit that is of sufficient toughness and resiliency. Preferably an apple. Do I have a volunteer, please?

Yes, you sir!

You have an... No, that's an orange. That's not going to work. I need someone with an apple. That's right, a crisp, crunchy, fresh, delicious, shiny, ruby-red apple. Do I have a volunteer? Yes? No?

Yes, you have an apple sir? You do? That's quite perfect! Come on up here sir, and let's all get to know you.

And what's your name sir?

MAN C *(shyly)* Cecil.

MAN A Cecil. What a lovely name. And that is a lovely red apple.

MAN C Thanks.

MAN A Thank you sir, for coming up here to facilitate my demonstration. Now if I could have the apple, please. If you could just sit on the floor here. Lovely, lovely. Right. May I? Thank you. *(He clambers onto a chair, and towers above Man C)*

Now Ladies and Gentlemen. Observe up here, a beautiful red apple.

And a man. Down there.

MAN C *(raises his hand shyly)* Excuse me, sir?

MAN A Yes?

MAN C You're not... Are you?

MAN A What?

Man C looks at the apple raised over his head. Man A follows his gaze, and then laughs.

MAN A Oh no, no. My dear man, what were you thinking? I wouldn't dream of causing you any pain.

MAN C No?

MAN A No.

MAN C That's good.

MAN A Of course not. I promise. Anything you may experience will be completely theoretical.

MAN C Yah?

MAN A Oh yes. In theory, this will be entirely painless.

Now as I was saying, ladies and gentlemen. The apple. And Cecil.

Two possibilities. Or maybe three.

When I release this apple...

A) It will fall downwards, and hit my friend Cecil on the head.

B) It will stay there suspended in mid-air.

C) None of the above. In other words, it could fly straight up like a helium balloon or an American bald-eagle. Or it could trace an elliptical orbit around my head. Or burst into flame. Or explode into a thousand little pieces.

There are a hundred, a billion things this apple could do. The possibilities are limitless. Why, when it could do so many other exciting things, should it fall?

Apart from this little theory that some of you may be familiar with.

In classical mechanics, it's known as the universal force of attraction that affects all matter. Some call it gravity. A law of physics.

And yet, what are laws but rules waiting to be broken?

I posit that this is what happened in the Asian currency crisis.

What went up finally came down, and came down spectacularly.

Did it have to? Of course not. It could have done a hundred, a billion other things. But did it do those billions of things? No. And why? I say gravity.

Shall we see the proof? Of course. Everything sounds good in theory. Hypothetically.

Now. In the words of Sir Issac Newton himself.

He releases the apple, and it hits Man C squarely on the head.

MAN C Ow!

MAN A I rest my case.

The music, which has faded to the background, gradually comes on again, until it drowns all other things.

ACT TWO: PANIC
SCENE 1: CHEERLEADING

The music for the Seven O'Clock News *blares on again, a little too loud and annoying. A huge trading screen is projected in the background, with the flashing green numbers of currency and share prices. This act has the frenetic energy of a busy trading floor. The three men hold bright, fluorescent pom-poms and cheer on their currencies like all-American cheerleaders. They are extremely hyper, as they go through their desperate, energetic cheerleading routine, and every gesture can be interpreted as a motion to buy/ sell. Isabel sits at her desk as usual, reading the news.*

ISABEL Good evening and welcome back. This is Isabel Cheong with more on the Asian currency meltdown.

Asian currencies plunged as confidence in the region deteriorates.

After more than thirty years of explosive growth, this crisis is taking the Asian Tigers by surprise. Investors are starting to panic.

MAN A Ready guys?

MAN B/C Ready!

MAN A Tell me, what's the bottom line?

MAN B/C The dollar sign!

MAN A I can't hear you! What's the bottom line?

MAN B/C The dollar sign!

MAN A The dollar sign?

MAN B/C The bottom line! Yeah!

ISABEL (July 2) Thailand floated the baht in a bold move which sent shock waves through Southeast Asia today. This resulted in a twenty percent plunge in the baht.

MAN A What are we waiting for?

MEN *(cheer)* You got the stripes! *(Clap clap)*

You got the claws! *(Clap clap)*

You got the stripes you got the claws!

Go tigers! Yeah!

ISABEL (July 24) Asian currencies plunged to new depths on Thursday. The Thai baht, which led the decline, hit a low of thirty-two-point-seventy to the dollar.

MEN I'm a tiger, hear me roar! I'm not gonna hit the floor! *(They roar)*

ISABEL (August 14) Indonesia succumbed to speculative attacks and floated the rupiah, which plunged by four percent after markets opened.

MEN Go tigers, go tigers, go tigers!

ISABEL (September 4) Asian currencies plunged on the news. The ringgit dropped by more than four percent in two hours as Malaysia renewed calls for a ban on currency trading.

MAN B Bloody foreign speculators!

MAN C Just get lost!

MAN A Stupid morons!

MEN S-O-R-O-S, what do you get?

M-O-R-O-N, that's what you get!

Who's immoral? Guess!

Who's a cheater? Who!

S-O-R-O-S the M-O-R-O-N!!!

ISABEL And now, a word from our sponsors.

SCENE 2: TIME OUT

[Playwright's Disclaimer: No numbers were actually hurt in this reconstruction.]

MEN Only the numbers plunge.

Only on paper.

Only those who believe.

That the numbers are real.

That you can wrap your arms around an eight hundred million dollar exchange rate loss.

That a five percent decline means your fingers are falling off.

A ten percent fall means you lose your arms up to your elbows.

A twenty percent drop means the amputation of both legs.

A thirty percent plunge means you lose all limbs.

You don't live beyond thirty percent.

You can't.

You start to lose your vital organs.

The liver, the kidneys, the stomach, the heart.

You lose eighty percent, and you're just a brain in a jar, on somebody's desk.

[End of Time Out]

Lights up on Ina onstage, watching the news on one of the TV screens perhaps.

INA Nowadays, very exciting times. You read newspapers, listen to news, hear what they say. Other worlds so different from me. Men in long-sleeve shirt and tie, making decisions, business deals. Not just thousands or tens of thousands. But millions of dollar deals. Sometimes even billions. Numbers so big, they don't make sense after a while.

And just like that. At the click of a button, just one word from their mouths.

That's why my father says, no point investing in the stock market. So risky, the wind change just like that. And people lose everything, it's out of their control.

He prefers to make money the old-fashioned way. Small business, hard work. You don't earn that much, but you get to know your customer well, and if you work hard, do things the right way, you'll be OK. You'll be safe.

And that's what's important.

Lights dim on Ina. They brighten again on Isabel at her desk, and the three men, who are taking a breather. The men wearily get back on to their feet again and prepare to do another round of cheerleading.

ISABEL Welcome back to the *Seven O'Clock News*. (Nov 17) We now turn to South Korea, where the currency was sent smashing through the one thousand won per dollar level this morning.

MEN You won, baby, won, baby, you want the won!

ISABEL (November 19) Determined to save its currency without turning to the IMF, the South Korean government announced a sweeping set of measures to stem the country's crisis.

MEN I won, baby, won, baby, I want the won!

ISABEL (November 20) The response to South Korea's self-rescue measures was not encouraging. After half an hour of trading the won plunged to one thousand, one hundred and thirty-nine won per dollar.

The men huddle discussing cheerleading strategies. They try again:

MEN Give me an I! (I!) Give me an M! (M!) Give me an F! (F!)

What do you get? Cash!

I can't hear you! Cash!

I-M-F! Cash!

ISABEL (December 4) Seoul stocks saw its largest single day gain after Korean officials and the IMF signed a letter of intent promising Korea fifty-seven billion dollars.

They start to sing and dance the I-M-F-Cash number below to the tune and in the style of the song 'Y-M-C-A'.

MEN We've got to go to the I-M-F-Cash

We've got to go to the I-M-F-Cash

They have everything there that you need to enjoy

We can hang out with all the boys.

It's fun to be at the I-M-F-Cash

ISABEL Labour unrest in South Korea has been sparked off by IMF demands for tougher laws on layoffs.

A factory worker at a South Korean shipyard died after setting himself on fire in support of a cancelled general strike.

The men's moods are dampened. Man C suddenly shouts at Isabel.

MAN C Are you happy now? Is that what you want?

Isabel ignores him and reads on.

ISABEL We now turn to Indonesia, where President Suharto has signed an agreement with the IMF that requires him to dismantle the monopolies and family-owned businesses that marked his thirty-two year rule. But markets were not impressed and the rupiah plunged through the fifteen thousand per dollar level. The currency has lost eighty percent of its value since last July.

MAN A Come on, you guys. Looks like the brain's in the jar, already.

The men try the I-M-F-Cash cheer again, more desperately this time.

MEN Give me an I! (I!) Give me an M! (M!) Give me an F! (F!)

What do you get? Cash!

I can't hear you! Cash!

I-M-F! Cash!

ISABEL (February 14) IMF has threatened to cut off funds for Indonesia over its controversial plans to establish a currency board.

MAN C *(sings)* Don't tell me what to do.

ISABEL (March 6) IMF delays a planned three billion dollar disbursement to Indonesia.

MAN A *(sings)* Don't tell me what to say.

ISABEL (April 21) Indonesia is launching a series of reform measures agreed to with the IMF.

MAN B *(sings)* When I get cash from you

Don't put me on display

As Isabel continues to read the news, the men react with increasing dismay at the news that she is reading, albeit in different ways.

Man B continues to sing the song, while Man A launches into another IMF cheer, and Man C rants and raves at her. Until they are all overtaken and dominated by the 'Three Blind Mice' nursery rhyme song that Isabel is singing.

ISABEL These measures include the removal of subsidies for fuel and electricity, which will lead to domestic price hikes.

MAN A Give me an I! (I!) Give me an M! (M!) Give me an F! (F!)

What do you get? Cash!

I can't hear you! Cash!

I-M-F! Cash!

MAN B *(sings)* Cos I'm strong and I like to be strong

I'm free and I like to be free
To live my life the way I want
To say and do whatever I please.

MAN C *(getting frustrated)* Why can't you leave us alone! Leave us alone! What are you trying to do? Shut up! If you'd just stop talking so much! Stop it, you moron! What else do you want from me? My blood? You idiot! You cheat!

ISABEL *(continues reporting in her normal tone of voice, even as the content of the news grows more ridiculous)*

And Asian currencies plunged again on the news. And Asian currencies plunged.

And plunged. And plunged.

And three blind mice. Three blind mice.

See how they run. *(Gradually picking up the tune)* See how they run.

They all run after the farmer's wife, who cut off their tails with a carving knife

Have you ever seen such a sight in your life, as three blind mice?

She continues singing, picking up speed as she goes, and the men, who ignore her at first, start to join in, one by one, singing in rounds. They get more and more frenzied. Lights gradually fade on her, and her voice fades away, until only the men are singing, and running in panic around the room. Finally, they fall down on the floor exhausted.

Lights come up on Ina.

SCENE 3: CRACK

INA We live without thinking.

Most of the time.

We live without choosing. Don't even know how to.

I sit at home and read the newspaper, watch the news. About other people.

Other people changing lives, changing things.

Other people making decisions for us.

And look at what happens.

Things can't go on like this. And they won't.

This is a chance. A crack in the floor.

And we're going to go for it.

My classmates and I have decided.

Tomorrow, after school. We're going to go for the protest rally.

I... I can't say I wanted to go at first.

But then, I thought about it.

All my life. I'm sitting there, watching someone else live for me.

This is the crack. The chance I have to take.

Lights dim on Ina, though we can still see her standing on stage.

Man A's voice comes on over the radio. He is a reporter, probably some US correspondent from CNN or something, live at the scene. His voice is breathless, a little hoarse from shouting to be heard, and generally excited to be in the middle of everything. You can hear the sounds of students chanting slogans etc in the background. Perhaps some of the television sets come on too, with scenes of the students rallying peacefully.

MAN A I'm now standing outside the campus of the University of Indonesia, where students are rallying peacefully against the recent price hikes as well as for political and economic reforms. Thousands of students are sitting on the road outside the campus, listening to speeches and chanting slogans.

Ina listens intently to the program. Lights now brighten on Ina, who is arguing with her unseen father.

INA No! No, Papa! I don't want to.

You cannot tell me what to do.

We are not going to fight. It is not for violence.

It is not for fun. You think we're so young, so immature.

What am I supposed to do? Stay at home, knit socks like an old woman?

You don't understand. I'm not going for myself, I'm going for all for us.

I'm 20 years old. I should know what I want.

I'm not being childish.

I'm not.

Don't be so narrow minded.

If you want to be a coward, go ahead.

Stay at home, lock your doors. Pretend the outside world doesn't exist.

I shouldn't even have told you in the first place.

But I thought you'd understand.

That this is important.

We cannot go ahead and let other people lead our lives for us.

Please, papa?

Please? (*Pause. Her father obviously disagrees*)

Aargh...

She picks up the note in frustration, crumples it up and flings it at her father. Then goes to the corner and sulks.

SCENE 4: THEORY B (BUBBLE)

[Panic Theory]

Lights suddenly come on very bright on Man B. It's his turn to play professor. Some bubble-gummish tune comes on. Preferably one with references to love, and bubbles or bubbly emotions. (e.g. 'I'm Forever Blowing Bubbles'.)

MAN B My respected colleague recently entertained you with his rendition of the Southeast Asian currency crisis. I wish to preface my presentation today, by saying that I have nothing but the utmost respect for my colleague. Unfortunately, this is an area where I beg to differ. Allow me to share my thoughts with you.

My beautiful assistant will be, of course, assisting me.

Man C comes up, dishevelled, rebellious, chewing his bubble gum.

Man B clears his throat, embarrassed.

MAN B Austerity drive. What can you do? Will you please get that thing out of your mouth? *(Man C looks mutinously at Man B. He scowls)* Or else. *(Man C grimaces, takes the wad of gum out and sticks it behind his ear)* That's disgusting. On second thought, please put it back in again. *(Man C smirks. Puts the gum back into his mouth)* Actually, you know, that works out rather well. *(Man B gives an unexpected smile)* My beau... My assistant will now blow a big bubble for you.

Man C ignores him, still chewing. Man B clears his throat, nudges Man C.

MAN B I *said*, my assistant will now blow a big bubble. *(Man C obliges. Man B shakes his head)* Nope, not good enough. You've got to be able to do better than that.

Man C takes a deep breath and blows a large bubble.

MAN B That'll do. Thank you. Ladies and gentlemen, if you will pay careful attention to this bubble. Note that when it was not so big, it was cloudy and pink.

Opaque, and almost impossible to break.

But pretend that it is bigger. And I mean much much bigger.

Imagine it twenty times the size of this really.

My beautiful assistant has somewhat limited lungs.

But if you can imagine the perfect bubble. About this big.

It would be as clear as glass. You can see all the way through it.

And the lightest, softest touch would cause it to shatter.

If I even breathed upon it, it would burst into a thousand pieces.

So that's how it happened. How the perfect crisis occurred because of the perfect bubble. Blown so big it is like fine Bohemian crystal.

But the harder you blow, the louder you burst.

And you're left covered in saliva and chewed up gum.

Man B takes a sharp pointed object, like a long knitting needle, etc. Man C looks worried but doesn't budge. He mumbles.

MAN C Mmm... mmm... mm.

MAN B Yes? You wanted to say something?

Man C shakes his head, shrugs his shoulders, tries gesturing, somewhat unsuccessfully.

MAN C Mmm mmm mmm.

MAN B My dear fellow, if you ever want the sweet taste of success, just once in your life, you've got to learn how to enunciate. That's what your tongue is for. Anyways... *(Shrugs his shoulders)* Education must go on. Boom.

Man B strikes at the bubble.

Instant blackout. Sound like a gunshot.

Lights come up on Ina who sits, looking very stunned.

INA They said zero. At first.

Zero. Then One. Or Two.

No. Four. Or Six? I don't know.

It's all numbers. I don't care. It doesn't make a difference.

Does it? Six. Or Sixty? Maybe six hundred even?

You hear people die in war. All the time. Somewhere in Serbia. Middle East. Somewhere else.

But this is not war. *(Pause)*

So why are there bullets?

Last I heard was six. But they could be lying.

Everybody lies nowadays.

People talk rubbish all the time. Especially people reading the news.

It's all rubbish. There should have been zero. Why six?

Out of how many?

It doesn't matter. Six out of six. Six out of six hundred. Six out of six thousand.

Only if you are one of the six. If you loved one of the six. Knew their name. Their face. Or shared a joke with them in class. Borrowed their notes.

Or kissed them on their forehead, like a blessing. Or a curse.

But just six. Not seven. Maybe.

Because I was here. Not there.

Later, at night. I couldn't sleep. But I lay in bed, thinking.

My father came into my room. So I pretended to be asleep.

He stood there for a while.

Then he whispered something. I'm not sure what it was, but I think it was my name.

He stood for a little while more and then went out again.

But before he left, he kissed me on my forehead. Like a blessing.

Ina continues to sit there slightly, as the television sets flicker on. The music for the Seven O'Olock News *comes on again.*

Isabel is on the television once more, reading the news. Ina barely registers it.

ISABEL The turning point in Indonesian President Suharto's thirty-two year rule came on Tuesday (12th May) when riot police opened fire on students from the elite Trisakti University. Six students were killed in the attack. This proved to be the catalyst for a wave of violence, riots and looting by angry mobs of poor Indonesians.

As Isabel reads the rest of her speech on the television set, Ina starts to react to what is being read out on the news, she addresses her monologue to Isabel, and the two speeches overlap.

ISABEL	**INA**
The trouble began with a protest by high school students that quickly degenerated into mayhem as people threw stones at anything breakable. The streets	Tell me that you are lying. It's not true. This was not supposed to happen. On the radio.

ISABEL *(continues)*

were littered with glass when marines and police arrived, firing into the air to send people running into side streets. Several major buildings in central Jakarta were still burning last night, after mobs of young Indonesians went on a rampage of arson and looting.

Major department stores, grocery stores, banks and petrol stations were vandalised and razed, as were businesses owned by the country's ethnic Chinese minority and the First Family.

Thick plumes of smoke enveloped the Indonesian capital and fires were raging late into the night. Fire-fighting services remained paralysed as officials were reluctant to send fire fighters onto the streets.

What began as anger against the killing of six students at a protest rally has deteriorated into an orgy of pillage and arson. Most of those killed have been youngsters trapped while looting shops in multi-storey malls set ablaze by other rioters.

INA *(continues)*

On the television.
In the papers.
Tell me that you are lying. Tell me!
They are not burning.
They are shopping. Right?
They are not looting.
Don't tell me these lies.
We want progress. Reform.
Not shopping centers burning down.
Not people stealing, and screaming.
And dying.
Not this.
Stop it. Stop it.
Tell me the truth.
Stop telling me these lies.
If you will just stop talking so much, it will be alright.
OK. OK, fine.
Say that there are protests.
There are rallies.
And the students are brave.
They stand, arm in arm.
Peacefully. Waving banners.
And all over the world, people watch them. And see what brave, peaceful people they are.
Don't... just don't...
Stop talking rubbish.
Shut up! Shut up!

Isabel pauses, looking slightly confused, as though she can hear Ina shouting. And then Isabel continues reading.

Ina runs to the television sets. Pulls out the plug. Starts disconnecting cables, etc. Starts banging on it, as Isabel's image on the television screens starts to flicker and die.

The men come up to Ina. Haul her away from the television set. And then, one by one, cart them off. Furtively, but with a sense of glee. They steal every scrap of material left on the floor. They shove each other to get it until there is nothing left on stage, except for Isabel's bare desk.

INA And when it is all over.

When you finally think it must stop. There is nothing left.

But still. It keeps burning.

Lights fade on the empty stage. Ina, looking lost. Alone.

ACT THREE: CONTAGION

The music for the Seven O'Olock News *blares on again, a little too loud and annoying. We are getting thoroughly sick of it. Lights come on over Isabel's desk. It is empty. We listen to the music for a while, look at the empty stage. The music fades away, then comes on again, insistently, a little louder than before, as if to make a point. Finally, we spot her, standing in one corner, clutching her stack of notes in her arms rather defensively. She opens her mouth, to say something. But she can't bring herself to do it.*

The music for the Seven O'Olock News *starts up again, even more insistently this time. Even louder than before. Isabel starts. She finally seems to remember where she is, and pulls herself together, striding confidently to her desk. She shrugs her shoulders and begins to read the news, articles on the May riots in Jakarta. Her voice sounds normal, controlled, but there is a tense edge to it, and her eyes are furtive as she glances around the room.*

As she goes on, she has more and more difficulty reading, and frequently stops, with uncomfortable pauses as she struggles to control her emotions.

ISABEL Good evening. This is Isabel Cheong with the *Seven O'Olock News* on May 17 – The death toll from violent riots across Indonesia continues to climb as rescue workers comb through several smouldering shopping centres.

ISABEL *(continues)*

A total of 499 people were killed in the Indonesian capital and its nearby Tanggerang district, with most of the bodies burned beyond recognition. All in all, rioters in Jakarta set ablaze to over three thousand buildings, nine hundred cars and five hundred motorcycles.

The military today issued a written statement apologising to the nation and to the Indonesian people for the current conditions.

(She pauses. Continues, slightly confused)

Meanwhile, rescue workers resumed their search of the rubble of Plaza Cileduk in southwest Jakarta. More than three hundred looters, mostly teenagers, are believed to have been trapped in a fire at the fourth floor of the shopping complex on Thursday night.

The 134 remains collected so far from Plaza Ciledug will be buried in a mass grave in Tangerang because there is no way to identify them.

(Finally responds to the voices)

No! I can't!

MAN A You start to see in the words. The faces of people.

MAN B You start to hear the voices. The screams.

MAN C You begin to feel the heat on your own back.

MAN A The fear in your own heart.

MAN B The sobs in your own throat.

MAN A You bite your lips so hard it bleeds.

MAN C You taste their blood in your own mouth.

MAN A You think these are nightmares. These are shadows.

MAN B You start to hear the voice of a young woman.

MAN C To see a face that looks like your own.

(She collects herself) I'm sorry. *(Beat)* The General Hospital's morgue has received at least 239 charred bodies collected from the rubble of shopping centers throughout the city. Hundreds of people flocked to the morgue in search of loved ones who had failed to return home after the shopping centre fires.

Suddenly, Man A shouts, startling Isabel mid-sentence.

MAN A NO!! You heard me? I said no!

He didn't.

He go shopping only.

He go with his friends. After school. He's a good boy. Always a good boy.

He never go there to loot. Never go there to steal. It's all a mistake.

ISABEL No. I didn't say that...

She steels herself again. Ignores him and continues reading her report. Man A also continues talking, muttering half to himself, half to Isabel, until the end when all the speeches converge to a climax. As the monologues start to overlap, we hear one monologue more clearly above the others.

Where the monologue is in bold, the speaker should be dominant (i.e. louder and more audible), while the other supportive monologues should form a collage of background murmuring.

ISABEL

Mr. Sani, whose son and daughter died in the ravaged department store, identified his son, Iwan, 21, but failed to find the body of his daughter Mulyani, 17.

The morgue received forty-four plastic bags containing the bodies recovered yesterday from the department store in East Jakarta...

MAN A

I ask him to stay at home.
I tell him not safe.
Nowadays, a lot of angry people.
May be dangerous.
But he say he arrange with friends already.
Short while only. They're only going shopping.
Come back in half an hour, he say.

MAN B *(Almost conversationally)* It's all over now.

Isabel is again surprised by this newest interruption, but takes it in her stride and keeps reading. But the pauses happen more frequently, are even longer, as she struggles to take in the monologues around her.

ISABEL	MAN A	MAN B
It was burned by rioters Thursday night and at least 198 bodies were recovered. Eleven bodies were found in the gutted shell of the Glodok electronics centre in West Jakarta.	You sure, I ask? Of course, he says. And he laughs at me. Why are you so worried? Nothing's going to happen. So I say OK.	**I'm not young anymore. Don't have the energy I used to have, but got experience. Got loyalty. These things count, you know. You can't write-off 25 years like that.**
The morgue also received two bodies from the Ramayana department store in North Jakarta and a further 18 bodies were found in a shopping centre in West Jakarta.	**And I wait. Half an hour. No boy. Maybe he's a bit late. Bus crowded or something. So I wait some more.**	25 years. That's how long I worked here. And you? You're not even twenty-five yet, are you? That's longer than you've been around.

Man C launches into his lecture (Theory C) at this point.

ISABEL	MAN A	MAN B	MAN C
Police said they had arrested 1,027 alleged looters, several of those were students, from various places all over the city. Jakarta Military Commander Maj. Gen.	He's a good boy. He doesn't know what to do. He's only 15 years old. Just a child. He's not a looter. He's not a stealer. **Why you say he steal? Why you say he**	Started work after secondary school to support the family. It's hard work, but I'm don't complain. I get on with my colleagues. Can joke with my boss. Got two	**Ladies and Gentlemen. Oi! I said, Ladies and Gentlemen!! Your attention please! I have something very important to say.**

ISABEL *(continues)*	MAN A *(continues)*	MAN B *(continues)*	MAN C *(continues)*
Sjafrie Sjamsoeddin said yesterday that the situation was under control and called for business to resume in the capital. Troops patrolled the city streets in armored vehicles in an obvious move to show they were serious in their threat to take stern action against trouble-makers... But... still I hear rumours of things. Echoes of rumours of things. I don't know what to believe. And now, all I can see is her face. Exactly like mine. But in flames. Or in tears. In pain.	**loot? He never loot. He just go there to meet friends. Go shopping. He's got money to buy things. He doesn't need to loot.** I said he's not a thief. Stop calling him a thief. I don't know. Why he never come back. I wait and wait and wait. It's the other people. That set the shopping centre on fire. That killed my little boy. It's not his fault. **He didn't go there to loot. He'll never do something like that. Stop blaming him. He died, okay? He died in the**	little girls. Primary Five and Sec 1. And my wife, also working part time. We got by. But now. **Kicked out like a dog. No warning, just sorry goodbye, forget about your 25 years. 25 years of sweat and blood you know.** Cost-cutting, restructuring. Big words that I can't understand. I never did anything wrong. But everything I have is gone. Like the floor just collapsed. And what about my two girls? My wife? I don't want the girls to suffer. I want them to study	*(Getting annoyed)* Oh come on... shut up?You know what this is? I'll tell you what it is. Contagion. It's the bloody flu! The Asian Flu! The Deadly Virus! **This is the real thing. The flesh-eating, man-killing stuff. Transmitted through saliva, the exchange of bodily fluids, or germs floating in the air.** You can also get it by petting strange animals. Or by holding hands. It's awful. You die. Symptoms are sudden wails of sheer agony. Liver soaked in cheap

ISABEL *(continues)*	**MAN A** *(continues)*	**MAN B** *(continues)*	**MAN C** *(continues)*
What can I do to save her? What can I do? I can't take anymore. I can't do this anymore. *(Screams)* Enough!	**fire.** Only fifteen years old. I went to the shopping centre later. When it was all over. Trying to find him. Maybe he's somewhere, confused, tired. Waiting for me.	hard, go to university. **Otherwise with me like that, how can they? Anytime they want to kick, kick. Who cares about you?** The worst is going home and pretending everything's okay. I don't want them to worry.	alcohol. A sudden drop in one's bank account. **Glass splinters in one's vagina. An abrupt retrenchment. A plunge from the tenth floor at the Shangri-la.**

The men are silenced. They turn to stare at her.

ISABEL *(almost pleading)* Enough. I can't see. I've learned not to. I have to, in this line of work. I can't get emotionally involved. Otherwise, it would be a fresh gunshot wound every day. One more blade in the belly. Another smashed up suicide. I read the news. I don't live it. All I hear is the hum of the air-conditioning. Nothing else.

The men start speaking again, softly at first, so that we can still hear Isabel. Then, gradually, they crescendo, until all three are fighting to be heard, except for Isabel, who is starting to falter.

ISABEL	**MAN A**	**MAN B**	**MAN C**
Not the screams, the wails. Not the heat, the rain. Nothing. Explosions	But there was nothing. Nothing to see. Nothing left. Not even the faces. Only the shape of the	Luckily I've got a bit of savings, but how long can it last? And how to find another job now? So old	You know what makes it worse? Smart-mouthed newscasters who think they know better than everyone

ISABEL

(continues)

without shrapnel. Floods without water. Accidents without broken glass. But then... I see this woman. With wounded eyes and a face like mine. I don't know what to do. I don't know.

(She can't go on)

MAN A

(continues)

blackened bodies. Are you happy now? He died. And there's nothing left of him. Isn't that enough for you?

Why you must keep scolding him? What's wrong with you? Why you tell lies about him? Shut up! Stop telling your stupid lies! I said stop it!

MAN B

(continues)

already who wants? It's not about kindness, about people. It's only about money.

Who cares if I starve, if they starve? Do you care? Of course not! You don't even look at me! You can't be bothered! Nothing to do with you, right?

MAN C

(continues)

else in the world. It's okay, they say. This is the bitter medicine. Tough love.

Well it ain't working, Missy! It's as effective as cyanide. So the best thing you can do is to shut up. Safest for you, and for everyone else. You got that? You know what's best for you?

During the last section, the three men approach from different corners of the room and begin to circle her, menacing.

Isabel looks up suddenly, as if aware of the danger she is in.

She stands up, clutching her notes to her chest, defensively.

And the men circle closer. One dives across the table, the other pulls away her chair, and she starts running.

But her voice continues reading the articles, across the loudspeakers, and we realise that it is not her speaking after all, but a taped recording. The recording continues to read the news impassively, as the men chase her around the room, knocking over the tables and chairs. It is a soundless struggle, intensified, as more and more newsreaders are layered over the single voice. Each with the same intense edge of controlled panic. All reading articles on the May riots. First, one and then the other voice, until you can barely distinguish individual words in the cacophony of sound. Climaxing, as the men catch Isabel and tear her jacket off her, pulling off her shoes, loosening her hair etc.

Lights gradually grow dimmer in the room, until it is completely dark and we can only hear the sound of voices, unbearably loud in the darkness.

As the lights gradually come on, the voices fade away to silence. And there is just Isabel in a crumpled heap on the floor. She tries to speak but her voice is hoarse, she only whispers. Only the people closest to her may be able to hear her. The rest may only hear her muttering to herself.

ISABEL I had a dream last night.

They came and took me, all of them. One by one

They pulled my panties down to my ankles.

And pushed themselves into me, one after the other.

I couldn't keep them out of me.

There was no door to shut.

They tore into me, large and expanding.

They stabbed me again and again with their penises. At least if they had pushed it into my mouth, I would have been able to bite them, with my teeth, but they didn't.

Two of them held my legs apart, as the third tore into me.

There is nothing now. There is nothing.

Only space inside me.

After a while it is not hunger, not anger anymore.

It is not human.

It is the beast come alive.

And I?

I cannot close the space between my thighs.

I cannot clamp it shut.

I will always have a gaping gash inside me.

I cannot shut it.

The gash like a mouth crying in soundless pain.

You shut my mouth with your flesh, seal it with your semen.

I cannot shut it.

I cannot keep it shut.

Don't know. Nothing inside me now. Only space, and tumbling air.

I plunge through the space, the hole inside of me. There is no end to this.

Why don't you say something? Why don't you do something?

Can't you see me? Can't you see?

She reaches out, and realises that she is still clutching a wad of notes in her hand. She uncrumples it slowly, smoothes it out on the floor and looks at it.

It is Ina's Chinese name.

She crouches in the corner, rocking on her heels.

Lights fade.

ACT FOUR: AFTERMATH (BODY COUNT)

The sound of gongs, chiming tunelessly. Narrow spotlight on the smoothed out piece of paper on the floor. Ina is crouched on the floor, in the dark.

INA It's all over now. Or is it?

There is nothing left.

But I saw your face in the mirror. And it could have been my own.

That is why I am here. That is why I am doing this.

Because I heard your voice.

Because the blood that seeps from the cuts in your arm is my own blood.

I will do this for you. I will be your voice.

I will make sense of this, I promise.

This will be my crack in the floor. This will be my chance to live. For you.

The projector throws up one empty rectangle of light onto the stage.

She moves into the centre of the rectangle of light. The light is stark on her face as she begins to speak, slowly gaining confidence as she does so.

She gives her presentation, perhaps she distributes photos, folders.

The following presentation is extracted from the report by the Volunteers Team for humanity, Early Documentation Number 3, entitled 'THE RAPES IN THE SERIES OF RIOTS'. Over the course of Ina's speech, she flashes four tables on the projector, one on each transparency.

As Ina speaks, the men stand in the shadows and recite the rape cases as detailed in Table B. At first, they are barely audible, but as her speech progresses, they get louder and louder, to the point of distraction.

INA Listen to me. I am here to tell you what happened. Someone has to put the pieces together. So that they make sense. So that you know what's going on. So that you can see.

Look. I have a report here, by Tim Relawan Untuk Kemanusiaan (or the Volunteers Team for Humanity). Early Documentation Number 3.

Please turn with me now, to the transparency on the screen.

Table A is flashed on to the screen.

[A. Locations of the Rapes]

These are the places where the rapes and the sexual abuses took place in Jakarta and the surroundings. Note the pattern. If the riot, the massive destruction and burning in May 1998 happened in all areas of Jakarta, the rapes only happened in West Jakarta, North Jakarta, and the other areas where a high concentration of Chinese live and work.

She flashes Table B on the screen.

[B. The Modus Operandi of The Rapes]

As mentioned above, the rapes and riots happened at the same time. The patterns of the rapes were very similar to the modus operandi used in the riot. Surely there must be a relationship between the two tragedies.

Another point to note is that the actors of the incident came from unknown places. They are different from the native residents. In some cases, victims were saved from the rapes by local residents.

She flashes Table C on the screen, even as the men start getting louder and more distracting.

[C. The Victims of Mass Raping]

Among the victims listed as shown, twenty died. The other ones physically and psychologically now are in a very bad condition. Till July 3, 1998, there are 168 persons who admitted that they were victims of mass rape and sexual abuse.

Ina flashes Table D on the screen, giving the noisy men a glare.

[D. Terror to Fact Finding]

Nor are many of the victims' ordeals over yet. Instead...

She pauses, distracted by the men.

Instead they...

She is too distracted to continue. She can't go on. Frustrated, she shouts at the men.

Can you please keep quiet! I can't... I can't concentrate!

The men glare at her, but they lower their voices, mutter sulkily to each other in hushed tones. It is obvious they cannot take very much more. They are on the point of pulling her off the stage.

Instead. Instead, the terror and intimidation continues, targetted both at them, as well as their relatives, volunteers, hospital staff and the doctors who treated them. The characteristics of terror and intimidation are shown in Table D:

Ina flashes the final transparency on screen. A photograph of one of the rape victims, such as the ones that were previously circulated on the Internet. The audience barely has time to register it, when the men dash out. One to shield the sight from the audience, another to tear the photograph off the projector, another to hold Ina back.

Now the following photograph shows...

What are you doing? I'm not done yet. Let me finish my... What.. Give that back. What are you doing? Stop it...

The men snatch her report and her photographs from her. Dart just out of reach even as she lunges for them. They circle her, as they start tearing up the photographs and the report, even as she watches in horror.

What on earth... Stop that! Stop it at once! That's evidence... my proof... Stop it

They keep circling her as they rip the photos into small pieces and fling them at INA, like confetti. As they do so, they spit out the words, one at a time.

At this point, Ina starts speaking as well.

INA

Yes! That is my proof!
What do you want?
No! Don't say that.
Don't talk rubbish. Don't...
That's not fair.
No! No... it's not.

She suddenly realises with a shock what is happening.

And her frustration turns into resignation.

Of course. How stupid of me. I should have guessed.
Why didn't I?
I can't fight with you. You don't even see. You don't even want to see.
That's the easiest, isn't it?

MEN

A Proof
B Evidence
C Facts

A Distortion
B Exaggeration
C Hysteria

A Lies
B Falsehood
C Fiction

INA *(continues)*	**MEN**
You just close your eyes and pretend this never happened. And you stuff your fingers in your ears and pretend you never heard.	**A** Excrement
So lucky, you. So lucky you can't see, can't hear. You're lucky you're blind. And you like being blind. Blind. Deaf. And dumb. So you don't have to worry anymore.	**B** Faeces **C** Manure
You can be happy now. Yes, you're right. The photographs are all fake. They are lies. They are rubbish. They are shit. Cow dung.	**A** Cow dung **B** Horse shit **C** Dog poo
Why do I say this word, rape? Why do I say this awful, terrible word? Don't throw around a word like that.	**A** Half chewed lump of pork fat
Why get so excited? Such ugly pictures. So ugly you can't see them. So ugly they're not true. No, they're not. They cheat. They lie. They're trash.	**B** Pulpy wad of used toilet paper **C** Decomposing heap of roadkill
No proof, no rape. No rape, no sympathy.	**A** Deformed cancer cell **B** Treacherous napalm
I'm sorry. I apologise.	**C** Radioactive waste
I should have screamed louder, so you could hear me.	
I should not have tried to wash the blood off my clothes, should have brought it to you first, yes	

INA *(continues)*

or no or maybe.

I should not have fainted. I should have stayed awake, so I could tell you what happened.

And what else? What else do you need?

You need to touch my body? Touch my scars, my blood, to know that it's mine.

You need to put your hand into my side, and put your finger into the holes in my palms.

You need to taste the tears on my face to check they're salty? So here. Go ahead. What are you waiting for?

Touch me. Taste me. Look at me.

Is this salty enough for you? Is it?

MEN

A Filthy compost-sucking maggot

B Tasteless wad of chewed gum

C Septic, mucus-filled blister

The men swarm around her, reaching towards her with curious hands. They finger her bruises, lick the sweat off her face, taste her tears.

And she finally collapses. The crackling sound of static is heard, louder and louder, as the lights fade down.

In the darkness, Man A is cradling a television set. We can hear faintly the crackle of a lone television screen. See the flickering static screen. No image, nothing. Just shapes that we might imagine in the blankness.

The lights gradually fade up, to show Ina standing alone, in a pool of light.

Man B and C start singing, this familiar old tune.

MAN B/C Smile, though your heart is breaking.
Smile, though you feel like crying.

Somehow, you'll get by...

Man A sits in a corner. He cradles a television set in his arms. The screen flickering with static.

MAN A I hold you in my arms.

When you were a baby, I would carry you sometimes, if your mother let me.

I remember the last time I carried you. You were three.

When your mother put you in my arms, you looked at me and started crying.

And I thought, this is not how it should be. She should be looking up at me, and smiling. But you screamed. And kicked me on the chest and arms. You were so angry. And I couldn't do anything about it.

I didn't want to touch you from then on.

Only when you were sleeping, sometimes. I go into your room, and kiss your forehead.

Scared you'd wake up, and start crying again. But now I'm holding you in my arms.

I can feel your skin and the warmth of your blood on my arms.

And you're not kicking anymore. Not struggling.

Just smiling at me.

And I am happy now.

If there are people shouting at me, I don't hear them.

If there is blood on your face, I don't see it.

I hold you in my blind arms. And kiss you on the forehead.

Lights slowly fade out on him, until all we see is the flickering television screen. We see the silhouette of Isabel/Ina standing alone. Her voice is crumpled with static and bad reception, as she speaks.

ISABEL/INA You had a dream last night.

You dreamt that you were walking through a hallway, full of shattered mirrors.

Every face spiderwebbed with grief. Your own face, yet not.

You reach out to touch the silvered surfaces and meet warm flesh instead.

Skin sticky with unexpected blood. Faces that wince at your touch.

Hands that reach out to catch your own.

And you realise, that these are not mirrors after all, but windows.

And you cannot live without seeing. Without speaking.

You will not live without a purpose.

Nor will you die without a purpose.

You will not.

You will fight until you have no more body left.

Speak until you have no more voice left.

These men that pick up your body, that push you out of your sixth floor window. They cannot stop you now.

There is fire behind you and your thighs are sore.

And you plunged.

Nothing else matters any more.

Only the wind against your cheeks, and the truth of your falling body.

All there is of you.

And you realise. It's not a dream after all.

You're awake. And falling.

Lights fade on Isabel/Ina. The sound of static grows louder and louder. Or perhaps it is the sound of the wind howling through your hair. All we see is the flickering square of static until even that fades into darkness.

Blackout.

The end.

JEAN TAY

Tay graduated in 1997 with a double-degree in creative writing and economics from Brown University, USA. Plays produced include *Senang* (2014), *Sisters* (2013), *Boom* (2008, 2009, 2012), *Everything but the Brain* (2005, 2007, 2013), *Plunge* (2001, 2009), *Hopper's Women* (co-written with Cindy Koh, 2000), *The Knot* (1999) and *Water from the Well* (1998). She has also written the books for musicals *The Admiral's Odyssey* (2005), *Man of Letters* (2006) and *Pinocchio* (2010). Her plays have been performed in Singapore, the US, the UK, and Italy. She attended the prestigious month-long International Playwriting Residency in 2007, organised by the Royal Court Theatre in London and has also participated in LaMama's International Playwrights' Retreat in Umbria, Italy in 2010.

In 2000, her play *The Knot* was awarded first prize for Action Theatre's 10-minute Play Competition and selected as a finalist for the Actors Theatre of Louisville's 10-minute Play Contest. She has been nominated four times for Best Original Script for the Life! Theatre Awards, and won for *Everything But the Brain* in 2006. For her fiction, she was awarded the Weston Prize for Fiction from Brown University, as well as the first and third prizes for the National Arts Council's Golden Point Short Story competition in 1995 and 2001 respectively.

Tay's most recent projects include being scriptwriter for the 2015 National Day Parade Golden Jubilee celebration and collaborating with Drama Box on the verbatim theatre piece *It Won't Be Too Long: The Cemetery* for the Singapore International Arts Festival 2015. She presented her latest play, *The Shape of a Bird* at the M1 Fringe Festival 2016. She was attached to the Singapore Repertory Theatre (SRT) as resident playwright from 2006–2009, and has been helming SRT's Young Company Writing Programme since 2012. She was also writer-in-residence at the Nanyang Technological University in 2013 and is currently an adjunct lecturer in playwriting there. Her plays *Everything but the Brain* and *Boom* have been published by Epigram Books, and *Everything but the Brain* is currently used as an 'O' and 'N' Level literature text for secondary school students.

Tay is the founding Artistic Director of Saga Seed Theatre, set up in 2015 to bring Singaporean stories to the stage, and provide a platform to showcase and nurture local talent.

Playwright's Note

I wrote *An Evening at the Opera* for three specific actors whom I have always admired. I could hear their voices, I could visualize their attacks, I could see them in rehearsal and in performance.

This may sound just a bit vain, but what I also wanted to create was a play that would bring the acting schools and styles of three very different companies together on the same stage: Ana for Repertory Philippines, Frances for Dulaang UP and Tad for Tanghalang Pilipino.

Now, since I could see and hear the actors already, I knew that if I ventured to direct the play, I would bring nothing new to the text outside of what I had imagined in writing. Instinct told me that a fresh eye, and a more daring touch was needed. Jomari Jose was the director I chose. Aside from being great friends, I always trusted his judgement as a colleague. He was my assistant director on many projects, from grand opera to pop concerts and fashion shows before he ventured out to directing on his own. I asked him if he would do it. I am so glad that he said 'yes'.

Jom brought a stillness to the play that made the piece all the more effective. This was particularly evident in the brutal scene where Bingo savages Miranda. In the text, he begins to maul her after she confronts him for his piggish ways. I had envisioned the hulking Tad throwing the frail Ana about as he said his lines. Jom made Bingo savage Miranda after his speech, after a moment of icy silence where Yolanda just glares at her social inferior of a husband. The effect was all the more chilling because the savagery came out of nowhere.

I often wonder if any other actors can play the roles of Miranda, Bingo and Mamang. I know that this must be a defeatist thing to say, since playwrights always hope that other actors will allow their creations to live on. But those who saw Ana, Tad and Frances in Jom's exquisitely elegant and brutal production, may agree with me that they are a tough act to follow.

Editor's Note

At times the characters break into Tagalog, revealing their native tongue. Meaning is generally clear and pronunciation can easily be found for a production. If more translation is needed, please discuss with the playwright.

AN EVENING AT THE OPERA

FLOY QUINTOS

First performed at Virgin Lab Fest, June 2011.
Directed by Jomari Jose.

Characters

MIRANDA BELOTO – the Governor's wife
BINGO BELOTO – the Governor
MAMANG – Miranda's mother

Cast

MIRANDA – Ana Abad Santos
BINGO – Jonathan Tadioan
MAMANG – Frances Makil Ignaciao

Time

The present. One evening.

Setting

In the master's bedroom of the Governor's mansion, in some distant, unspecified province of the Philippines.

The only set pieces needed are a woman's dresser and large bed, on which have been laid out a man's suit and a jusi barong Tagalog.[1] *At the foot of the bed, a polished pair of men's evening shoes. Both set pieces must help to convey an atmosphere of intimate luxury.*

1. A woven man's shirt, usually translucent silk, often embellished with embroidery. Worn outside the trousers.

Miranda is sitting at her dresser, doing her face. She is of an undetermined age, well-preserved and stylish in a simple evening gown.

Mamang sits at a corner of the bed, watching Miranda as she does her make-up. Miranda never looks at her during the conversation.

Somewhere in the house, Bellini's 'Casta Diva' from 'Norma' is playing softly.

MAMANG He's late again, hija.[2]

MIRANDA He'll be here in a while, Mamang.[3] Huffing and puffing and making a scene...

MAMANG He will make a scene? He's the one who's late.

MIRANDA He'll put the blame on everyone. His aides, my aides... he'll swear a blue streak and maybe even throw a few things around.

MAMANG Que horrible.[4]

Naku[5]... naku, baka[6] naman he did something again. Something awful...

MIRANDA Mamang, he has people like Ponce to do it for him.

MAMANG Aber, what does he do then?

MIRANDA He makes... calls.

MAMANG Same thing.

That last scandal... Hesus![7] A radioman... gunned down in front of his own family. For saying things against the governor, allegations... And you? You went to the wake–

MIRANDA – and paid for the funeral and gave the children scholarships.

MAMANG That didn't stop the talk, Miranda. That's what I mean, hija... your role. You make him look good again.

---

2. Hija – daughter; derived from Spanish language
3. Mamang – mother; commonly used for mothers of well-to-do family
4. Que horrible [Spanish] – how ugly; expression of disgust
5. Naku – Filipino expression, no direct translation
6. Baka – maybe
7. Hesus – Jesus; also used as expression

MIRANDA I was just following your advice, Mamang... remember?

MAMANG Oh – yes. Should I say I'm sorry, hija?

MIRANDA Too late for that, Mamang.

MAMANG We needed the Belotos, hija. You understand?

MIRANDA Yes, Mamang.

MAMANG How was I to know he'd turn out to be such a monster? I mean, even in your Papang[8]'s day... it was never so... so vulgar. And you're alright? He doesn't beat you?

MIRANDA He doesn't hit me, if that's what you mean.

MAMANG So, you're alright?

Miranda does not answer. She goes on doing her face.

MAMANG Why not leave without him? Go by yourself.

MIRANDA I could. But... it wouldn't look right. You would never have gone alone, Mamang.

MAMANG You're right, hija. It would cause talk. I haven't been the best example, I know, but–

MIRANDA – Go away, Mamang.

MAMANG – Your own mother. Well, I'm not surprised. You think this is all my fault. You don't understand.

MIRANDA I didn't have a choice.

MAMANG Oh you did, Miranda. Even I had a choice. But what did we choose? *(Beat)* Your lipstick is too red, Miranda.

MIRANDA It's the opera, Mamang. Nothing can be too red. Now, go away please.

MAMANG I am always here for you, Miranda. Now, that I'm gone, I can always be here for you–

A noise, outside the bedroom.

MIRANDA He's coming, Mamang. I can hear the racket.

MAMANG If he even tries to hit you, I'll... I'll–

---

8 Papang – father; commonly used for the father of a well-to-do family.

MIRANDA Rise from the dead and hit him back? Please Mamang... *(Beat)* Now, go away, be a good, dead mother and just fade away into the shadows... I can handle him...

MAMANG You had a choice, hija. You could have said no. You could have run away.

MIRANDA You didn't.

MAMANG And look where I am now.

MIRANDA Good bye, Mamang.

MAMANG Tell him what you know. That always gave me the upper hand, with your Papang. Are you listening, Miranda?

MIRANDA Yes, Mamang. Now go away, please. The Governor is in the house...

Mamang recedes into the shadows. All throughout the ensuing scene, she remains present. When she joins in the conversation, neither Miranda or Bingo ever look at her.

MIRANDA ... Big Boss Bingo Beloto... in five... four... three... two...

Bingo suddenly enters. A huge swaggering male presence. There are sweat stains on his rumpled shirtjack, and his hair and face are greasy. As he speaks, he disrobes leaving his clothes on the floor and on the bed. He has a .45 gun tucked under his belt, which he also throws on the bed.

BINGO Hon'? Miranda? Ya... ya, okay, I'm late again. 'Tang inang mga tao yan.[9] Ayaw akong pakawalan. I had to shake every hand, pose for pictures with everybody.

You know, Miranda, even the poorest people in the barangays have cellphones... with cameras ha!

Shet,[10] I had to beg off... "Ma'am Miranda is waiting for me. Alam niyo naman si Ma'am Miranda niyo. Always so proper. Never na-la-late yan. You want to know the truth about Big Boss Bingo ha? Isa lang ang kinatatakutan ko [There's only one I fear. Your

---

9. 'Tang ina or putang ina – a Filipino curse; literally means 'bitch mother', or 'your mother is a whore'

10. Shet – shit

Ma'am Miranda] Si Ma'am Miranda nyo!" Putang ina, that always gets them.

Miranda does not respond. She doesn't even look at him, she goes on unperturbed, fixing her make-up.

BINGO I'm here, okay... don't be angry na[11] at me. I was trying to call you to say that I might be late, but you weren't picking up. So, I called Narcing na. He said that you were with the singers, but I told him to tell you that I'd be late.

O, let's go?

Bingo has stripped down to his equally sweaty undershirt and boxer shorts. Miranda gives him a look of withering contempt.

Then she looks away.

BINGO Okay, okay! So I told Ponce to call Narcing. Eh, he called him naman daw. Narcing got the message naman. He didn't tell you? Your aide didn't tell you? Aba eh,[12] that's not my problem. What do I pay that person for, if he can't get my messages to you? 'Namputcha,[13] I'll fire him! But you don't like naman. O, I'll fire him na. tomorrow. I'll do it. 'Namputcha, I can do it even if you don't want.

Miranda...? Miranda! *(She remains silent)* Ah, okay... I get the point. Cold shoulder ha? So, what if I said I don't want to go out tonight? What if I said, putcha,[14] I'm tired. I don't wanna go out and smile and wave at people. I'm tired.

He sits on the bed.

BINGO I told you naman[15] yesterday. I had to meet with the leaders of the Beloto Youth Association this afternoon. Tell them how to be on guard against leftist elements out to destabilize our province. 'Namputcha, Miranda, you should have come with me. I asked you to come with me but you were too busy organizing this...

---

11. Na – no direct translation; use to stress something in a sentence
12. Aba or aba eh! – an interjection meaning Well!
13. Namputcha or anak ng puta – Filipino slang for son of a bitch
14. Putcha, namputcha or anak ng puta – a Filipino slang for son of a bitch
15. Naman – generally used as a prefix; could also mean again

this palabas[16] in the capitolyo. 'Tang ina, you should have seen them, the Beloto Youth brigade!

'Tang ina... naka-tsinelas at t-shirt na punit lahat! [Everyone is wearing slippers and torn shirts!] Putang. And these were the leaders ha? Punyeta...[17]

Hoy... Hoy! I'm talking to you!

Miranda lets out a sigh and looks at him. But as soon as Bingo begins talking, she goes back to her make-up.

BINGO I thought, baka naman [maybe] you should ask some of your fancy Manila friends to donate uniforms. Just so my Beloto boys will be presentable. That's something you can do for me, Miranda. Something we can work on together.

Putres naman,[18] Miranda, talk to me. Help me dress. You know I hate getting all dressed up.

Miranda...? Miranda!

Miranda finally gets up. She moves to the bed and picks out the suit jacket and throws it at Bingo.

BINGO Tux? Eh punyeta, I'm not going to wear a tux in the capitolyo. That's not me... that's not my style.

If you want, I can go in my dirty shirt jack, so the people will see that their governor is a working man... a real working man. Not some phony. "Look at Gov, even at the musical play his wife brought into town, he still looks our Big Boss Bingo."

I'm not wearing that shit tux. (*Bingo throws the jacket on the bed. Non-plussed, Miranda gets up and hands him the barong tagalog)*

BINGO Long sleeves? Polo barong nalang. You want? I know... I know. I'll look like my own goddamned bodyguards. You always say that, hindi ba? [right?] O, for you... for you, Miranda... for you...

---

16. Palabas – show
17. Punyeta – often used to express agitation or disappointment
18. Putres or putrages – Filipino slang for damn; used when someone is agitated

Bingo tries to get the barong over his head. But he is too impatient. It rips. He tries to maneouver himself into the barong, as it continues to rip. All the while, he continues to fume.

BINGO Putang ina naman. If you're going to be angry at me... aba, eh, puta... I won't go with you. You go alone. You and your amigas enjoy that musical play. See if the common tao [people] like it. See if they understand it. See if they care. See if they stay when they see that I'm not around to escort you.

Buti nga.[19] They can see how you forced me to spend a million pesos to bring them some art and culture. Musical play, leche...[20]

Leche, it doesn't fit! 'Tang inang yan!

Bingo gives up and throws the barong on the bed.

Miranda finally faces him.

MIRANDA It's an opera, Bingo! (*She grabs the suit jacket and holds it up*) And this is not a tux! (*She grabs the poor, mangled barong*) And this was a perfectly beautiful barong until you mangled it. And Ponce didn't call Narcing.

Narcing was calling Ponce, and only because you weren't picking up your phone. I called, Bingo, from the reception for the singers... at the rehearsal, where I told them you would come... and you never picked up. Ponce didn't pick up his phone. No phone... no radio... I mean, where were you?

BINGO Punyeta, you go alone. I'm staying home...

From where she stands, Mamang joins in.

MAMANG Tell him what you know!

MIRANDA Where were you? You were with Eva!

BINGO No!

MAMANG He's lying...

BINGO I told you I don't see her anymore! Puta naman–

MAMANG – Oye, the language...

---

19. Buti nga or mabuti nga sa yo – meaning 'good for you' (used sarcastically here)
20. Leche – curse word – derived from the Spanish, it literally means 'milk', but is also slang for 'semen'

MIRANDA Oh my God! Bingo, did you just hear yourself? Did you really just hear yourself? Punyeta... milagro! [miracle!]

BINGO Milagro?

MIRANDA You didn't tell a lie!

BINGO How do you know?

MAMANG Tell him now!

MIRANDA I called her!

BINGO You called Eva?

MIRANDA Yes, Bingo. I called Eva. I asked her, "Is my husband with you? What time did he leave? Is he on his way here?"

MAMANG Huli ka! [Gotcha!]

BINGO Punyeta kayo–

MAMANG Kayo? [You?]

BINGO – ni Eva! Talking to each other.

MIRANDA – I mean, why not? I thought Eva was the only one I really liked. The only one I felt I could talk to... I mean, she went to school in Manila. Those other girls? My God, don't get me started. Bagabag High School? And that other one, Adriana... the one from Pegasus? I thought for a while, stupid me, that Pegasus was a school. A modelling school, finishing school... something?

... I don't know... but Ponce told me. Or he told Narcing... when I asked Narcing to find out where Pegasus finishing school was so I could talk to the director about that Alyssa... or Adriana... Or something? I don't know anymore...

MAMANG Hesus. You know, your Papang would never stoop that low!

BINGO You talked to Adriana?

MAMANG – His women were all collegialas...

MIRANDA – And the one before her... and the other one, Miss Bagabag High School.

MAMANG – Hesus, mga mambubukid! [Jesus, what peasants!]

BINGO – You're crazy!

MAMANG My beautiful Miranda, competing with the daughters of the mambubukid! [peasant farmers!]

MIRANDA They never told you? Of course, they never told you.

MIRANDA I told them not too. After all... I only wanted to know if they were clean...

BINGO Clean?

MIRANDA Of course, clean. I can't stop you, Bingo... I know that. So, it matters to me that they are clean.

BINGO What's clean?

MAMANG Hay, que bobo [what an idiot] this husband of yours...

MIRANDA Clean! Haaay...

BINGO Ahhh... You called Eva?

MIRANDA You can say we've become... close.

BINGO Shet, Miranda... that's invasion of privacy.

MIRANDA No. I'm just–

BINGO Just what?

MIRANDA Just being a good... politician. My mother used to do that.

MAMANG Yes, I would!

MIRANDA She would call Papang's queridas [mistresses] and try to make them friends. Okay, maybe not close friends. Just keep them near enough to know what they were doing, what Papang was doing. What they did in private, Mamang never asked...

MAMANG – That would have been vulgar.

MIRANDA – So it's not what you think.

BINGO – Not what?

MIRANDA Invasion of privacy. You just said it. Mamang told me that when we were married. "Hija, you're marrying into a political family. Just like ours, but not as old. Warlords, hija... can you live with that? Well, you must – "

MAMANG For you and me, hija–

MIRANDA – Your Papang needs the alliance with the Belotos. That Bingo Beloto will be governor of this province in a few years. I know, hija he's... a bit of a goon. Right now, it's not important.

MAMANG We never had sons, and you always felt that politics was beneath you. What are we to do, you and me, when your Papang goes? Someone has to take care of us.

BINGO Mamang called me a goon?

MIRANDA That's not the word she used, of course...

MAMANG – Sanggalo! That's what I said! Not goon! Hija naman

MIRANDA It's not important. She said, "Miranda... you must give your husband Class!"

MAMANG – Respectability!

MIRANDA And even if you don't love him now... well, you will learn–

BINGO – learn?

MAMANG – to love him nga! Oye, que bobo...

MIRANDA – "And if you don't, at least keep a good public face. Never fight in public. Represent him well in front of the voters... and make sure you know his queridas. Invite them to your bridge club... or make them members of your ladies' committees... or something – "

MAMANG The best way... the most civil way, hija, is to keep an eye on them! It worked for me!

BINGO Ladies committees... ha!

MIRANDA Mamang was wrong there–

MAMANG – I was?

MIRANDA – Boy, was she ever wrong. I mean, Miss Bagabag High School on my Cultural Committee? Miss Adriana Pegasus in the Ladies for Barrio Literacy Association!

MAMANG Tama nga naman. [Yeah, right.] They'd look...

BINGO Stupid.

MIRANDA The others, yes. Eva, no. Eva has class. But she says you don't call her anymore.

BINGO Putcha, you think I want to call her now? After what you told me?

MIRANDA Bingo, she is the only one I can talk to. In English. Straight English. That's beside the point. Eva's decent.

MAMANG – If you can call any querida decent–

MIRANDA But no. You want them cheap and tarty. And young. *(Beat)* Keep Eva.

MAMANG I would say that too...

BINGO Shut up...

MIRANDA I don't mind... I promise, I do not mind. She's a good girl.

BINGO You stop talking like that, Miranda...

MIRANDA – I tell her how to handle you. And she promised not to embarrass me in public, and to keep herself clean.

BINGO Putcha, shut up!

MAMANG No bastards, remember!

MIRANDA – And no babies. Never.

BINGO Shut up, godammit! I said, shut up!

MIRANDA And she loves you too. Did you know that? You said you would buy her a house in Los Angeles.

MAMANG No!

MIRANDA She asked me if she should accept it. And I said, all the houses we've bought are in San Francisco and the Bay area. So Eva would be just a drive away. But she said she would never accept it.

BINGO I did not buy her a house in Los Angeles!

MIRANDA No. You bought her a condo in Manila. That, she accepted.

MAMANG Aba naku! Que es aventurera! [What a golddigger!]

BINGO – We're late–

MAMANG Miranda, that's your money too! So that's your condo!

MIRANDA I told her to accept it. I said "Eva, Bingo will never marry you. He can never leave me. Take the condo."

A beat.

MAMANG Good point.

BINGO Leche kayo!

MAMANG The language in this house!

Bingo fumes for a minute Then changes the subject.

BINGO So, are we going out tonight or not? We're late for the musical play! You're stupid, asshole musical play!

MIRANDA It's an opera, Bingo.

BINGO 'Tang ina...

MIRANDA – in Italian.

BINGO So, how will the masa [masses] understand it? Will the voters appreciate it?

MIRANDA I had programs printed, with the synopsis in Filipino.

BINGO You think they read?

MIRANDA If my Ladies for Barrio Literacy Association is doing their work, then that shouldn't be a problem.

BINGO Putcha naman, Miranda... Italian opera. Fat singers? Why not pop concerts? Good, catchy music that they hear on the radio or on television?

MAMANG He has a point. The constituents...

MIRANDA I'm so, so tired of that–

BINGO – Beauty contests... Miss Gay...

MAMANG – something entertaining–

MIRANDA Please... I've crowned enough rural beauties in my life.

BINGO – Basketball All Stars! Boxing exhibition...

MAMANG – Dog show! Fashion show! Horticultural exhibit!

BINGO – What's wrong with good, old-fashioned sports! Something manly! Bagay sa image ko. [Something that suits my image.]

MIRANDA Done to death. Every birthday of yours.

BINGO – Something they like, something I like! Something we understand!

MAMANG – He has a point, hija. The voters.

MIRANDA But it's *my* birthday! *(A stunned silence)* My birthday, Bingo...

MAMANG Oh, my dear... oh my darling dear Miranda... I forgot...

Bingo hems and haws for a while, then finally, blabbers.

BINGO Shit...! Shit...! 'Tang ina! Why didn't Ponce tell me? Or Narcing? They didn't remind me... Putang ina yang dalawang yan. [Damn those two.] They're fired... I promise. Patay sila sa akin... [They're dead to me.] I'm sorry...

An awkward silence, which Mamang breaks.

MAMANG I'm dead! I don't remember birthdays... but your husband!

BINGO I'm sorry, Miranda... I'm really sorry... hon?

MIRANDA Forgiven.

BINGO I... I... don't have a gift...

MIRANDA Oh, but you do.

MAMANG Hija, ask for something... something expensive...

BINGO – I do?

MIRANDA You paid to bring the entire Manila Philharmonic here, and a full-length production of Mascagni's Cavalleria Rusticana. Right here, in the capitolyo.

MAMANG That's what you wanted for your birthday??

MIRANDA What? Another house in San Francisco? Another condo in Hong Kong?

MAMANG More jewellery?

MIRANDA What do I need that for? Please, Bingo...

BINGO But that's good investment of our money!

MAMANG – Only if it's a joint account! They're joint accounts, aren't they, Miranda?

MIRANDA But I want to hear singing, Bingo! *Bel Canto*...

MAMANG The properties are in your name? Well, are they?

BINGO What the fuck is *bel canto!*

MIRANDA Beautiful singing!

MAMANG You wanted to study opera? But you never told me... when you were young, you liked the Madonna...

MIRANDA – An evening of beautiful singing...

BINGO In Italian?

MIRANDA You don't understand, Bingo.

BINGO Since when did you like opera?

MAMANG You never told me! I would have sent you to study–

BINGO Since when ha?

MAMANG – In Milano! In the conservatory–

MIRANDA It just occurred to me, when I went to watch the opera at La Scala. With the speaker's wife... last summer. It was beautiful...

MAMANG What did you watch, hija?

MIRANDA I don't remember what it was we saw. Isn't that funny? But it was a tragedy... a woman deceived, her lover killed... I'm not sure anymore. But I know how it made me feel, Bingo.

BINGO You don't speak Italian.

MIRANDA It doesn't matter. I understood it... somehow. The scenery, the costumes... the music. The music, above all. And all that hatred and deception and anger in the story. All made beautiful, dramatic... All that ugliness in human nature made bearable.

MAMANG My daughter, a patroness of the arts... I am so proud...

MIRANDA I just connected. And I said, this... this is something I want to bring to the province. No matter the cost... the people, our people should experience this.

BINGO They'll laugh–

MIRANDA They'd be too scared to do it out loud. And when you and I applaud, they'll all applaud. It will be a success. And good for your image.

BINGO I paid a million pesos... for Italian songs?

MIRANDA I told you! You never listen. It doesn't make the slightest dent in your budget, Bingo. You know that.

BINGO 'Tang ina, I could have built classrooms with that money–

MIRANDA You could, but you didn't... so the opera it will have to be.

BINGO *Okay...*! Okay. It's your birthday, hon'... I'll do this for you. O, let's go.

Bingo pulls on a shirt, and the jacket, all the while fuming. As he does, Mamang speaks.

MAMANG O, he's making up to you. He's conceded na. You won!

BINGO 'Tang ina, kundi mo lang birthday... [Damn, if it's not only your birthday...] O, I look good enough for you? Do I? Do I live up to your standards ha? Because you look really classy, hon'...

MAMANG Say something nice. He's trying to be nice.

BINGO Sabagay [Anyway], you always look classy...

MAMANG – Quick before the mood passes. Say he looks guwapo [handsome]... Lie!

Except for his shoes, Bingo is done dressing. He presents himself to Miranda.

BINGO O, okay na? [Oh, OK now?] Let's go...

Miranda does not move.

MIRANDA So where were you today?

Bingo pauses a moment. He cannot look at Miranda.

BINGO I told you. With the Beloto Youth Association leaders.

MIRANDA And what did you talk about?

BINGO – The leftist threat.

MIRANDA and?

BINGO and how to eradicate it.

MIRANDA – through?

BINGO ... education.

MIRANDA ... hmmm...

BINGO – and good moral values.

MIRANDA – values...

BINGO and sports... exercise...

Miranda starts to laugh.

BINGO What the shit are you laughing at? 'Tang ina...

MIRANDA Bingo! Big Boss Bingo! You and I know, your Beloto Youth Association leaders in their tsinelas [slippers] and torn t-shirts know, this whole province knows that education, good moral values, sports and exercise can never eradicate the leftist threat. There is no leftist threat here. At least, none that's too dangerous for you to care about. You just shoot anything that moves up there–

MAMANG – In your Papang's time, there was no NPA[21]–

MIRANDA – Shoot anything that moves!

MAMANG – Everyone in this province was happy and content–

MIRANDA – That way, there's no one around to stop you from selling everything–

BINGO You know what? You may know some things about that bel canto shit, but you don't know how to run this place!

MIRANDA Oh, but I do, Bingo. It takes fear!

BINGO It takes real discipline, and an iron fist – my iron fist!

---

21. NPA – New People's Army.

MIRANDA – and deals!

BINGO 'Tang ina, I have what it takes to run this shithole province–

MIRANDA – private armies in tsinelas and torn t-shirts–

BINGO – Shut up!

MIRANDA Everyone on the take!–

BINGO – Don't question me. You have no right to question me!

MIRANDA I don't? I don't? Big Boss Bingo naman, you're talking to me, Miranda, your wife, your partner, your lady! I know everything, baby!

I'm a good wife. I do the laundry–

MAMANG You do the laundry?!

MIRANDA – And you know what I mean by laundry, don't you?

MAMANG Oh.

MIRANDA I always know when you've been a bad boy, Bingo. Because you suddenly turn – nice. "Hon," – Hon? – "Hon, we have some extra money from logging" – from logging! As if Papang left any logs in the mountains–

MAMANG Your Papang was not an illegal logger–

MIRANDA – "We need to get it into the account in San Francisco. Or Macau. Or Florida. Would you like to travel, hon? Take a vacation? Go shopping?" And I know what it is you really want me to do, and I know how to do it without looking suspicious. Without being conspicuous. People take one look at me at the airports and at the banks, and they don't suspect a thing. "She's the daughter of a governor. Her mom was a famous society figure. Of course, Miranda Beloto travels frequently. Of course, she banks internationally. She's done it all her life!" Stupid, stupid blind people...

I give you class, Bingo. That's what I do, that's my primary, wifely duty to you. I give you class. Miss Bagabag High School and Adriana Pegasus could never, ever walk through an airport or go into a bank without people thinking – or laughing out loud.

BINGO Enough, putcha! I said enough–

MIRANDA – And this opera you don't want to go to? Listen, Bingo, one day, one day when all this comes toppling over your pig's head, you can always say, "What corruption? What graft? I used the money to bring opera to my province! Art and culture at one million pesos a pop! I even have the papers to prove it! My wife, my beloved Miranda, it was her program for Arts and Culture. Opera in the capitolyo! What graft? What corruption? I gave my province... an Opera Season – "

BINGO That's your plan ha? That's your stupid plan?

MIRANDA – You want to hear another one? Maybe, Eva and I should work together? You see, that's why I want you to keep her, Bingo. She can do it too! She can tag along with me for a while until she gets the hang of it and then, she can do it on her own. No suspicions. Can you see it now, Bingo? The two women in your life most likely to hate each other, traveling together, laundering together! Co-conspirators! Big Boss Bingo's laundry bimbos! The classiest lavanderas around!

BINGO 'Tang ina, I said enough–

MIRANDA So where were you, huh? Making another deal? Who with, Bingo? Army? Big business? Foreign investors? Did you sell more offshore fishing rights? Strip mining in the mountains? Oh, but you've done that already.

I know! A nuclear reactor that'll blow this province apart one day! But you and I don't need to be afraid because we'll be in San Francisco! How much did you make on the deal today, Gov? How much am I suppose to launder this time, Bingo? I need to know. I'm your wife, and I do the dirty work too. I have a right to know!

BINGO 'Tang ina ka! Why are you doing this to me?

MIRANDA Because 'tang ina ka rin. Sometimes, someone just has to give it to you, Bingo! In the face! Yes, someone has tell you how rotten you are. You and your goons and your deals and your pig ways! Rotten to the core, baby! To the core!

Bingo has had enough. He grabs Miranda by the shoulders and shakes her violently.

BINGO Leche ka, alam mo? [You're a bitch, do you know that?] Ha? I took you and your broken-down family that this province was so tired of, and we made a deal, your Papang and I! Cover up his mess, take over his deals, his concessions. And you knew, you, you little shit, you knew you'd be a part of it. You knew! So don't come around now and try to lecture me. Not me... not Big Boss Gov. Bingo Beloto. You hear...?

Ako pa, [me] Miranda? Putang ina! Ako pa?

He throws her down on the bed and straddles her, pinning her hands down. Miranda tries to struggle.

BINGO Class? Putang ina, you got class, pero you wanna know something? You're rotten too, Miranda. More rotten than I am! At least, I don't hide behind any shit class.

Where's your class now ha? Ha? Here's some class!

Bingo raises his hand to strike her. Miranda cowers and covers her face with her hands. Bingo stops suddenly, and slides off the bed, onto the floor.

BINGO Why do you do this to me? Why do we have to fight like this? We have to be partners, Miranda – just like your Papang and Mamang wanted us to be. Let's be partners, so we can build a better future for this province...

I'm sorry... I'm sorry... I'm sorry. I won't do it again... just don't push me, OK? Not me... I'm sorry...

He rises from the floor and gets into the bed, trying to hold Miranda.

BINGO I love you. You know I do, hon... I do. I'm sorry. Just don't push me...

Miranda pushes him away. She gets off the bed and staggers to her dressing table.

Bingo gets up.

BINGO Get fixed up. We're late for the opera. The people want to see the Governor and his lady. We'll all sing 'Happy Birthday' to you...

He puts his shoes on, and prepares to go. Then, he stops.

BINGO Sya nga pala.[22] About the opera? I get it. I like it. The season... that's not a bad idea. That's real class, huh? I think I may get to like it. You'll teach me, hon'.

You'll teach us all.

He starts to walk off. Miranda stops him.

MIRANDA Bingo, where were you this afternoon?

Bingo turns and smiles broadly.

BINGO Surprise! Later, hon, we'll talk about later. After our evening at the opera... Now, hurry up. Our people are waiting for some Art and Culture.

Bingo walks off.

MAMANG Hija...

MIRANDA Go away, Mamang.

MAMANG Why do you do this to him? Why? You bring it on yourself.

Miranda speaks as she smoothes her hair and retouches her lipstick.

MIRANDA It only happens once in a while... when we need to know how awful we've become. You know, he's right, I'm rotten too, Mamang, deep inside.

MAMANG This is my fault...

Miranda does not answer. She is almost ready to go.

MAMANG I know this will sound stupid... coming from me... But you can go, hija. You can walk away. I would. Your Papang – he never, never treated me that way... hija–

Miranda turns suddenly and slaps Mamang in the face.

MIRANDA Please, Mamang. We're late for the opera.

Miranda turns and goes.

Lights down.

The end.

---

22. Means 'by the way'

FLOY QUINTOS

Writer/Director Floy Quintos is well-known for his plays and musicals. He is the owner of the Art Gallery Deus in Manila. He has also been involved in the *Songs For Heroes* concerts and has written screenplays such as *Wating* (*The Tough Guys*) 1992, the last film directed by Philippine National Artist for Film Ishmael Bernal. He directed *Ang Bagong Harana*, a showcase of Filipino music for the Philippines Opera Company.

His plays include:

St. Louis Loves Dem Filipinos – First produced as a straight play in 1991, then as a full-length musical in 2005.

Atang: Dulang May Musika – A full-length play on the life and times of Atang De La Rama, star of the zarzuela and wife of nationalist Amado Hernandez.

Isang Panaginip na Fili – A daring, revisionist take on Rizal's *El Filibusterismo*, juxtaposing the plot of the novel with Rizal's tortured process of writing.

Fake – An examination of the various hoaxes that have become a part of the Filipino psyche. From religious visionaries, to the Tasaday, to the controversial Code of Kalantiao. The play asks, 'When is a lie better than the truth?'

Ang Kalungkutan Ng Mga Reyna – First Prize, Palanca Memorial Awards for Literature One-Act Play in Pilipino, 2008.

An Evening At The Opera – First Prize, Palanca Memorial Awards for Literature One-Act Play in English, 2011.

Suor Clara – Second Prize, Palanca Memorial Awards for Literature One-Act Play in Pilipino, 2010.

Shock Value – A biting, unapologetic look at the world of television. The lies, the fabrication, the delightful madness. A circus of a show.

Fluid – Second Prize, Palanca Memorial Awards for Literature Full-Length Play in English, 2005.

THE NIGHT OF THE MINOTAUR

TEW BUNNAG

Characters

MINOTAUR/MAN – a creature with the head of a bull and the body of a man.

OLD WOMAN – an old blind woman, once maid to Pasiphae.

OLD MAN

MINOS – King of Crete.

PASIPHAE – the King's wife.

THESEUS – a legendary hero.

PRIME MINISTER – to the King (PM).

CHORUS – 3 young homeless citizens (2 male, 1 female)

OVERTURE

In the darkness there is the sound of a timpani drum roll, faint at first then steady rising to an almost deafening pitch.

(On a big screen) The image of a giant tsunami wave crashing down. Cities destroyed.

Darkness once more. Silence.

Stage begins to lighten.

Out of the darkness at the back of the stage and into the light, the strong figure of a man in rags slowly walks towards the audience. He has a faded red scarf wound round his head, long, white hair sticking out of the sides, and a straggly beard. He carries a stick and a shoulder bag. He mumbles to himself and hums a tune as he looks around him. Finally he sits on a rock and slowly unwinds his red scarf. Now he kneels to the ground, pats the earth, takes a handful of soil, brings it up close to his face, smelling it and letting it run slowly through his palm. Then takes a big breath and looks around him. He keeps shaking his head in puzzlement, as though he half-recalls where he is. Finally he gets up onto his feet and speaks to no one in particular.

MAN It's all gone! All gone. They told me what had happened. I didn't believe it. Had to come back to see for myself.

Again he turns this way and that as though to establish his bearings.

MAN But I never imagined the senses could bring back such memories. After so long, the scent of the pine resin, the taste of the sea in the morning breeze! It's as though I never left. Ah, what simple pleasures!

Especially when one has come full circle. *(He smiles)*

I went away looking for what I thought I was deprived of. I went after knowledge. I travelled the world. I lived the endless round of experience. I tasted the pleasures of love, the horrors of war. I visited magnificent cities. I conversed with famous and important people...

He pauses and scratches his head.

MAN You know what? When it comes down to it, ignorance and desire are the same everywhere.

When I was tired of it all I turned away from all the earthly distractions and I looked inward. I did strange practices. I used substances. I had visions beyond our limited minds. I followed wise men even though I couldn't understand half of what they were saying.

He laughs.

MAN And the freedom I so longed for? My conclusion? Freedom is really here, *(points to his head)*, here, *(points to his heart)*, here, *(points to his balls)* and so is the prison, by the way.

He walks around in silence.

MAN You know, sometimes, we have to go a great distance to see what is in front of our eyes.

He gets up and begins to execute a slow dance in front of the rock.

Fade out on the man.

End of Overture.

ACT ONE
SCENE 1

King Minos' ante-chamber. Daytime.

The King sits by a small table, on which there is a jug of wine and some goblets. He is slightly turned away from his wife Queen Pasiphae who stands tense and upset as she waits for him to respond to her question.

MINOS *(angrily)* No. The whole plan has been set in motion.

PASIPHAE Then change your plan!

MINOS It cannot be changed. Besides, I have no choice.

PASIPHAE Please, I beg you to reconsider. Is it really necessary?

MINOS *(his anger rising)* Why do you keep insisting? I don't have to explain to you things you do not understand.

PASIPHAE But why now? What will it solve?

MINOS *(turning to her)* It will solve everything. It has to be done. Call it destiny!

PASIPHAE Ha! We both know destiny has nothing to do with it. It's not his fault he became what he is. He had no say in the matter. You forced it upon him, as you forced it on me.

MINOS Yes, because he was the fruit of your lust...

PASIPHAE No, it was because of your greed! Your ambition! You needed him for your own purposes. Now, he's no longer useful to you. But I'm not sure you have thought it through.

MINOS You question me, whore? I could have had him slaughtered when he came out of your womb, and you along with him. But I spared him. And you. That made the god Poseidon angry. Now it's time for your offspring to play his part in the story. That is the end of it.

PASIPHAE But he is the one innocent in your scheme. He cannot go anywhere. You've made sure of that. And you've made good use of his presence. In fact, he has been invaluable to you. You've told me that many times. What's changed now?

Minos turns away from Pasiphae, who is slowly shaking her head in disbelief. Minos turns back as she is about to speak.

MINOS Enough! Enough! It has been decided. This conversation is over. Get out of here. Go! Go!

He dismisses her with a violent brush of his hand. She moves backwards as if to protect herself from a blow and rushes to the door.

Pasiphae leaves. Minos gets up and pours himself a cup of wine and drains it in one gulp.

His Prime Minister enters. Minos pours another cup and hands it to his minister.

PM I saw the Queen in the corridor. She didn't greet me. She looked terrible. I hope she won't do anything to compromise our plan.

MINOS Don't worry about that. Her shame has always outweighed her decency. But tell me. Is everything going according to schedule?

PM I've talked to the Athenian ambassador. They will pay a great deal to cancel the debt. He said "one way or another".

MINOS Aha, he will try to get the best agreement for his people. It's natural.

PM Did you manage to persuade Theseus to accept the challenge?

MINOS Of course! I pointed out how he would go down in history as the saviour of those poor young Athenians who have gone on being sacrificed to the Minotaur over the years. He seemed to like that. All heroes are vain. I only hope he lives up to his reputation. They talk of him as though he were some kind of demigod. I pray he doesn't turn out to be some fraud or an idiot.

PM Does he know the truth?

MINOS He doesn't need to. Not until after the deed is done.

PM Have you considered what would happen if he failed?

MINOS He cannot fail. We need that gold. We have no other options. Our people are scared and they are losing faith in us.

Pause.

MINOS Where is Theseus now?

PM Ariadne is showing him round the palace. They seem to be getting on well.

MINOS Yes... I've already spoken to her. She's told me that she will help our cause.

The two men exchange knowing glances.

They raise their cups and touch them.

SCENE 2

Pasiphae's bedroom in the Palace.

OLD WOMAN But my Lady, he is your son!

PASIPHAE He is also the Monster.

OLD WOMAN How can you say that? It was you who gave birth to him. You cannot let him be destroyed now.

PASIPHAE Believe me, I am at a total loss. I sense what Minos has up his sleeve. But I don't know what I can do to stop him. What do you think?

OLD WOMAN I think Minos wants to finish with his guilt. This is what it's all about.

PASIPHAE I wish it were that simple. But I fear it's more complicated than that. It's a political move and the stakes are high.

OLD WOMAN I'm aware of that. But we also both know that all this mess started with Minos, not you.

PASIPHAE It makes no difference. He is the King, the absolute ruler. He decides. Besides, he would never admit to anything he has done wrong.

OLD WOMAN Unless it suits him! He is covering things up and transferring the blame on somebody else once again.

PASIPHAE The Minotaur has always been his scapegoat. You knew that something like this could happen one day. You knew it from the day I delivered him to you. I did everything in my power to prevent this. I have a strong feeling that Minos has been plotting and planning this for some time. I know him well.

OLD WOMAN Is this why the Athenians are here?

PASIPHAE I'm certain of it. But exactly what is being agreed between them, I don't know. Minos is keeping me in the dark as always.

Now she is agitated and eager to end the uncomfortable conversation.

PASIPHAE Anyway, I didn't summon you here to discuss Minos or his motives. I just want to help my – my – the Minotaur.

OLD WOMAN But you've already told me you cannot stop Minos' plans.

PASIPHAE That is exactly why my son's only chance is to escape from the labyrinth.

OLD WOMAN But he would never do that. He is trapped. You know that, as well as I do. If he disappears, Minos will kill me. They made that clear to him on the first day of his incarceration. They hold him with my life as a ransom.

PASIPHAE Yes! And I know how much he has always loved you – and hated me.

OLD WOMAN He does not hate you. He doesn't know you. Neither of you know one another. You had no choice at the time but to hand him to me to raise him.

PASIPHAE Yes! It has been your kindness and affection that has kept him going. So now it's up to you to convince him to free himself.

OLD WOMAN *(her frustration and despair rising)* I will do my best. But I know he will refuse. Besides, how could he escape the labyrinth? It is not as though he can become invisible.

PASIPHAE Calm yourself, woman! I have something for you to give him. But there is no time to lose if what I've heard is true.

She goes over to her table and extracts a small cloth bag from the drawer.

PASIPHAE Here, take this. I went to great lengths to steal it from Minos' room. He would kill me if he knew. Anyway, this will make things a lot easier for you both.

She hands the cloth bag to the Old Woman who carefully touches it before putting her fingers inside, feeling the contents.

Suddenly her face lightens up with a look of pleasant surprise and recognition. She nods.

OLD WOMAN You have done well, my lady. Let us hope he will make use of it.

PASIPHAE He must – or he will die.

Lights fade out.

SCENE 3

In a backstreet of Knossos. Daytime.

The city is in a state of confusion. Chaos and conflict everywhere.

There are discordant sounds of hysterical laughter mixed with cries of anguish, angry shouts, and sobbing.

Above the noise, a Young Man's voice is heard shouting angrily:

YOUNG MAN *(off-stage)* You filthy pigs! Trying to rob an old Woman! Have you no shame? Are you that desperate?

From backstage, two young men dressed in rags are approaching. They are accompanying an Old Woman, to whose rescue they have just run.

Behind them walks a Young Woman who keeps looking back warily as if expecting the attackers to pursue them. She is carrying the Old Woman's small cloth bundle, recovered from the gang.

The Old Woman is walking with the aid of a stick tapping the ground as she goes. From the use of it we realize that she is blind. The young people lead the Old Woman towards a torn carpet and they all sit down by the makeshift shelter where the three young people spend their nights, the three of them lie back exhausted.

The Old Woman sits upright as though nothing has happened. After a while the young people recover their breath and energy.

OLD WOMAN Are you alright my children?

1ST YOUNG MAN *(sitting up)* Well, I don't think they'll be back. I kicked one of them in the balls so hard, he's going to be hurting tonight. *(Leaning towards her, says in a sweet tone)* I finished what you started!

All three laugh.

2ND YOUNG MAN *(turning to the Old Woman)* You're a tough one. I saw you with your stick. How can you do it without having sight? Very impressive!

YOUNG WOMAN And what are you doing in this part of the city? Don't you know it's not safe anymore?

OLD WOMAN *(answers slowly)* It's been some time since I've come here. Everything has changed. It's all becoming so strange and unfamiliar.

YOUNG WOMAN *(astonished)* You can sense that, can you? Even blind as you are?

OLD WOMAN A person doesn't see only with the eyes...

1ST YOUNG MAN *(looking puzzled)* But what are you doing here at all? Are you lost?

2ND YOUNG MAN You look as though you've come from the mountains. That's a long way, isn't it? Where were you headed?

The Young Woman takes the Old Woman's bag and looks inside it.

YOUNG WOMAN My, my! There's bread, cheese, olives and wine! *(She pulls out a skin bag of wine and waves it in the air)* Country wine! Whoopee! Don't tell me. You're going to a party!

The Old Woman looks agitated and worried and tries desperately to snatch her bag back from the young woman.

1ST YOUNG MAN Don't worry, granny. She is only playing.

The Young Woman puts the wine skin back in the cloth bag and hands it to the Old Woman.

YOUNG WOMAN Here you are. We're not going to rob you, if that's what you think. We're not thieves. We haven't sunk as low as that mob you ran into today. Not yet, anyway. Who's it for?

OLD WOMAN It's for my son.

1ST YOUNG MAN *(incredulous)* Your son? And where does he live? Somewhere nearby? There's nothing in this wasteland but the cemetery, the labyrinth and the palace. Nobody comes here anymore, especially now, with the gangs moving in.

YOUNG WOMAN This used to be our neighbourhood. It was one of the best, but now we too have to leave it.

OLD WOMAN I sensed it. You are decent children.

2ND YOUNG MAN *(laughing)* I don't think that we could be described as 'decent' anymore. We are not children of slaves, that's for sure. And we were educated after a fashion. But we are hardly 'decent'. At least, not in the eyes of society!

YOUNG WOMAN Not since our families lost everything in the crisis. We've given up trying to live the 'decent life.'

1ST YOUNG MAN Or you could say that, 'decent' life has given up on us.

They laugh.

OLD WOMAN And how do you make your living? How do you put food on the table?

1ST YOUNG MAN Our folks are struggling to keep up with their debts. But it gets harder by the day. There is hardly any work. They are trying to make ends meet and save the little dignity left in them. As for food, thank the gods for the food rations that are handed out in the market place.

OLD WOMAN *(half to herself)* We are cursed. Our land is divided and sinking into despair! You poor young people are paying the price for greed and stupidity. And those who rule, they live like gods.

YOUNG WOMAN *(with a shrug)* It's just that we have lost faith. We don't know who or what to believe.

2ND YOUNG MAN Like that nonsense the minister was declaring in the market place this morning. He said everything is about to change, and that this crisis is nearly over. And that the Athenians' part in it will be crucial. See, this is what I don't get – how are the Athenians going to help if we cannot help ourselves? Anyway, how did we get into this mess in the first place?

1ST YOUNG MAN You fool. Don't you remember the stories we used to hear from the elders about Minos sacrificing the wrong bull? That's why everything has gone so badly in recent years. This is what they are trying to rectify now. This is their way out. A new order will be implemented. And we will have a brand new treaty with the Athenians...

2ND YOUNG MAN *(spits on the ground in disgust)* And, as if by magic, I suppose, the rains will come back, the harvest will be good and the market place will be bustling again. I wonder, do they think we are so simple-minded? And what is the story with the Minotaur? They've been trotting him out as long as I can remember. The monster justifies all their laws to hold us down. What a load of horseshit! Nobody has ever even seen him.

1ST YOUNG MAN Maybe we've never seen him, but I've heard his roars from over there and it's scared the shit out of me.

Pause.

OLD WOMAN I feel the sun is beginning to go down. Why don't you start a fire or you will freeze to the death.

The two men get up and begin to prepare the fire. The Young Woman, fascinated by the Old Woman, takes hold of her hand and keeps stroking it. After a while, the Old Woman pats her shoulder. Then the Old Woman smoothes down her long tattered skirt, adjusts her shawl and takes hold of her stick, looking as though she is preparing herself to leave.

YOUNG WOMAN *(helping her onto her feet)* But you can't be thinking of leaving now, granny. Why don't you spend the night here with us? It's getting late.

OLD WOMAN Thank you! I'm grateful for your help, but I have to go. Now that the sun has set, it's time for me to run my errands.

2ND YOUNG MAN What kind of dark errands can you possibly be thinking of running at this hour, granny?

The Young Man laughs at his own remark.

OLD WOMAN *(straightening her back)* I have to save my son.

The young people exchange confused glances and shrug.

1ST YOUNG MAN *(disbelieving)* And what if you come across some gang again?

OLD WOMAN It's kind of you to concern yourselves with an old woman you've only just met, but I'm not afraid of them or anyone else.

YOUNG WOMAN It will be curfew very soon. The city guards will arrest you.

OLD WOMAN Do not worry about the city guards. They know me only too well. I am no threat to anyone.

YOUNG WOMAN You are so brave, let me at least take you out to the roadside.

OLD WOMAN Thank you, my daughter! *(Addressing all of them)* You are all good people. I wish you well in your life. Your time on earth is precious. Don't waste it.

1ST YOUNG MAN/2ND YOUNG MAN Good night, granny. Go well on your way.

The Young Woman leads the Old Woman off into the background. Upon her return to the shelter, the lights dim on the three young people.

Out of it the cry of a bird. Moonlight and shadows.

Darkness.

We have now three parallel actions in dim lighting:

One with the Minotaur walking in the shadows at the far end of the scene; one with the Old Woman walking towards the palace tapping her stick, singing a melancholy song; and one with the three young homeless citizens preparing to go to sleep.

After a while the lights fade out firstly on the Old Woman (only her song and tapping are heard until the total blackout), then on the Minotaur and lastly on the young people.

Silence.

Blackout.

SCENE 4

In the shelter, on the outskirts of Knossos.

Later that night. Darkness.

Under the moonlight, the three young homeless citizens are lying down in their shelter huddled up to keep warm. The fire is still smouldering. Suddenly the Young Woman wakes and sits up sensing a presence. Above her there are many shadows thrown by the firelight. She looks around frightened, doesn't see anyone and goes back to sleep.

Cry of a bird.

Darkness.

SCENE 5

In the Labyrinth.

We are in the inner sanctuary. It is an open space with a huge rock in the middle.

Out of the darkness there comes a single long, horrendous cry (of pain, anguish, anger). It is a strange voice, hardly human.

A faint light starts to creep into a corner of the labyrinth. Out of the shadows the Minotaur, a terrifying looking figure, approaches with a small burning torch in his hand. He places the torch in a receptacle then paces around slowly in front of the rock like a stalking animal, stops, cocks his head to one side to listen, then finally crouches down. He groans, snorts and scratches himself then sits still as if meditating, staring into the space in front of him.

He suddenly jumps up, roars theatrically, towards no one in particular, then he laughs ironically. Then he starts addressing the audience as if talking to himself. After years of solitude he has become accustomed to voicing his thoughts out loud.

MINOTAUR I smelt danger in the air. I felt the anxiety in their hearts. I sensed it on my skin. I tasted falsehood in my mouth. And then I heard them talking about it, with my own ears. They are plotting against me.

He gets up to do a crazy, grotesque, lewd jig.

When he sits down again he puts both hands on his head as though he is deep in thought and rolls his head around for a while like a wounded animal who is suffering. Then he hangs his monstrous head in a gesture of defeat, his body bent and collapsed. When gradually he straightens up he stares ahead in anger. He has the look of someone who has been driven crazy by what he has had to endure. He starts to cry until he is screaming his pain. Then eventually he recovers his composure.

MINOTAUR Well, here I am, flesh and bone like you, confused like you, in need of love and healing, like you. I am the living product of Greed and Lust. That's the mixture that conceived me. Greed and Lust, and then a good dose of Deception. I am their bad dream made flesh!

He flops onto the ground like a wounded beast and twitches his body this way and that as if in agony. Then he sits up again slowly.

MINOTAUR They could have slit my throat and dropped me off the cliff as soon as I appeared. Maybe they should have. But Minos was clever. He saw what I was worth to him. He made me the figure of Fear. The Monster. I am the threat of darkness and destruction – of chaos itself. That's how he rules his people.

He gets up on his feet again and this time executes a weird Tai chi like movement, then stops and laughs. He speaks to the air again in a mad sing-song voice.

MINOTAUR And now with the same might and power that they used to invent me and imprison me here they are now planning to destroy me and replace me with another myth...

A shout from the shadows interrupts him.

OLD WOMAN *(off-stage)* Little one, little one! Where are you?

The Minotaur, shaken out of his solitary ranting looks pleasantly surprised and jumps up. He goes to the back of the stage and returns guiding the Old Woman on his arm.

OLD WOMAN How are you, my son?

MINOTAUR I'm alright, mother. I'm alright. Did you have any trouble coming down here?

OLD WOMAN I was attacked by a gang who tried to rob me. But some young people came along and helped me. I am not harmed.

MINOTAUR *(angry)* You should not wander alone in the city. It is my fault you have to come here at all.

OLD WOMAN *(dismissing the Minotaur's concern with a wave of her hand)* I had a bad dream. And then the Queen sent for me.

The Minotaur is now seated beside the Old Woman who strokes his back while he hangs his head in silence.

OLD WOMAN *(tenderly)* I have missed you. Have you been hungry? *(The Minotaur shakes his head. The Old Woman's face shines)* Today, I have something to give you much better than food or wine. But first, let me tell you what I have discussed with the Queen.

MINOTAUR *(putting up his hand to stop her)* I already know the news, if that is what you have come to tell me. I am about to be executed by the famous Athenian, Theseus.

OLD WOMAN *(incredulous)* You know this already? How?

MINOTAUR *(sarcastically)* Like I know everything. Yes. I heard the guards discussing the whole plan. I even learned that the sword with which he will try to kill me is a famous one. It belongs to his father.

OLD WOMAN I am amazed that you don't seem worried. He has a mighty weapon and all you have is your bull's strength.

MINOTAUR *(amused)* Yes. But I am the wicked Monster. Why should I be disturbed by all of this?

He gets onto his feet and jumps around wildly like a mad bull, mocking himself and making grunting noises. The Old Woman cackles with laughter. He then performs an elaborate ritual, stamping his feet on the ground in a fierce rhythm, like flamenco. It is explosive, like a war dance. She follows his antics with jerky movements of her arms, as though she can sense what he is doing.

When the Minotaur finishes he sits down by her.

OLD WOMAN *(nostalgically)* You used to do that dance as a child when the moon was full.

MINOTAUR Yes, it was my war dance. It will scare the hell out of Theseus!

OLD WOMAN Do not take it lightly, I beg of you!

MINOTAUR *(still in the same mood)* Do you forget? I have devoured all those lovely young Athenian boys and girls. I have drunk their blood like the best wine. I gnawed their bones till they were clean. *(He wipes his mouth with the back of his hand)* Anyway, you said you have something for me. What did you bring me that's so precious?

The Old Woman puts her hand in her shoulder bag and brings out the small cloth bag that Pasiphae has given her. She hands it over to the Minotaur.

OLD WOMAN Here! This is for you. It is from your mother. She risked her life to get it for you. I am only sorry it has taken her so long to get hold of it. Use it now if you are to escape your fate.

The Minotaur puts his fingers inside and feels its contents with his back to the audience. All we hear is the clinking sound of something metallic.

MINOTAUR *(astonished and pleased)* Ah! Is this really what I think it is? Is this the key to my freedom? Thank you! Thank you! For years I have been dreaming of holding this in my hand. And you say the queen gave you this?

OLD WOMAN Yes! She stole it from Minos. She took a great risk. It was a brave thing to do.

MINOTAUR *(laughing)* Never too late to lend me a hand! Thank you, Mother!

Waving the key in the air he performs a short dance of celebration.

OLD WOMAN Now, you can finally leave this place. I want to see you free.

MINOTAUR But Mother, I can come and go anytime I please. Thanks to you I learned to use my senses early on. As you know, I found the way long ago.

OLD WOMAN That's not what I mean. The situation is different now. You can really leave this place!

As he finishes his dance, the Minotaur takes the Old Woman in his arms and swirls her around.

MINOTAUR Oh Mother, you don't know what a gift you brought me! This will help me to complete my own plan!!

OLD WOMAN What plan? What are you going to do about Theseus?

Slowly he releases her.

MINOTAUR *(still in a joyful mood)* This time I am using my brain not my instincts, as you taught me. Anyway, tell me. Why should I be afraid of some handsome young preening upstart?

OLD WOMAN He is not just a fine looking nobleman who goes everywhere saving people, making men follow him and women desire him. He has charisma.

MINOTAUR *(confident)* Let him come. I've been preparing all my life for a chance like this!

OLD WOMAN *(raising her voice)* He's a great warrior. Do not underestimate his experience!

MINOTAUR Aah! But you see, I have the advantage here! I am on my turf. The labyrinth is my home. He is on uncharted ground. The labyrinth is all new and mysterious to him. And unlike me, he is not trained to smell his way here like an animal, not as you have taught me.

He leans over to hug her as he tries to ease her worries.

OLD WOMAN I don't know what you have in your pretty little head. But it worries me to see you so joyful and confident.

MINOTAUR Don't worry about me, Mother. I know what I'm doing. I have had plenty of time to figure things out. But the circumstances have never been favourable. Not until now. Suddenly, everything is coming together. My time has come. Minos is desperate to find a solution in this crisis and I will provide with him one – my version of it! And now this!

He holds up the small cloth bag triumphantly.

MINOTAUR This is going to make everything so much easier!

He kisses the bag.

OLD WOMAN My poor boy, none of what you say reassures me. I can't stop my worrying.

MINOTAUR I'm glad it's come to this. But now you must rest, Mother. You must leave this place soon. I don't want you anywhere near here when Theseus comes looking for me.

OLD WOMAN I hope you know what you are doing.

The Minotaur caresses her and sings the lullaby she has taught him. The Old Woman begins to sob gently and the Minotaur keeps consoling her, hugging her to him and then laying her down on the ground.

MINOTAUR Shush. Lie down now. I will explain everything when you have rested. I'm going out for a while. I need some air. I won't be long.

The Old Woman lies down and the Minotaur covers her tenderly with a blanket. Then he wanders off into the shadows.

SCENE 6

The young people's shelter.

Slow movements in the young people's shelter. The first to wake up is the Young Woman, shivering from the cold air. She starts to stoke the fire. Soon after, the 2nd Young Man stirs. No sight of the 1st Young Man.

2ND YOUNG MAN *(stretching and then shaking his limbs, trying to warm up)* Good morning.

YOUNG WOMAN *(grumpily)* Morning...

2ND YOUNG MAN *(realizes that she's a bit moody)* Are you alright?

YOUNG WOMAN I didn't sleep well... I had this funny feeling and I woke in the middle of the night and...

2ND YOUNG MAN *(continuing his warm up more vigorously)* And what?

YOUNG WOMAN I saw a shadow last night... The shadow of a very peculiar figure – lurking in the woods, far out there. I think... I think it was the Minotaur...

2ND YOUNG MAN *(stopping his movements)* No way!

YOUNG WOMAN Yes, it was the Minotaur! I know what I saw.

2ND YOUNG MAN No way, I'm telling you. He cannot escape the labyrinth. You must've dreamt it... *(Looking around)* Where is our friend?

YOUNG WOMAN He's gone to the market to get some rations. I tell you. I'm sure of what I saw. It was a man... but no ordinary man. His head was covered by his cape, but it was huge head... and he was carrying something on his back.

2ND YOUNG MAN And I'm telling you that it couldn't have been him.

1ST YOUNG MAN *(entering in a rush)* You won't believe what I heard when I was queuing up!

The other two ignore him, still arguing on the Minotaur.

YOUNG WOMAN Yeah, and why not?

2ND YOUNG MAN Because, silly, if he could leave that place any time he pleased, then why not leave it altogether?

1ST YOUNG MAN Hey listen to me!

YOUNG WOMAN I don't know about that. What I know is that it was... it was weird – out of this world, you know, the whole feeling...

1ST YOUNG MAN *(putting down the bag of food he has brought)* Hey, I'm talking to you!

2ND YOUNG MAN *(resuming his warm up exercises)* Maybe you were cold or hungry and you had some nightmare or something... Once you eat something, you'll be OK.

YOUNG WOMAN I'm telling you, it was–

1ST YOUNG MAN Will you *listen* to me?

They finally turn to him.

2ND YOUNG MAN/YOUNG WOMAN What!?

1ST YOUNG MAN We don't have to worry about him anymore! Theseus is going to kill him! It's all been arranged!

2ND YOUNG MAN Who? What – How?

1ST YOUNG MAN The Minotaur. This is why the Athenian delegation is here. They came with their hero and... their gold.

YOUNG WOMAN I caught a glimpse of that Theseus yesterday, when he came out on the balcony with Princess Ariadne.

2ND YOUNG MAN And?

YOUNG WOMAN Well, he's a strong, good-looking man; looks like a real hero–

2ND YOUNG MAN *(interrupting her)* I wouldn't want to be in his shoes. He may be a hero but our monster's eaten all those people in his time.

YOUNG WOMAN Nah! There's nothing to worry about. Heroes never fail.

1ST YOUNG MAN Hey! Enough with the Minotaur and your hero. What really matters is that all this Athenian gold will be put in our economy – all our troubles will be over. It's being discussed all over the market place.

2ND YOUNG MAN And you believe it? They have lied to us again and again. We're always the suckers.

1ST YOUNG MAN Maybe it will be different this time. Even just the killing of the monster will be enough. All this time, just the thought of him being around... *(Shudders)* I just hope Theseus succeeds.

YOUNG WOMAN Still, I can't help pitying the monster. Everything was against him. Kept in that labyrinth for so long. We'd all turn into monsters...

2ND YOUNG MAN Don't tell me you're getting soppy about the Minotaur... Now, enough of that, let's enjoy our royal breakfast!

They all laugh and begin drinking their tea and eating their bread.

SCENE 7

The inner sanctuary of the Labyrinth.

The Old Woman sits up slowly, shivers and pulls the blanket round her shoulders. After a while she throws the blanket off and begins to fold it up. She is humming the same lullaby as the Minotaur sang to her.

At this point the Minotaur returns out of the shadows carrying a big heavy sack which he hides behind a rock. Then he goes and sits down next to the Old Woman who strokes his face tenderly.

OLD WOMAN Where have you been, my son?

MINOTAUR I needed to clear my head and I had something to do. I went to the palace. I wanted to find out more about what they're planning for me, so I climbed up to Ariadne's bedroom window and I heard them speaking.

OLD WOMAN Who?

MINOTAUR Theseus and Ariadne.

OLD WOMAN You shouldn't have been so reckless.

MINOTAUR *(slightly bitter)* I heard my own sister flirting with the enemy – plotting against me. Siding with our father to kill me. She told him she's afraid of me. Just the thought of me makes her tremble. The poor flower!

OLD WOMAN Give her some credit. Minos is just using her.

MINOTAUR I dont't think it is just that. She's more than willing to do his bidding. She's fallen for Theseus, I think, and it's obvious to me that he is her ticket out of here. I heard her tell him that she wants to sail with him, far away from here. Anyway, she gave him the ball of thread to help him in and out of the labyrinth – I bet she even took the plans of the labyrinth from Daedalus himself.

OLD WOMAN That old fox has always been part of the set-up.

The Minotaur stretches his arms upwards, in weariness. He stands erect, he flings open his arms wide and he lets out a long, frightening roar.

MINOTAUR There, they all know now. The Monster is famished and angry, needs blood. So let Theseus, the monster slayer, the world saviour come if he dares! Bring it on! *(He calms down)* Here, Mother, I will take you to the gate. I will tell you what I have in mind.

They walk out of the Labyrinth together.

Darkness.

End of Act I.

ACT TWO
SCENE 1

Minos' Palace. Midday. Minos is standing with his Prime Minister.

MINOS How is everything with the Athenian ambassador? Did he agree on the terms?

PM Yes! He was particularly satisfied about the part where it says that the destruction of the great common enemy will herald a new beginning in the relationship of our two states.

MINOS I would be surprised if he weren't! No more dead Athenian youngsters and he can take part of the glory.

PM He said he will sign the deal once he has proof that the Minotaur is dead.

MINOS That goes both ways. One more thing, make sure that the gold stays with us.

PM Pragmatic as always. I will do my best.

MINOS Let us hope Theseus will do the deed. I will give the people a juicy myth this time: The great young hero overcoming the evil monster. The generations to come will feast in my name and sing his praise.

SCENE 2

Pasiphae's bedroom. She sits by the window pensively sipping wine out of a goblet.

Darkness. An owl's long screech.

SCENE 3

In the Labyrinth.

Lit by torchlight. Two shadows carefully stalking each other in the twisting maze but just missing each other.

Darkness.

SCENE 4

The Minotaur's sanctuary inside the Labyrinth.

The Minotaur, holding a wooden club, enters the area first and then hides behind the rock. Theseus, who has been carefully lured into this unfamiliar space enters cautiously. He is in armour and wearing a helmet. He is holding a torch in one hand and his sword the other. He looks around him and for a brief moment kneels down and puts his sword on the ground. Then he takes the ball of thread that he has attached to his belt and carefully puts it down before retrieving his sword. As he now approaches the rock the Minotaur comes at him from behind. He hits Theseus' arm with his club so that Theseus lets go of his sword. Hurt, he fights back skillfully and manages to get the Minotaur to let go of his club. Both now unarmed, they struggle furiously. Finally, the Minotaur manages to trip Theseus to the ground and to hold him round the neck in a vice-like grip. Theseus is on the point of losing his life when the Minotaur rolls away and picks up the hero's sword which he now holds up in the air menacingly.

Theseus is exhausted from the fight. But he pulls himself up into a straight sitting position and opens his arms to his adversary. It is a formal gesture of surrender. He is resigned to his fate, accepting that this is his final moment on earth. The Minotaur who has now stood up, points the tip of the sword at Theseus' chest. He shifts his weight forward as if he is about to plunge the point into the hero's heart.

MINOTAUR I've been expecting you.

Theseus freezes, astonished to hear the Monster speaking.

MINOTAUR Take off your helmet. I want to see your face.

Theseus hesitates to make a move at first. He is in shock. But eventually he takes off his helmet.

The Minotaur stands over him with the brandished weapon and turns his head this way and that, examining his captive. Finally he nods approvingly.

MINOTAUR At least you're worthy of your fame. (*Still holding the sword high)* Are you surprised that I can speak the language of men?

THESEUS But how can you...?!

MINOTAUR Are you afraid?

Minotaur again looks as though he might plunge the sword into his captive. Theseus makes a backward move. Then he nods his head.

MINOTAUR Good. All warriors need to know fear. Otherwise they are dangerous. To themselves. *(Pauses)* Are you an honourable man?

Theseus hesitates. Then he nods again.

The Minotaur now lowers the sword and points to Theseus to sit by the rock. Theseus does so.

MINOTAUR Why are you here? Is it for your personal glory?

THESEUS *(hesitates then finally answers)* As far as my people are concerned, it is about time to finish with all this... Athens has paid long enough.

MINOTAUR Well, you shouldn't have killed Minos' son back then – over a stupid race too!

THESEUS That was a long time ago, it was about time we renegotiated the debt.

MINOTAUR *(distractedly)* Yes, yes, of course. So here we are... You, a renowned hero, descended from a royal line, fighting for his country, and me... What am I?

Theseus shakes his head, more bewildered than ever.

MINOTAUR A monster, the result of a freak coupling between a queen and a bull from the sea. Together you and I, we make the best ingredients for a myth.

THESEUS *(confused)* I am only here in the interests of Athens.

MINOTAUR I know that.

THESEUS I've brought gold to buy the Athenians out of the debt.

MINOTAUR But Minos had another agenda.

THESEUS Yes.

MINOTAUR So Athens will pay no more taxes to Crete – you have agreed on that. And the gold you brought Minos? I bet the king wants to keep that for himself as well.

THESEUS I was not informed of the details. It is not my place.

MINOTAUR But it is! Did you know that Minos would demand that you kill me?

Theseus shakes his head.

MINOTAUR Still, you did not question his motives?

THESEUS I follow orders.

MINOTAUR Is that all a hero does? Follow orders?

THESEUS I do what is expected of me.

MINOTAUR Yes, yes... So Minos wants to kill two birds with one stone. He has found a way to appease the troubles of his people –

through me! I am to blame! I am the curse on this island! He has convinced his people I am the cause of their suffering. *(He laughs ironically)* The best way to manipulate the masses, divert them from the problem!!

THESEUS Go on...

MINOTAUR Who is really the cursed one here? Minos or I? *(Beat)* Haven't you heard about Poseidon and his gift of a precious bull?

THESEUS Maybe...

MINOTAUR The story goes that Minos should have sacrificed my so-called father the White Bull in his honour. But instead, he switched him for a common one. He tricked a god. Isn't this a cause for punishment?

THESEUS We agree on that. *(Pensively)* And he has imprisoned you here...

MINOTAUR First he sent me away to the mountains as a child in the keep of an old blind woman. And then, when I came of age, he constructed this prison especially for me.

THESEUS And you've been here ever since?

MINOTAUR All my adult life.

THESEUS And how do you know so much when you have been stuck here in this labyrinth all this time? How can you speak a human language at all?

MINOTAUR You think that a labyrinth is enough to keep someone imprisoned?

THESEUS I should think so.

MINOTAUR Why? What is a labyrinth? The place itself or a state of mind?

THESEUS I haven't given that much thought...

MINOTAUR Why should you? You were never faced with a similar situation. What is asked of you is a practical matter. You have to go out there and perform some heroic deed. No time or place for inner contemplation.

THESEUS It is true that you and I are standing in the opposite poles in life... But how did you come to be so philosophical?

MINOTAUR Firstly, I was brought up by a good person, to think and to question. Secondly, there's plenty of time here to do just that. It's an ideal place for contemplation, don't you think? A healthy spot too. I have fresh air and the sea nearby and oh, the beauty of these rocks that surround me. What a comfortable, simple existence...

THESEUS The sea? How can you know anything about the sea except how it might sound on a stormy night?

MINOTAUR Ah but you don't think that I've spent all my time in here, do you?

THESEUS You mean, you can leave this place?

MINOTAUR I can and I do, all the time.

THESEUS But how?

MINOTAUR Easily enough. And I certainly don't need a ball of thread to guide my way. My blind mother trained me well to use all my senses. So when I want to bathe, I go out and swim with the dolphins. At night I lie on the beach and look at the stars. I drink water from the springs.

THESEUS *(puzzling over the Minotaur's answer)* Since you can leave, why do you come back? Why not run away to the mountains?

MINOTAUR Because Minos has threatened to kill my mother – my real mother, not the one who gave birth to me...

THESEUS You have no choice but to remain!

MINOTAUR You are beginning to get the picture...

THESEUS And what about all the young Athenians over the years?!

MINOTAUR You mean the ones I tore limb from limb and whose flesh I devoured? Do you want the truth? Minos had them slaughtered right in front of me. Do you believe me?

Theseus slowly takes this in and nods.

MINOTAUR By the way, I am a vegetarian, brought up as one by my wise mother. The thought of eating flesh repels me.

THESEUS *(still trying to take it in)* But, this prison...? What you've had to endure...

While Theseus's is talking, the Minotaur carefully puts the sword down by his feet and takes up the small cloth bag he received from the Old Woman. Out of it he extracts a metal key that he now inserts into the back of his mask. Then very slowly he begins to take the bull's head mask off, lifting it over his head. He puts it on the ground and looks at it for a long while.

Then he touches his straggly beard, the contours of his rough face, his blotchy, pale skin, and runs his fingers through his tangled, wild curly hair. He twists his features this way and that, opening his mouth wide, baring his teeth, sticking out his tongue. He pulls his ears, pats his cheeks, he makes grotesque faces... Finally he shrieks out a yell of victory.

During the revelation, Theseus becomes even more confused.

THESEUS My God!?

MINOTAUR And what? Haven't you ever seen a man who has been wronged and abused before?

THESEUS You are... you are human?

MINOTAUR As human as any other man.

THESEUS But how...?

MINOTAUR Let's say that my real father was a bull of a man. In fact, he was one of Minos' bodyguards. Or so I was told.

THESEUS Then the White Bull was not your father? So Minos invented you. The Monster.

MINOTAUR That's exactly what happened. And thanks to him I will remain the Monster for the rest of time.

THESEUS So tell me. Why didn't you free yourself from the mask before and disappear into the crowd along with your mother?

MINOTAUR Because I did not have this key before today. *(Ironically)* My dear mother, the queen, has only just stolen it from the king.

THESEUS And she knows that Minos wants you dead?

MINOTAUR Monsters are needed by kings to terrorise the people so that those who govern can be the protectors. When they save the people, order and normality can prevail. But you know how that always turns out.

THESEUS How could you stand it all these years?

MINOTAUR The mask? Being stuck in this forsaken place?

He pauses. There is a moment of deep regret.

MINOTAUR Yes, the king, my father, wants me dead. But not quietly, using some cheap assassin from the ranks. And this is where you come in, Theseus. Don't you see? You are a crucial pawn in the game.

THESEUS I don't like to be anybody's pawn.

MINOTAUR Then what happens next, my friend, is a way out for the three of us – you, my mother and myself. The only thing that saddens me, is that Minos will get off the hook too easily...

Pause

THESEUS What do I have to do?

The two men look at each other for a moment. Then the Minotaur takes up his bull's head mask once more and walks over to where Theseus is sitting and puts it on the ground in front of him like an offering.

Then he takes hold of the hero's sword, holds it up ceremonially above his head before placing it down by the mask.

MINOTAUR Then you, the hero, must do the honourable thing. And I, the Monster, must go to its death.

THESEUS *(surprised at the proposal)* I don't follow you...

The Minotaur takes out the cloth bag with the food the Old Woman has brought him and invites Theseus to sit across him.

MINOTAUR Here, let us feast. I will let you in on my plan.

Darkness.

End of Act II

ACT THREE
SCENE 1

Daytime. The city is in celebration. There is the sound of flutes and drumming. Music and laughter fill the air. Flags are flying. Confetti is being thrown. It is like a carnival. Theseus comes out on a balcony of the palace in his shining armour and waves to the crowd. He holds up the head of the bull that is dripping blood in one hand, and in the other he is brandishing his sword in victory. We can hear the people cheering in the background and shouting their approval.

1ST VOICE The Monster has been killed. You are a true hero.

2ND VOICE Things will be different from now on.

3RD VOICE Athens and Crete can now be allies again. Theseus, we worship you...

Theseus receives all this adoration gracefully, like a true champion, raising his hands and saluting the crowd. Then, even as the roar continues he bows and disappears into the palace.

SCENE 2

Minos' ante-chamber. Daytime. They pour wine and drink.

PM *(raising his cup of wine)* Congratulations, sire. I must say, I feared that Theseus would abandon the deal once he realized the truth.

Minos stops drinking, looks at the Prime Minister.

MINOS We met at the gate of the labyrinth. All he did was to hand over a bloody sack to one of my men and said, 'Here is the head that will solve all our troubles'. He looked me in the eye for a moment or two and left with his companions.

PM Surely you checked the sack?

MINOS The sack contained a common bull's head.

Pause.

PM What do you make of it?

MINOS I didn't think twice about it, nor did I ask. That look of his said it all. So, as far as everyone is concerned, the Minotaur is dead. We have what we wanted. Theseus fulfilled his role.

PM So – we must forget all about the gold?

MINOS You cannot win them all.

PM Aren't you afraid the truth might come out?

MINOS How? Not from Theseus and certainly not from that bastard who gains his freedom. If he did open his mouth I would have him killed... So that leaves us only with you.

He looks threateningly at the Prime Minister. The Prime Minister is silent, fearful.

MINOS No, I didn't think so. Everyone has played their part. The myth is now set in stone. Nobody will doubt it. We can move onto a new time of prosperity.

They touch goblets.

SCENE 3

Daytime. Sounds of a city in celebration.

Out of the crowd, away from the noise of the marketplace walks the Old Woman, led by a clean-shaven man in a simple, worn cloak. They look like beggars. After a while they sit down by the roadside and share food from a basket.

MINOTAUR Are you sure you'll be alright?

OLD WOMAN I have survived this long, haven't I? Don't worry about me. There are still good people around.

MINOTAUR I can't help feeling I am abandoning you when we could do the things we couldn't enjoy all those years...

OLD WOMAN Listen to me, my son. This age has passed for the both of us. And despite everything we had our share of happy moments, though they were few. Do not dwell on the sad ones. A new era dawns for you and you must live it.

MINOTAUR I only wish you could be a part of it.

OLD WOMAN The gift of your freedom will keep me going until the end of my days!

There are sounds of more shouting and cheering in the distance. Out of the crowd, two men and a woman run over to them. They are the same homeless dropouts who helped her the day before. They stop and look at the Old Woman surprised to find her there. Then they look at the Minotaur.

1ST YOUNG MAN Is it really you, Granny? So you found your son.

But they are too drunk and excited to stop their celebration or wait for her reply.

2ND YOUNG MAN This is a great day. The Monster is dead! And the best part of it – free wine for everyone!

He laughs. Then turning to the Minotaur

2ND YOUNG MAN What are you doing here? Everyone in the city is celebrating. Come with us. Come!

He takes the Minotaur's arm. The Minotaur resists at first but the Old Woman waves to him to go. So, still reluctantly, he follows the two Young Men.

YOUNG WOMAN *(merrily drunk)* Don't worry. Go on. Have a drink. I will look after your mother.

The Minotaur lets himself be taken by them into the background where the city has erupted into a frenzy of celebration. A faint smile of joy slowly replaces his reluctance.

The Young Woman sits down by the Old Woman's side and takes her hand. Then she slides herself down and rests her head on the Old Woman's lap.

YOUNG WOMAN *(sleepily)* I'm so drunk and sleepy. I just need to rest for a while. Tell me a story, granny...

The Old Woman start to stroke the Young Woman's head. The latter has fallen asleep instantly.

OLD WOMAN Once upon a time, in a faraway land, there lived an evil king. So mighty and sure of himself that he thought he could defy everyone, even the Gods...

Her voice fades into the background noise. A cacophony of sound drowns her voice. On a large screen we see a montage of wild celebrations and street carnivals taking place.

After a while the images fade. Now the Minotaur returns alone, with his face flushed red and slightly out of breath. He is both surprised and pleased to see the Young Woman with her head in the Old Woman's lap.

MINOTAUR They have put Theseus on a tall chariot and are driving him round the city like a great conqueror. He is still holding onto the bull's head. He has a fixed smile on his face. I mean Theseus, not the Minotaur.

They both laugh.

OLD WOMAN That's the image Minos wanted. He'll win their hearts back now. Agh, they don't see what is right before their noses. But the good thing about it is, they're all convinced that you are dead.

The Minotaur puts the food and wine back into the Old Woman's bag. The Old Woman releases herself by laying the Young Woman's head gently on the ground and with the help of the Minotaur, she stands up.

OLD WOMAN Tell me my son, have you made up made up your mind where you will go? Have you planned things carefully?

MINOTAUR Don't worry mother, I have had plenty of time to do so, I will be alright. But I can't tell you where I will land up.

OLD WOMAN Do you think will you ever come back?

MINOTAUR I don't know, Mother. How can I? I'm only starting out. But I know it will be a long journey.

OLD WOMAN Farewell then, my son. Go with my blessing. Go! My friend the captain is waiting for you to sail away.

MINOTAUR Good bye Mother, thank you for everything. Be well.

OLD WOMAN Wait. Take this.

From her shoulder bag she takes a long red scarf and hands it to him. The Minotaur holds it up and slowly winds it round his head and his neck. Then he gives a last embrace and walks away holding his small cloth bag without looking back.

The old blind woman turns her blind gaze to follow him as he fades into the background. Just before we lose sight of him, she puts her palms around her mouth and shouts out:

OLD WOMAN Do not forget to remember!

Lights down.

The end.

TEW BUNNAG

Bunnag was born in Bangkok in 1947, and educated in the UK where he studied Chinese and Economics at Cambridge University. He has been a teacher of t'ai chi and a lay teacher of Buddhist meditation since 1975, and has given courses in England, Spain, France, Switzerland, Greece and the US. In Spain, where he lives most of the year, he also contributes to the Palliative Care Movement, running workshops on issues concerning Death and Dying, and he is the current president of the Asociación Vinyana.

In Bangkok he works in Klongtoey, the biggest slum situated in the port area of Bangkok where he is one of the directors of an NGO that helps street children, and adults and children who are HIV positive (The Human Development Foundation, Mercy Centre). The funds that he helps to raise in Europe go to these projects.

His fiction works in English include *Fragile Days, After the Wave, The Naga's Journey, Curtain of Rain*, and three published short stories (*A Most Generous Uncle* for the *Asia Literary Review, The Mistress Wants her Freedom*, for the *Bangkok Noir* collection, and *Eyes of Karma* for the *Asia Literary Review*). All deal with the contradictions and anomalies thrown up by the confrontation of traditional values and the modern aggressive materialism that has become a feature of Asian society. He writes both as an insider and an observer using his ability to slip in and out of the different strata of Thai society that are usually inaccessible to both Thai and foreign outsiders.

His work has been serialized in Thai magazines and translated into Spanish and Greek. *The Naga's Journey* and *Curtain of Rain* have been translated into Italian.

He is married to a British artist, has three children and five grandchildren. His eldest daughter lives in Italy with her family. His son is a filmmaker based in Paris and Bangkok and his youngest daughter is a musician. Because of these family commitments he divides his time between Europe and Thailand.

TARAP MAN

ANN LEE

Tarap Man was first produced by Kuali Works/Dramalab at the Annexe Galleries, Central Market, Kuala Lumpur from 5–9 December 2007.

Produced by Wyn Hee and directed by Zahim Albakri.

Translators/Dialogue coaches: Petronila Maurice, Fenella Jinu (Kadazan); Prakash Rao Kudathala Atchana (Telugu); Peggy Chan Mu Shen, Lee Ling Chin, Callyn Leow, Simon Woo (Hakka).

Characters

AASHI – a senior journalist, female, quick-tempered and quick-witted.

CORNELIA – a young trainee-journalist, female, sincere, casual and confident.

LEONG KIN – a senior journalist, old friend of Aashi's, male, modest demeanour.

REGINA – editor and senior journalist, female, stern but open.

OLD MAN – in his 60s.

HAMID – a lawyer, old contact and friend of Aashi's, easy-going.

RUDY – a male nurse, young and fit, keen to help but unreliable.

PRISONER – in his 60s.

GUARD 1 – late 40s, male.

GUARD 2 – mid-30s, female.

INMATE – in his 60s, male.

MESSENGER – early to mid 20s, male or female.

BOY – aged 14.

VOICE ENSEMBLE (optional) – any age or gender.

Cast

AASHI – Anne James
CORNELIA – Mia Palencia
LEONG KIN – Thor Kah Hoong
REGINA – Christina Orow
BOY/OLD MAN – Vernon Adrian Emuang
HAMID/GUARD 1/VOICE ENSEMBLE – Megat Sharizal Yusoff
RUDY/PRISONER/VOICE ENSEMBLE – David Lim
GUARD/INMATE/VOICE ENSEMBLE – Abdul Qahar Aqilah
MESSENGER/GUARD/VOICE ENSEMBLE – Fariza Ariffin

ACT ONE
SCENE 1

Wartime 1940s, Sandakan.

A boy, aged about 5, runs around, free and laughing. He plays in a drain, trying to dam it with wood, stones, a shoe, amidst the sound of monsoon rain, thunder and lightning. He wears oversized khaki shorts that look a bit comic on his skinny legs.

SCENE 2

1994. Open plan newspaper office, Kota Kinabalu.

Leong Kin (modest demeanour) and Cornelia (casual, confident, perhaps a little too much) sit close to each other. Aashi (physically striking, given to rhetorical outbursts) sits up stage. Leong Kin and Aashi, clearly good friends, enjoy 'toying' with Cornelia. While writing, they talk at a heightened pace, almost on top of each other.

LEONG KIN Drinks on you tonight.

CORNELIA Orange juice, can.

LEONG KIN That's not a drink. It's a toy.

CORNELIA Whatever!

LEONG KIN Congrats.

CORNELIA I liked your story about watches in Switzerland. It was... timeless.

LEONG KIN It was well written.

CORNELIA Story was already there, bah. I just picked the right one.

AASHI *(from the back, raising her voice)* Leong Kin! They never had such awards for journalists before. How on earth did we know we could write back then?

LEONG KIN Hallo, why spoil the girl's party?

AASHI Who wants to spoil?

CORNELIA *(to Leong Kin)* Who's that?

AASHI *(still loud, sarcastic)* 'Well done, keep up the good work'.

LEONG KIN *(to Cornelia, as if to explain the rude interruption but lightly)* Dari Semenanjung...[1] go introduce yourself.

Cornelia walks over to Aashi's desk and extends her hand. Aashi shakes it.

CORNELIA Cornelia... Did you read it?

AASHI What?

CORNELIA My story.

AASHI Your award-winning story?

CORNELIA Yes!

AASHI No.

CORNELIA Would you like to?

AASHI No!

CORNELIA *(taken aback)* OK.

AASHI I can guess what it's about: how fragile the ecosystem. How evil the company. How pitiful that everybody, but everybody, is screwing the environment. *(Beat)*

CORNELIA I don't use that kind of language.

---

1. Peninsular Malaysia

AASHI 'See How They Spoiled Sipadan',[2] wasn't it?

CORNELIA 'The Death of Our Coral Islands' actually – brain, boulder, spaghetti coral too.

AASHI Spaghetti coral?

LEONG KIN Looks like worms going lenggang lenggok[3] in the water.

CORNELIA Latin name, Euphyllia. It's dying. So many islands are in danger.

AASHI Of what?

CORNELIA Disappearing.

AASHI I thought that's what coral does; come and go.

CORNELIA It's vital for ocean life.

AASHI I never knew that.

CORNELIA *(not getting her)* Yah, a lot of people don't.

AASHI So you think, if they knew, they would care?

CORNELIA Of course. No awareness, no understanding.

AASHI Better we don't know, then we don't have to care.

CORNELIA *(sincerely)* Malaysia is a caring society, aiming to be.

AASHI *(to Leong Kin)* Someone's actually read Vision 2020? *(To Cornelia)* Just now, you said the word 'dying'. And spaghetti what?

CORNELIA Spaghetti coral, yes.

AASHI But dying as in, say, 'our justice system is dying'?

Leong Kin clears his throat, as if to warn but Aashi continues.

AASHI As in, say, a recent report claims migrant workers in Malaysian camps have died of 'beri beri'. Last seen in survivors of Japanese prisoner-of-war camps! As in, people in Malaysian prisons can spend years in remand so they might as well be dying in wait before they get to court! Or perhaps you mean dying as in, it seems these days, there are more deaths in police custody than during the British?

---

2. World-renowned island for scuba-diving
3. Walking with a sensuous hip-movement

LEONG KIN *(to Cornelia)* Ignore her, bloody eel, hides behind rocks, just comes out to bite.

AASHI Are you calling my office a rock?

LEONG KIN It's between a rock and a hard place. And it's 'during the time of the British' or 'the colonial period', not 'during the British'.

AASHI *(smiles briefly)* Leong Kin, amateur historian. Can debate a detail to death and miss the point entirely.

LEONG KIN *(to Cornelia)* My point was grammatical not historical.

AASHI You see? Now really, Ms. Award Winner. Haven't you noticed something about these greenie stories?

CORNELIA You mean? I'm proud of them.

AASHI Oh yes, poor dear flying squirrel, splat. Devote pages to it, of what even looks like analysis. But on issues closer to home? Quiet as a bloody mouse.

LEONG KIN There was a story once about a mouse, glowed in the dark.

AASHI The story or the mouse?

CORNELIA But the environment is home.

AASHI So much squid ink. *(To Cornelia)* You know almond jelly?

CORNELIA Yes...

AASHI You like almond jelly?

Cornelia hesitates, getting Aashi by now.

AASHI Who doesn't like almond jelly? *(Then)* Your kind of story is like almond jelly. Comes at the end of the meal, goes down well, just doesn't taste of anything. Tasteless. Everybody is too full to think about what's really *(looks at Cornelia)* at sea.

CORNELIA Haven't you heard of global warming?

AASHI 'Haven't I heard of global warming'? Oh yes, I'm familiar with that multinational, Greenpeace. And I understand the anxiety about existence. But my idea of salvation is not a Philips energy-saver light bulb. The sun is getting hotter. Can't do much about that. And this planet is a six billion year-old star.

LEONG KIN Planet or star?

AASHI It's going to close shop one day whether you 'off' your aircon or not. You think, because you burn vanilla candles, everyone is dancing bharatanatyam with joy up there in the ozone layer? You can't catch rainbows in the palm of your hand! Immediate realities, please. We used to focus on real crimes and stay with them.

CORNELIA S... screwing the environment is a real crime.

LEONG KIN I wonder why red herring? They're silver.

AASHI *(still at Cornelia)* Why does it get so much coverage?

CORNELIA It doesn't.

AASHI Of course it does. Neck and neck with rape and sexual abuse. Because that's almond jelly too. Who's going to disagree, you see? Somebody's got to ask the tough questions. And count the boats out and back in. It really is a journalist's calling.

CORNELIA *(as if it has just come to her)* I know. You're being a professional cynic.

AASHI No, 'professional native'. The PM once called greenies selfish, and I agree. 'All they want is for the Penan to be wandering around the forest – blowpipes, bogel[4] – for the tourist cameras. Like professional natives.'

CORNELIA Pardon me but you're not native.

Aashi looks bemused at Leong Kin who responds with a shrug.

CORNELIA Have you even seen any coral?

AASHI Sure. Looks like bird bones. What's the big deal?

CORNELIA I mean, alive.

AASHI Cannot afford to scuba dive.

LEONG KIN Port Klang Achi. Cannot even swim! Table tennis, can.

AASHI We've evolved for millions of years to get out of the bloody water, and you want me to get back in. I will not. I'd rather stay with the muck I know than the muck I don't! Ya, table tennis can. Just stand and deliver and spar.

---

4. Naked

CORNELIA Let me take you sometime.

AASHI Spare me any fucking underwater beauty crap.

CORNELIA Hey! Respect for elders but if they just swear and...

AASHI *(interrupts)* Who are you calling elderly? My dear sumandak penampang[5] and I mean this with a poppadom of sincerity. How wonderful that you chose journalism. Or did our superlative university lottery select 'Mass Comm' when all you wanted was Nuclear Physics?

CORNELIA That's my business.

AASHI Oh dear, my talent for accuracy.

CORNELIA But I had to go to Semenanjung to study. We're not big enough for a university yet.

AASHI *(to Leong Kin)* Let's see, together with Sarawak, that's what, 70% of the whole country? *(To Cornelia)* You can go much further than that silly little peninsula!

CORNELIA What are the sources for what you said earlier?

AASHI Why, you going to check them?

CORNELIA You used them like the truth bah.

AASHI Find your own bloody sources.

LEONG KIN She was asking.

CORNELIA You said deaths in police custody more than during the British. How do you know?

AASHI One, I said it 'seems' like it. Two, I urge you to find out. And three, it's 'during the time of the Brit–'

Enter Messenger.

MESSENGER Boss wants to see you. Now bah.

They all react differently. Cornelia is interested. Leong Kin looks worried. Aashi hesitates.

MESSENGER Cornelia.

AASHI Uh oh. Better you than me.

Cornelia leaves. The conversation is less heightened now.

---

5. Innocent village beauty

LEONG KIN You know, you should lie low.

AASHI I'm in Sabah! How low do you want me to go?

LEONG KIN You're the one picking on easy targets. Stop shooting your mouth off.

AASHI Multimedia morons. If we had flowers in our hair, this lot has rafflesia for brains. Once a year, they'll have a thought. Is that what we deserve?

LEONG KIN I thought, for a moment there...

AASHI What? I report car thefts and accidents now. And when did you ever get so gutless?

LEONG KIN Yah, yah, you got enough for all of us.

AASHI A tidak apa[6] attitude leads to dictatorship and tyranny!

LEONG KIN Don't be ridiculous!

AASHI We used to work for an independent paper!

LEONG KIN Arm's length.

AASHI OK, but now we're down to editors who can't spell, wandering the corridors in double-breasted suits, little anchor signs on the gold buttons, like so many *laksamana*[7] wannabes. This country's going down alright! *(Leong Kin sighs)* How do you do it, Leong Kin.

LEONG KIN What?

AASHI Switch off.

LEONG KIN I don't! I cannot just up and leave. Besides, I want the kids to know Selingan island, off Sandakan not Rottnest, off Perth. When we know where we come from, we know where we're going.

AASHI Oh, please lah. Look at all those temples in Bujang Valley. Hindus were here over 1,500 years ago. So what? I know where I'm going – to build temples, is it?

LEONG KIN Proves that's 1,500, not just 150 years of pendatang![8]

---

6. 'Couldn't care less'
7. Malay title, akin to Admiral
8. Derogatory word, meaning foreigner

AASHI Right, temples, rubber and railways, three splendid careers.

LEONG KIN Santayana says 'those who cannot remember the past are condemned to repeat it'.

AASHI Which bloody past? In Bujang, did they speak Telugu? That would be good news for mother. She's never cared for bloody Tamil.

LEONG KIN Pick and choose! National Geographic says we all came out of Africa.

AASHI Tell that to the UMNO General Assembly. If you ask me, it should be 'those who know their history are inspired to repeat it'. Look at the ethnic cleansing in Bosnia Herzegovina. Centuries of it. Our Melayu Ultramen would do it too, if only they dared.

LEONG KIN Oh, toxic cynic. I leave it to the next generation. And *takdir*[9].

Aashi is silent; seems rather disoriented.

LEONG KIN But ya, immediate realities. Lunch?

Leong Kin gathers his things and doesn't notice Aashi who is still disoriented.

AASHI Yes?

LEONG KIN Lunch. How about the Western food stall? Got pork chop, coral spaghetti...

AASHI Later. Work to do.

LEONG KIN How many car accidents can there be in one day?

AASHI Ha.

Lights out.

SCENE 3

Soundscape of forest, bullets and rough sex.

9. Fate

SCENE 4

A Sports club. Hamid in golf gear; a half-filled glass of beer on the table. Aashi walks in hurriedly, carrying a bottle of Bubble Up with a straw.

AASHI Hamid, so sorry I'm late...

HAMID It's OK but I must pretend to play golf soon.

AASHI At least they let you in.

HAMID *(laughs)* Still takes a damn passport! What lah buggers. Not until Noah builds another ark is it?

AASHI I finally read the Twenty Points of 1963 – 'unfettered control' for immigration!

HAMID Foreigners in our own country.

AASHI I know. Talk about exotic. Number Two: 'While there is no objection to Islam being the national religion of Malaysia, there should be no State religion in North Borneo, and the provisions relating to Islam in the present Constitution of Malaya should not apply to North Borneo.' And Number Four: 'The Head of State in North Borneo shall not be eligible for election as Head of the Federation.' It *is* a different country.

HAMID I should be able to practise anywhere.

AASHI They're not stupid.

HAMID So inconvenient.

AASHI Pairin has held out well. But it must be like watching the waters rise. The Weatherman of the Peninsula will start a storm soon.

HAMID But you, got your toes in the sand? How's everything?

AASHI Compared with?

HAMID Well, heaven and hell are clear enough. What's purgatory like?

AASHI It has its seafood. I can't believe how many Catholics there are here. It's like Jalan Gasing Road on a Sunday. Times ten. Even Moses lived in Sabah, you know.

HAMID Eh?

AASHI Charles Lee Moses, American ambassador, 1800 something.

HAMID Wah, your new 'home state'?

AASHI Must make an effort...! So how?

HAMID Your Mother asked me if you're taking your medication.

AASHI *Bubble up.*

HAMID What's that?

AASHI *(hands Hamid the bottle) Bubble Up.*

Hamid sips the Bubble Up.

HAMID It's just like *7-up* or *Sprite*. Even that must be different!

AASHI I feel like I moved to the baby pool. Tell me some real news.

HAMID OK, OK. There will be an official report, after all.

AASHI When?

HAMID About a month's time.

AASHI Who knows about it?

HAMID *(shakes his head as if to say, nobody)* It's yours. He got to see remand prisoners.

AASHI Where?

HAMID Seven in Taiping, five in Alor Setar and another seven in Johor Bahru.

AASHI How did he get to them?

HAMID *Ada cable lah!*[10]

AASHI But how come they let him in?

HAMID Because nobody will believe the report? I don't know.

AASHI You lawyers uh, ten a penny but act like the British Mint itself.

HAMID Ya and who kept me waiting, like the tide coming in?

AASHI Sorry la... In Taiping, how many are up for murder?

---

10. 'He has connections!'

HAMID All. Except one for ganja trafficking, Melayu. Rest, all Cina.

AASHI What kind of delays?

HAMID Five or six years, mostly. One guy said he had to make forty-three trips to the Kuala Kangsar Court before the Prelim Enquiry was completed!

Aashi takes notes.

AASHI And then?

HAMID The Melayu fella has been in a kind of solitary confinement for the past eight years. Allowed to *mandi*[11] and wash a tin for his toilet needs. Locked in his cell otherwise.

AASHI You have the names la.

Hamid nods.

AASHI What about Alor Setar?

HAMID All up for drug or ganja trafficking, murder. They complain about the defence counsel who never visits them. Judges get it too in the Report. One guy's prelim enquiry ended five years ago. Still waiting for a hearing. Another guy, his hearing was postponed eleven times.

AASHI What about Immigration overstays?

HAMID Interviews were done with Vietnamese, Thais, Nigerians and... I mean...

AASHI What?

HAMID Some of it, hard to believe. One fella, detained five years ago, said he was a Captain of the South Vietnam Army. Surrendered to the Malaysian army, along with two others. Case was handled by Immigration. He was sentenced for three months, served it, but he's still in remand, five years later. He organized a hunger strike with the others. Prison department got them to call it off, but one guy tried to commit suicide. In fact, another tried to hang himself, he's now a mental case... Of the Thai buggers, one fella tried to slit his throat with a tin can. Another fella hung himself, but also didn't get it right. He's now a mental case...

11. Bathe

AASHI I can believe. You're sure, ya?

HAMID Scout's honour.

AASHI Oh God.

HAMID Just because I joined to sit next to my favourite Brownie, Hayati! Now, there's this one guy *(leans forward, voice low)*. He's not in the Report. Nobody knows how much about him, I thought you should know.

AASHI Who, where?

HAMID Your new home state lah! Seems he was in Kepayan at one point.

Aashi listens.

HAMID *(builds the tale up)* This guy. From Sandakan. Murdered his own mother. Cut her eyes out with a kitchen knife. Plucked the eyeballs clean, not eyebrows you know. Eyeballs, clean out of their sockets. She was a fruitseller, chicken seller, something. Seems he removed the eyeballs from ten people he killed – five men, three women and two mak nyah.[12] Collected all the eyeballs in a small Milo tin, it seems. Or was it two Milo tins...

AASHI Oh come on!

HAMID Serious! Set fire to his fingers to lose his fingerprints. Swallowed paraquat[13] and survived, it seems.

AASHI Really.

HAMID They call him Tarap Man.

AASHI Tarap?

HAMID Can talk Moses, but don't know tarap. It's a fruit lah, head size, skin very easy to push open, inside are not the biji[14]. Smells like cempedak[15].

AASHI So?

---

12. Transgender (male to female)
13. Herbicide, poisonous to humans if swallowed
14. Seeds
15. A kind of breadfruit

HAMID Seems he was eating tarap when they found him next to the mother's body... He may have swallowed the eyeballs, biji about the same size.

AASHI Sounds like a wild goose chase.

HAMID Well, that's it, end of story. The guy who told me, trying to scare me or what. Anyway, nah the names.

Hamid hands Aashi a file and gets up.

AASHI Eh, you're leaving already?

HAMID I can't tell my irons from my woods, and they still ask me to play. Like one hand tied behind my back.

AASHI Oh, the non-bumi [16] handicap.

HAMID Please pray I get a pretty caddie.

AASHI Don't get marooned with one again.

Hamid exits. Aashi eats Hamid's leftover sandwiches as she writes in her notepad.

SCENE 5

In the dark, at first we hear a male voice, aged about 14, speaking low, almost a whisper... Then the silhouette of a boy can be just made out, walking back and forth within a cramped space. He speaks in Hakka (Maoyen dialect), mostly, but counting and left, right in Japanese.

BOY *(calling out)* Sui'ga! Sui'ga! San'chuk [Watermelons! Watermelons! Mangosteen]

Mok'ga! Monggoh! Pat'chai [Papaya! Mango! Guava]

Hiongjau! Hiongjau! Niulen! [Bananas! Bananas! Durian!]

Bo'loh! Taisu Bo'loh [Pineapple! Jackfruit]

Ta-lap! Ta-lap! Ta-lap [Tarap! Tarap! Tarap]

---

16. bumi, short for 'bumiputra' ('sons/princes of the earth'); a political term for the Balays, Orang Asli and other ethnic groups considered indigenous to Malaysia and who therefore stand to benefit from particular 'special rights' in the Malaysian Constitution and/or a national affirmative action policy

Yit, ngee, sam, see, ng [One, two, three, four, five]
Lieu, chit, pak, qiu, sip [Six, seven, eight, nine, ten]
Hidari, migi, hidari, migi [Left, right, left right]
Hidari, migi, hidari, migi [Left, right, left right]
Ngai miang heh [My name is...]
Sze Sze, Sze Sze, Sze Sze
Sui'ga! Sui'ga! [Watermelon! Watermelon!]
Kamchai, kamchai [Oranges-green skin, oranges-green skin]
Yit, ngee, sam, see, ng [One, two, three, four, five]
Roku, chit, shichi, pak, qiu [a mix of numbers]

SCENE 6

Hawker Stall. Cornelia and Leong Kin at lunch.

CORNELIA Those how-to-be-a-journalist books never say must have sarcasm bah.

LEONG KIN You have to remember, she's a giant.

CORNELIA A skinny old harimau![17]

LEONG KIN Once, she wrote a commentary on affirmative action – ours compared with Australian aborigines, North-American Indians, women. You never saw eight hundred words of more poetic punch... spiked.

CORNELIA *(bored)* Oh I see.

LEONG KIN I don't want to be patronizing so I'm sure I will be.

CORNELIA I mean, OK, good, but about the N.E.P.,[18] right? Cari pasal sahaja![19]

LEONG KIN *(sighs)* Once upon a time, there was a fourth estate.

CORNELIA Where?

---

17. Tiger
18. New Economic Policy (1971–1990) The first name for a national affirmative action plan designed to eradicate poverty and eliminate identification of race by occupation. Has been extended and re-named.
19. 'Asking for trouble'

LEONG KIN "Burke said there were Three Estates in Parliament, but in the Reporters Gallery yonder, there sat a Fourth Estate more important far than they all"... Thomas Carlyle.

CORNELIA *(peeved)* Coba ulang dalam BM bah.[20]

LEONG KIN Maybe there's a Dewan Bahasa translation somewhere – typo errors to cripple your eyesight and grammar to rot your gut. Her column was simple, elegant, and provocative. Not like those who think they can hold two 'thots' in their head. But she got too big for her boots.

CORNELIA Cannot imagine that bah.

LEONG KIN *(smiles)* She had support you see – at first. Thought she was immune. Then she criticised more names in high places that had friends in higher places...

CORNELIA Oh, she got fired! That's why she's here.

LEONG KIN She was put in cold storage. That's the way. Aashi has integrity to make you blush. But the ego, that's the problem.

CORNELIA I thought it was her bad breath.

LEONG KIN You can learn a lot from her.

CORNELIA Swear words and bad manners? Not all journalists are like that.

LEONG KIN Thick skin, foul mouth – industrial injuries.

CORNELIA How come you're not like her?

LEONG KIN *(smiling)* I'm not as good. We were jobless once, 'in between' jobs, in PR.

CORNELIA *(as if, beneath her)* PR? You?

LEONG KIN Yah, why not? A lot of bright and beautiful women in PR...

CORNELIA Is she here for long?

LEONG KIN Some people wash up here like flotsam and jetsam, but don't be rude bah.

CORNELIA Hey, no, sorry, I didn't mean you. Thanks for your help with my article. My family is so proud.

---

20. 'Yes but, what about a reference in Malay?'

LEONG KIN Don't mention it. It's a great start.

He takes her hand. She responds. Then they remember they are in public.

SCENE 7

Prison. Zon Kepayan, Kota Kinabalu.

Aashi walks up to the guardhouse. Guard 1 looks at Aashi who remains calm, deferential. Guard 2 is pleasant enough, asks for her Identity Card (IC). The scene has comic potential given characters of the Guards (one of whom 'sounds Indonesian').

AASHI Saya nak jumpa Encik Rosli. [I want to meet Mr. Rosli.]

GUARD 1 Ada surat? [Do you have a letter?]

Aashi passes a letter over the counter. Guard 1 looks at the letter then shows Guard 2.

GUARD 2 Tunggu sebentar. [Wait a moment.]

Guard 2 makes a call/disappears then returns, looks at Guard 1 as if there is a problem; whispers something. They confer for a while.

GUARD 1 Sorry, not possible today.

AASHI Not possible? Tetapi tadi sebelum datang, saya sudah confirm dengan pejabatnya Encik Rosli. [But before I came, I confirmed things with Mr. Rosli's office.]

GUARD 1 Sorry, no visitors.

AASHI But you took my IC.

GUARD 2 Yah, you can have it back *(returns her IC)*.

AASHI But I have an appointment! Tak perlu surat ke? [The letter isn't necessary?]

GUARD 1 Ya perlu. [It's necessary.]

AASHI Then?

GUARD 1 Today cannot!

AASHI Why?

GUARD 2 You want to make trouble, is it?

AASHI Why people cannot just call to cancel?

GUARD 2 Which people?

AASHI *(improvising, naming the furthest place she can think of)* I came far you know – from Kelantan.

GUARD 1 *(as if he too is from the same state)* Kelantan, oh! Dari mana? [From where?]

AASHI Let me try and speak to his secretary. Puan Lim.

GUARD 1 You cannot use this phone.

GUARD 2 If *he's* in a meeting, then *she's* in a meeting.

AASHI *(awkward with the parlance)* Come on. Bah, Sir.

GUARD 1 Cannot help you. Sorry.

AASHI Yah, I'm sorry too.

Aashi takes the letter back.

GUARD 2 Kurang ajar. [No manners.]

SCENE 8

Open Plan Office. We see Cornelia reluctantly sit in a chair and desk next to Aashi's desk where there was no place before. Aashi arrives.

AASHI What are you doing here?

CORNELIA I'm on the Crime Beat.

AASHI Over my dead body.

CORNELIA Wasn't me... There was a memo.

AASHI Don't tell me.

CORNELIA I'm not such a problem bah.

AASHI Your mother's the editor and that's not a problem?

CORNELIA *(surprised)* Huh? She's not...

AASHI *(interrupts)* She might as well be. Such mollycoddling – sorry – 'career guidance'.

CORNELIA I have a lot to learn from you, it seems.

AASHI Since when did I look interested to teach?

Cornelia is starting to know Aashi better and does not respond.

AASHI *(busying herself at her desk)* I know what purgatory is. It's a fresh graduate!

Cornelia sighs.

AASHI Don't expect to follow me like a shadow.

CORNELIA I won't, don't worry.

AASHI Been to the courts?

CORNELIA Yes.

AASHI Good, then you can get there by yourself.

CORNELIA ... What should I do, actually?

AASHI *(explodes)* You see, it's questions like that! Just a waste of breath! Questions are priceless! Not like any old dead rubber seed lying on the ground. Diamonds – shine, polish, take care. So, what do you think? And if you can't think, sit there and listen!

CORNELIA You want me to go now to the courts?

AASHI You have to go first thing in the morning.

CORNELIA Yah bah I know!

AASHI Then don't ask me what you already know. Use your common sense.

CORNELIA *(sarcastic)* This is what they call in-house training.

AASHI I don't get paid to baby-sit. Baa baa black sheep. *(Then)* By the way, when is tarap in season?

CORNELIA Not sure these days. Why?

AASHI Just asking.

Aashi exits, leaving Cornelia to herself.

SCENE 9

Editor's Office. Regina (friendly but somewhat intimidating, and with a strong Kadazan[21] *accent) sits opposite Aashi who looks smaller in her chair somehow.*

21. Main indigenous ethnic group in Sabah

REGINA It's a measure of my faith in you, Aashi.

AASHI As a dumping ground!

REGINA She has potential!

AASHI Everybody has that.

REGINA Just a small request.

AASHI I'll see what I can do, to put her off.

REGINA She's the only one of her batch to finish. Training is tedious, I know.

AASHI Some batch.

REGINA Oh, stop growling.

Things are a bit uncomfortable between them but not unfriendly.

REGINA Need any help?

AASHI *(she does not mean Cornelia)* No, you've given me enough.

REGINA What are you working on?

AASHI Mental health and mental hospitals. What they're like these days.

REGINA Oh. World Mental Health Day soon?

AASHI Yes, could be good for that. *(Beat)*

REGINA Please don't be a musang[22] and leave a stink.

AASHI Smells clear to me.

REGINA I hope so, Aashi.

AASHI Yes ma'am!

REGINA No need any 'ma'am' business.

AASHI Just trying to show respect for my elders.

REGINA *(chuckles)* Where did you get *that?*

AASHI Thanks.

REGINA You're welcome.

---

22. Civet, a nocturnal mammal found commonly in parts of Malaysia

SCENE 10

Man 1 stands next to young Boy/Man who is blindfolded. The Boy/Man is expecting something pleasant.

In walk Man 2 and Man 3, with a single cup cake and candle, singing 'Happy Birthday'.

MAN 1 Selamat datang ke Taiping!

They take the cup cake away and kick him to the ground.

SCENE 11

Aashi meets Rudy at a hawker stall. Aashi tries to please Rudy who is pleasant enough.

RUDY Not many people want to become male nurses!

AASHI Must be quite dangerous.

RUDY Not really. I like to help people.

AASHI A cousin of mine got sick one time, we didn't know what to do. Nobody liked to talk about her in the family. If we did, then we might get sick too. Thank God for somebody like you.

RUDY Yeah, it's not easy.

AASHI To be honest, Rudy, thanks for this. But I'm also trying to find someone. I don't know if he's in Sim Sim or not.

RUDY A member of your family?

AASHI Not directly.

RUDY Nobody can help, unless you're a family member.

AASHI No, it's OK, I'm not asking you. I'm just saying that I'm looking for someone. I need help to find him.

Rudy is silent.

AASHI He's 50 plus. From Sandakan also...

RUDY Where are you looking?

AASHI The homes, care centres.

RUDY What's his name?

AASHI ... I only know his nickname. Tarap Man.

Rudy shrugs.

AASHI I want to help him.

RUDY *(cutting)* Just because I said I like to help people?

AASHI I'm investigating something. I cannot do it by myself, and you must know a lot of people... You've been so helpful, so... I'm just trying my luck lah.

RUDY I can see what I can do but you don't hope.

SCENE 12

Open plan office, Aashi's desk. Cornelia walks in. She sits down, puts bag around chair, looks around her, then sits in Aashi's chair, tries it for size. Enter Aashi.

AASHI Somebody is slouching in my chair.

CORNELIA Oh, sorry.

She hurries to sit in her own chair. Aashi notes this as well as her subsequent lack of energy as she attempts to look busy. There is a rare moment of quiet. Aashi starts to type as she talks.

AASHI So tell me. What was it you wanted to study originally?

CORNELIA Syariah law.[23]

AASHI Oh! That's much more advanced than multimedia. Tun Suffian once said, he sees an Islamic judiciary in 30 to 40 years time. Is your family Muslim?

CORNELIA No. And my second and third choice was law.

AASHI So what did you get?

CORNELIA Hotel management.

AASHI Oh dear.

CORNELIA It's OK, this way I stay close to my family.

---

23. Sharia Law – rules for those living under a legal system based on Islam

AASHI Why, are they in danger of disappearing too? Sorry, I meant disappointing. It must have been disappointing for you.

CORNELIA It was, but I got work at the Hyatt. Helped out with the newsletter. Then came here.

AASHI Great thing about journalism. Attracts anything and everything.

CORNELIA I never understood that until now.

AASHI *(turns back to typing)* So, what have you been doing?

CORNELIA You said, cover the courts.

AASHI Oh yes, I did.

CORNELIA Nothing very interesting...

AASHI I'm not a crime reporter, by the way. Don't have the stomach for it – graveyard shifts, hobnobbing with the police to get the scoops they want you to get...

CORNELIA I'd like to work on a big story.

AASHI Big?

CORNELIA I've got data on how many prisons, rehab centres, which ones for women, young offenders, categories of crimes...

AASHI Why prisons?

CORNELIA Because you're interested in them. I heard you were researching them...

AASHI Don't listen to everything Leong Kin tells you.

CORNELIA Our prisons and repatriation camps don't conform to international standards.

AASHI Says who?

CORNELIA The latest International Crime Commission reports. There are Minimum Rules for the Treatment of Offenders and not all our prisons or camps have them.

AASHI Oooo. 'International' reports. Must be good.

CORNELIA There are local NGO. reports too.

AASHI You trust them?

CORNELIA And news from the Bar Council.

AASHI Their everlasting quorum conundrum.

CORNELIA A report on remand prisoners, by a Jagjit Singh–

AASHI How did you get it?

CORNELIA Email...

AASHI They don't all conform with Minimum Rules because prisons come under the Prisons department but the camps come under the Immigration department. And since when did a fella who chops passports know how to run a prison!

CORNELIA The *camps* don't conform then. I thought, should compare sources.

AASHI Read them. All. Good. But use your own head! Prisons in other countries don't always conform either, and I don't just mean Somalia. Is this your 'big' lead?

CORNELIA I thought I'd wait for your OK first.

AASHI What's your key question?

CORNELIA What's wrong with our prisons?

AASHI Nothing's wrong with them!

CORNELIA But you just said...?

AASHI People are in there who shouldn't be in there. You can't print that.

CORNELIA But Thursday's editorial. It praised our Minister for wanting to cut down the crime rate, said the public should help...

AASHI You read editorials? You do read a lot, don't you? As for the public? The dear public? Screaming blue murder for handbag thieves to get longer sentences? Think again, you have to think again.

CORNELIA If you're not a crime reporter, how come you got crime? It doesn't make sense.

AASHI Regina doesn't expect me to put my foot in my mouth. But I will tell you... that I need to know more about criminal law in the 1950s.

CORNELIA The 1950s?

AASHI Ancient history, I know.

CORNELIA For what?

AASHI Back then, how old was a minor? Aged 10, 12, 16? And what exactly is doli incapax?[24] I need Acts that relate to mental health. The Juvenile Courts Act 1947; Protection of Women and Girls Act, 1937. Am looking for someone who might be in prison or mental hospital. *(Beat)* Bring on the coral spaghetti!

CORNELIA You mean I research with you?

Aashi is experiencing disorientation again.

AASHI Sorry?

CORNELIA We research this together?

AASHI Yes, yes... *(Recovers)* What am I, deaf? You know how, don't you? There's a Lunatics Act, 1951. For Sabah only... imagine that.

CORNELIA Funny.

AASHI Get me the Acts. *(To herself)* I could use the help.

CORNELIA Sorry?

Aashi tries to say something that sounds like 'the Acts, the Acts' but this is said with some difficulty; doesn't sound like her usual self.

Cornelia hesitates but then gets into action.

Aashi snaps her fingers near Cornelia's ears as if to test her hearing.

SCENE 13

Zon Kepayan. Aashi and Cornelia walk up to the guardhouse. The same Guards are on duty. Same Identity Card (IC) ritual. Same comic potential as earlier scene with Guards (Act I, Sc 7).

AASHI Kami nak jumpa Encik Rosli. [We want to meet Mr. Rosli.]

GUARD 1 Ada surat? [Do you have a letter?]

Aashi passes a letter over the counter. Cornelia smiles. Guard 1 looks at the letter then shows Guard 2.

GUARD 1 Eh...

---

24. Means that a child is 'incapable of crime' under legislation or common law.

AASHI Yah, kami nak jumpa Encik Rosli. [We want to meet Mr. Rosli.] Boleh tak? [Can we?]

Guard 2 looks at letter and shakes her head to Guard 1. Guard 1 indicates that Guard 2 should check first, go make a call. Guard 2 does so.

GUARD 1 Encik Rosli baru keluar! Dia ada meeting di Bandar. [Mr. Rosli just left! He has a meeting in town.]

AASHI Baru keluar? Tetapi saya baru panggil pejabatnya! [Just left? But I just called his office!]

GUARD 1 Uda keluar bah. [He's already gone.]

AASHI Sekali lagi. [Yet again.]

GUARD 1 Encik Rosli selalu sebok. Kadang kadang orang panggil dia 'Short Notice'. [Mr. Rosli is always busy. Sometimes people call him 'Short Notice'.]

Guard 2 comes back and shakes her head again. Aashi stands, frustrated.

AASHI *(to Cornelia)* Can you believe it?

Cornelia takes the initiative and leads Aashi away from the guardhouse.

CORNELIA OK, terima kasih, Encik, Cik, terima kasih. [Thanks Mr., Miss...] *(To Aashi)* I'll just try to talk to them...

Cornelia returns to the guardhouse.

CORNELIA Maaf bah, saya nak tanya, Encik Rosli pulang pukul berapa? [Sorry, but I'd like to ask: what time will Mr. Rosli return?]

GUARD 2 Tak tahu. [Don't know.]

GUARD 1 Besok pagi... mungkin. [Tomorrow morning... maybe.]

CORNELIA *(to Guard 1 who seems warmer)* Boleh tak, kami tunggu sini? [Is it OK if we wait here?]

GUARD 1 Tunggu? [Wait?]

CORNELIA Kasian dia. Dia nak tanya Encik Rosli satu soalan sahaja. Dia udah tunggu udah lama bah... [Pity her, she just wants to ask Mr. Rosli just one question. She's been waiting for a long time.]

Silence from Guards.

GUARD 1 Apa soalannya? [What question is that?]

CORNELIA Ingat tak Mat Salleh, Antanom, pahlawan tua? [Do you remember, Mat Salleh, Antanom, those old warriors?]

GUARD 1 Yah...?

CORNELIA Dia tengah research pasal orang-orang terkenal bah, pahlawan da orang kriminal juga... macam Botak Chin... [Well, she's doing research about well-known people like that, warriors, criminals... like Botak Chin.]

GUARD 2 Kamu bekerja dengan dia? [Do you work with her?]

CORNELIA Ya... junior bah! Dia jumpa satu orang terkenal di Sabah. Kamu pernah dengar pasal Tarap Man? [She's found out about a famous guy in Sabah. Have you heard of Tarap Man?]

GUARD 2 Tak pernah dengar pun. [No, never heard.]

GUARD 1 Siapa? [Who?]

GUARD 2 Tarap... Man...

CORNELIA ... from the 1970s...

GUARD 2 Takda. [No]

GUARD 1 Tak tau pun. [I don't recall, either.]

CORNELIA Dia bunuh mak dia bah! [He killed his own mother!]

They both shrug.

CORNELIA Dia korek mata maknya. [He gouged out his mother's eyes.]

GUARD 2 Mata? [Eyes?]

CORNELIA Iya... lepas tu dia simpan dalam tin Milo. [Yes, and after that, he kept them in a Milo tin.]

GUARD 1 ... Oh ya saya ingat... dia terkenal jugak *(to Guard 2)* Dia dulu di sini. [Oh yes, I remember. He was well known, that's right. He was even here at one point.]

Guard 2 nods.

CORNELIA Di sini, Kepayan? [Right here?]

GUARD 1 Sebenarnya, dia masuk mata tu dalam satu tin susu cap junjung! Selepas tu, dia tanam tu dalam utan. [Actually, he cooked the eyes in a tin of condensed milk! After that, he buried it all in the forest.]

CORNELIA Kamu pernah jumpa dia? [Do you know how we can meet him?]

GUARD 1 Tak, kawan saya. Dah lama tiada. Dia sudah pindah... Buli Sim Sim. Oh ya, ia terkenal. [No, my dear friend. He's long gone. He was sent to Buli Sim Sim mental hospital. Oh yes, he was famous.]

CORNELIA OK, ah... Dah lama tunggu kat sini. Terima kasih Encik, Cik, bye. [OK, well, we've been waiting here long enough. Thanks Mr., Miss.]

GUARD 1 OK...

Cornelia leaves the Guards and heads off towards Aashi.

GUARD 2 Siapa kawan kau yang kenal dia? [Who's your friend that knows him?]

SCENE 14

Aashi's desk. It is late at night. Leong Kin casually comes in, looks at things on the desk. He takes keys from under a drinks mat. Opens a locked drawer, finds something, looks around to see if anyone is listening, and then makes a short call.

LEONG KIN Well there's a tube of Smarties... *(Serious)* Uh, no. Something you might be interested in... I know she has been out several times there. Yes, both of them were out today.

Aashi enters. Listens, curious but then suspicious.

LEONG KIN Don't know where... Sure, sure, I'll let you know if they go anywhere. I can't keep an eye out all the time you know.

Leong Kin puts the phone down.

AASHI Who was that?

Leong Kin jumps a little.

AASHI Who were you talking to?

LEONG KIN Oh, someone from Accounts.

AASHI Accounts!

LEONG KIN Yes.

AASHI *(laughs)* Use your own phone for your office affairs... Have you got my keys?

LEONG KIN *(ill at ease)* I thought you said I can raid the hamoi[25] jar any time I want.

AASHI Don't fuck with me, Leong Kin.

LEONG KIN What are you talking about?

AASHI Who wants to know if you can keep an eye on me?

LEONG KIN Who said anything about you?

AASHI You can't even lie properly.

LEONG KIN Look, not everything has to be about you.

AASHI Don't give me that.

LEONG KIN My daughter has a tie. She's painted 'DTA' on it: Don't Trust Anyone. Where'd she get that idea? Must have been some school spat.

AASHI Must have been.

LEONG KIN You're being paranoid.

AASHI I don't need a nanny.

Aashi takes her keys and leaves. Leong Kin shrugs but he is disconcerted.

SCENE 15

Old Man appears in plain clothes eg black trousers, white T-shirt. He has a shock of white hair/crew cut. He tends to his fish tank in a small, makeshift but neat garden. The lighting suggests shifts and waves of breathtaking colour, of refractions of the sea, and colourful fish and coral in the tank writ large. The effect is magical.

25. Preserved white plums (an equivalent English expression might be jam jar or cookie jar)

Inmate joins him. More lights appear.

ACT TWO
SCENE 1

Recreation Centre. In the newspaper office. Cornelia and Aashi, in office clothes, set up the net on a table tennis table.

CORNELIA In 1952, no stomach purge would have been done. No expertise bah. So they wouldn't have checked whether he swallowed anything or not.

AASHI *(disagrees)* Stick a finger down your throat!

CORNELIA Well, Dr Mahadzir said they didn't do such things.

AASHI Who?

CORNELIA Head of forensics department. *(Moving on, keen to impress)*... In the Juvenile Court, all records were sealed to protect the minor, anyone under the age of 16. Doli incapax is the age that a child is 'held to be incapable of murder'.

AASHI Under 16 seems high.

CORNELIA It says 'less than 10 years old'.

AASHI And if you're aged 10?

CORNELIA I'll have to find out. If there were no guardians or family, the magistrate would have signed the final order to send him to Henry Gurney School.

AASHI Which one?

CORNELIA Melaka.

AASHI I thought there's one here?

CORNELIA No.

AASHI If he was there until his 21st birthday, then what?

CORNELIA Probably sent him to Taiping. They still go from the school to prison, if they haven't been pardoned. Permission to transfer prisoners from Semenanjung to Sabah and vice versa only started last year.

AASHI Started or officially started?

CORNELIA Our prison systems were aligned in 1975.

AASHI You own the prisons, is it? Stop the 'our'.

CORNELIA The public does own them.

AASHI *(dismisses)* How and when did he get back here?

CORNELIA *(shrugs)* ... Maybe parole?

AASHI Cannot be, there's none... That's why I went to Sim Sim. Was a bit of smoke and mirrors.

CORNELIA Maybe I should go.

AASHI No, I already know someone in there. But you could get some patient records.

CORNELIA But they're just for family members. Or someone with standing... Though the AG[26] can order records to be released.

AASHI Look into that option.

CORNELIA I wonder if anyone else has ever asked for his records?

AASHI Nobody will ask. They all want to blame.

CORNELIA You underestimate everybody.

AASHI No, not disgruntled residents associations!

Aashi picks up a table tennis bat, challenges Cornelia to play.

CORNELIA How come you play pingpong?

AASHI It's table tennis. I played it at school a lot! *(Then)* If you make a case that a person was not insane, can they re-open it?

CORNELIA Not on whether he was not insane in the past, but can, if he's not insane today.

Aashi picks up two table tennis balls, and holds them up to her eyes.

AASHI Aaarrgh! That was at least two horrifying double negatives.

CORNELIA You're sick bah!

AASHI Thanks for reminding me... *(Takes her pills)*

CORNELIA What are they for?

---

26. Abbreviation for Attorney-General, the country's highest ranking public prosecutor

AASHI Guess.

CORNELIA I don't know...

AASHI Don't be shy!

CORNELIA Heart condition, stress, high blood pressure?

AASHI What – all three?

CORNELIA Sorry!

AASHI Must be nice to be born with a silver snorkel in your mouth. When you go diving, do you use Daddy's boat?

CORNELIA Anybody can hire equipment. Hey, I can pick on you too, you know.

AASHI What makes you think those who fight for democracy are democratic themselves?

CORNELIA Have you ever been married?

AASHI Of all the diamonds in the world, you cut that one.

CORNELIA Well? I can't imagine.

AASHI I can tell you no.

CORNELIA Divorced or just not married?

AASHI The frigid spinster.

CORNELIA Oh yes. What does your name mean?

AASHI Smile.

Cornelia giggles.

AASHI My name means smile.

CORNELIA Your parents, too funny.

AASHI There's a history of depression in my family, you see. Wasn't in my father, Tamil union man. Sunny fella – no, make that blinding with hope. Even had time for uppity Jaffna tamils. My Telugu is from my mother's side.

CORNELIA Aashi, honestly, I can't tell when you're telling the truth bah... What's telugu?

AASHI Language from Andra Pradesh in Timbuktu.

CORNELIA Where's that?

AASHI Let's get to safer ground then. What else?

CORNELIA If we wanted to reopen a case, then his lawyer, or someone, would have to apply for a habeas corpus. The AG would then appoint three or four doctors to decide. Dr Mahadzir said our definition of lunacy...

AASHI That 'our'!

CORNELIA Medical and legal terms of mental health have changed but according to Dr Mahadzir, in the Lunacy Act–

AASHI Ordinance, no?

CORNELIA Ordinance... there's only lunacy. The definition hasn't changed since about 1890.

AASHI So, is he in Sim Sim?

CORNELIA Let's ask Leong Kin.

AASHI Let's not. *(Aashi gets ready)* Leaving now.

CORNELIA Game over?

AASHI Game over.

Cornelia is a little startled but follows.

SCENE 2

Mental Hospital. (Two scenes can interplay here, side by side. The other scene is of Leong Kin and Cornelia working in the office, getting closer)

Aashi is sitting opposite Inmate, a man, aged 70, in simple trousers and t-shirt. But they are silent. Rudy keeps an eye on them. After a few minutes, Aashi gets up and shakes Inmate's hand. Inmate leaves and Aashi joins Rudy.

Aashi shakes her head.

RUDY What's the problem?

AASHI He's not the right guy.

RUDY Eh?

AASHI Says they never spent time together.

RUDY Is it?

AASHI Don't lah bugger me about.

RUDY Sorry bah.

AASHI You said you could help me.

RUDY I said I would try only.

AASHI Then?

RUDY Why want to kacau?[27] You think you can help, is it?

AASHI I'm not trying to kacau... Why have you changed your mind? Are you in trouble?

RUDY No bah! But you cannot simply expect.

AASHI We agreed, what. *(Beat)*

RUDY No interviews.

AASHI You know where he is.

RUDY I know!

AASHI Then why did I waste my time with...?

RUDY No interviews.

AASHI I need to talk to him, not look at him! *(Beat)*

RUDY What can you do actually?

AASHI I'm not saying I can 'do' anything. I need to meet him first and talk to him. *(Beat)*

RUDY If you come again, don't buy tarap.

AASHI But I thought he likes it?

RUDY I like it but he doesn't.

He exits.

SCENE 3

Aashi is at her desk. Regina walks by.

REGINA I just got a call from a director of the Prisons department.

AASHI What about?

---

27. 'Stir things up'

REGINA Exactly. I thought you were onto mental health hospitals.

AASHI I am. What's the problem?

REGINA Why would they call me?

AASHI I don't know. I'm following a guy caught for stealing a Holden in 1965. When I have something, I'll run it by you.

REGINA A Holden in 1965? What are you working on?

AASHI *(hesitates)* What am I working on?

REGINA Whatever you're doing, it's not funny.

AASHI Actually, I... What time is it?

REGINA 5.15 pm. Aashi?

AASHI What day is it?

REGINA Aashi...

Aashi's mobile rings. She walks away, leaving Regina standing. As scene continues, the light slowly comes down around Aashi.

AASHI *(worried as never seen before)*

(In Telugu) Hallo? Hallo...? Amah? Oh Ammah. Nenu konthachepu mathleh kuntha poyannu! Nahku okthi Eenabadha lethu mari mana Regina munthikeh.

[Yes, mother, yes. I've been taking them... I can't. I didn't know what to do. For a moment, everything just... fell away. I felt the phone, saw your name and then I remembered. I was right in front of Regina.]

(Aashi listens)

Nakhu okithi Theliyalehthu. Antha oka mayalagah Jeriginthi.

[But I'm OK now, I'm better now, really, I'm sorry. Don't worry, it will be alright Mother.]

Nenu bhaga yunanu Ammah. Nagurinchi Bayapadharathu.

[I'll talk to you later. Mother. Yah, OK, I'll be fine. Bye.]

SCENE 4

Leong Kin and Cornelia are alone in the office.

LEONG KIN Come on, I'll give you a lift.

CORNELIA No, it's OK. I have a car today.

LEONG KIN Are you OK?

CORNELIA Yah sure, I'm fine.

LEONG KIN Haven't seen you... in some weeks.

CORNELIA I've been busy. Have to follow Aashi here and there bah.

LEONG KIN Of course.

CORNELIA I'm learning a lot. You were right.

LEONG KIN Just be careful.

CORNELIA About Aashi? I don't really care if she knows.

LEONG KIN No lah, she's not interested in such things. Her purpose is much bigger. She wants to save the world.

CORNELIA I admire her. She's brave.

They hug. Leong Kin with his back to audience, Cornelia facing audience, eyes open.

SCENE 5

Old Man is asleep, next to his fish tank. A Guard comes to wake him. We follow Old Man getting dressed. Before he leaves, he checks on his fish, aware of the Guard. He lifts the lid and puts it back carefully, twice. He then leaves and walks some way before coming into the light to meet someone...

As he approaches the person, we see it is Cornelia, dressed older and wearing an unlikely wig. She approaches Old Man who does not recognise her and becomes distressed.

Suddenly pandemonium as Old Man fights off the Male Nurse/ Guard (note, not Rudy). But he is soon overpowered and taken away. Cornelia is also taken away.

SCENE 6

Editor's Office. Regina and Aashi are standing in a face-off.

REGINA I told you, damn it!

AASHI I had nothing to do with it!

REGINA You didn't put her up to this? *(Shows file)*

AASHI *(acknowledging it)* I did say I could use some help.

REGINA You used a gung-ho guinea pig!

AASHI I did not! She's smart. You said so yourself.

REGINA You threw her in the deep end.

AASHI Come on, she can swim. Scuba-dive, for God's sake!

REGINA You're supposed to be her mentor.

AASHI Not twenty-four-seven! I was in a bloody temple. Nowhere near her half-baked scheme.

REGINA You were in a temple? *(Aashi doesn't reply)* I thought you got the point.

AASHI *(not a question)* Which particular one.

REGINA The lying low one. I created the crime desk just for you.

AASHI Yes and I've been doing that. Here is a man who has spent nearly 50 years inside. He was never found guilty or a lunatic!

REGINA From what I've read, you don't know that for sure.

AASHI Half a century at His Majesty's Pleasure! Full nine of their Majesties' Pleasures.

REGINA But there are serious gaps.

AASHI There's enough to take a stand.

REGINA On what! We can't run it just because it suggests some kind of 'epic miscarriage' of justice. Where is he now? It's not a story. It's a patchwork quilt.

AASHI And what if we got an interview with him?

REGINA Well then, that would be something. Pairin is at the residence waiting to be sworn in but the Head of State is suddenly unwell... That is our story.

AASHI This is big!

REGINA This is bigger! Aashi, come on, you must know, this on-going mistreatment of Pairin.[28] *(To herself)* Do they think we are idiots who dance the sumazau[29] every day before breakfast? Or maybe we ride horseback on our way to church, via the Niah caves? The election was legitimate! What are they trying to do?

Regina and Aashi have an imagined conversation with one another, or separate monologues. They speak in their respective mother tongues.

REGINA *(In Kadazan)* Asang zou titi tuhun Malaya! Manangsangi nopo om minggaga, om mokiazou dau.

AASHI *(in Telugu)* Manishi yoka Brathuku oka Bhayam tho yunthi. Manaki jeevitham mukium. Mari raajium mukium lethu.

REGINA *(in Kadazan)* Moboos ko pasal esai ti? Okon ko koinsan nogi hia... tuhun maiga diau popohomus boos kaka, mingkamamaha do popogingoh ngan nu di au songkuo di. Au no otuhid ginavo nu ti...

AASHI *(in Telugu)* Nena? Na maytha meeku namakamuletha?

REGINA *(in Kadazan)* Ee... ziau no tuhun! Au kou nangku kosoupingkuo topuimanan tokou songian tuhun suvai mopi pia ga tokou ngavi.

AASHI *(in Telugu)* Anteh! Kadazan variki, Dusun variki yeh behtam lethah? Allagah aiteh, Donald Stephens varini jayamponthincharu. Allagah aiteh miru Bajau varini, Indon varini, Filipino varini, thesaysthera? Miru mondithananga yunaru!

Above dialogue has been translated from following dialogue in English. Either version – original or translated – may be shown in subtitles, line by line. Alternatively, the actors could speak their mother tongue sections, non-stop, and untranslated on screen, and then speak the dialogue in English afterwards; the sound

28. Joseph Pairin Kitingan, a Malaysian politician and founder of PBS, the United Sabah Party, Chief Minister of Sabah (1985–1994), currently Deputy Chief Minister.
29. A traditional dance to mark the harvest

and meaning of their mother tongues is important and should be incorporated rather than using only English.

REGINA *(in Kadazan)* I can spot a Semenanjung[30] foreigner by the sneer. See how it stands, imperious in its complacency and arrogance.

AASHI *(in Telugu)* A human life is at stake here, not just a bloody state.

REGINA *(in Kadazan)* And whose life are we talking about? It wouldn't be the first time that a journalist used good intentions like a fresh nappy to clean up his soiled reputation.

AASHI *(in Telugu)* Me? Well, it is not a 'son of the soiled' reputation, if that's what you mean.

REGINA *(in Kadazan)* You of all people should understand what it's like to be a 24-hour stereotype.

AASHI *(in Telugu)* Me?

REGINA *(in Kadazan)* The Indian wordsmith, vocal, shrill, hysterical with injustice, carrying the weight of the third class world on her shoulders!

AASHI *(in Telugu)* Oh the spurious distinction between Kadazan and Dusun and who cares whether it was Donald Stephens! Oh sorry, Tun Fuad. You just want to ride roughshod over the Bajau and root out the bloody Indons and Filipinos! Smell a Semenanjung foreigner from afar, is it? Brothers-in-arms!

Phone rings/lighting snaps them out of their 'interior dialogue'.

REGINA You're on probation, remember.

AASHI You should support me. You're Editor. Not Managing Director.

REGINA Oh, Aashi. Slip on your own banana skins and blame it on others! But you're not the victim here.

AASHI Damn right I'm not! As a matter–

REGINA *(interrupts)* Cornelia will get a brown IC[31] for her little impersonation stunt! Nobody will ever hire her.

30. Peninsular Malaysia
31. Identity Card

AASHI Then keep her here. She's a good reporter.

REGINA I would have thought...

AASHI *(interrupts)* I'm a reporter, let me do my job.

REGINA I trusted you. Now I'm getting calls from everywhere and this is not the time. I thought we understood each other.

AASHI We do!

REGINA Then why can't you be practical?

AASHI About what!

REGINA Cornelia!

AASHI *(almost loses her voice)* Practical? *Practical??* I'm so bloody practical, I'm on my knees with it! I've been making a living, despite everything. And now that we have an exclusive, my editor wants to spike it.

REGINA I know you think he's been in for a long time. But what proof? *(Aashi is silent)* You can't risk everything on this. *(Aashi is silent)* Aashi.

AASHI This is one of those times when I think I'm going mad... Really. Am I hearing right? Is it gone? *(Then, to Regina)* Who will stand up for him? That's it, pure and simple as Hazeline Snow.[32] Where's your humanity?

REGINA I gave you a job, didn't I?

AASHI Oh bloody hell. I'm not asking for pity! Why are you asking for gratitude?

REGINA You should respect my opinion. Pairin is being refused – again, even though he won – again. A Chief Minister elected by the people! This is the story.

AASHI I get it, I do.

REGINA Then what?

AASHI You can do this. I wasn't sure you had it in you but you can! *(Beat)*

REGINA Wow, thank you for the faint praise. You think nothing of telling people how to do their job. Even me!

---

32. A kind of moisturising cream.

AASHI Somebody's got to do it.

REGINA OK, Aashi! Have it your way. Please take your things and be out of the office in 48 hours.

AASHI What!

REGINA I won't tolerate lack of respect. You ignored my express request.

AASHI I'm entitled to an opinion!

REGINA I've already told you to leave.

AASHI You're just like the rest of them.

Aashi exits. Immediately outside is Leong Kin who leads Aashi into a separate room/space. The lights become brighter.

SCENE 7

AASHI *(still hoarse)* What do you want?

LEONG KIN Stupid idiot!

AASHI Stupid bitch! I made a mistake.

LEONG KIN Always a bloody hero!

AASHI *(as if to herself)* It was a simple mistake... I didn't think she would go that far.

LEONG KIN Her parents have been told. They're very upset.

AASHI I'm talking about Regina. Who are you talking about?

LEONG KIN What's wrong with your voice?

AASHI We just need the interview. There's a boy, stuck in no man's land, for fifty years. I'm sure his name is Yew, Yew Chong Sze but he's in Sim Sim.

LEONG KIN Why didn't you tell me earlier?

AASHI Why should I? You haven't been honest with me.

Aashi falters a bit.

LEONG KIN Look at you... Have you called your mother?

AASHI What? Of course not. I just walked out from Regina's bloody office.

LEONG KIN She asked me to keep an eye on you.

AASHI Regina? I knew it.

LEONG KIN Your mother!

AASHI Oh bloody hell.

LEONG KIN Calm down.

AASHI I feel giddy.

LEONG KIN Calm down.

AASHI Stop saying that already.

LEONG KIN Come, sit.

Leong Kin finds Aashi a seat and she sits.

AASHI OK, OK... Can you do something for me?

LEONG KIN What?

AASHI Interview him. I'll give you the whole file.

LEONG KIN But I can't. I cannot get involved.

AASHI Oh for heaven's sake!

LEONG KIN No, I can't. I cannot put my family in jeopardy.

AASHI *(hapless)* Please. Please. If not us, then who?

Aashi exits leaving Leong Kin opening the file.

SCENE 8

A small room or dark space. Aashi interviews Old Man, who should not be portrayed as a 'madman' who makes no sense. He plays with words and still makes sense, like a storyteller keen to capture the attention of children. He's always watchable though we never know what to expect. Aashi tries various tacks to get answers. They speak a pidgin of Hakka, English and Malay. Images on screen may serve to suggest meaning and narratives from the Old Man's words.

AASHI *(in Malay)* Ingat tak? *(Then, in Hakka)* Ngai tdidao hao giuyi qen geh si, haodoh du mm gidet. [I know it was a long time ago. Many cannot remember.] Ngi junggi mm gidet? [But what can you remember?]

Old Man pauses for a long time and just looks at Aashi. Aashi takes her pen and paper out and puts it on the table. Old Man watches Aashi. Aashi takes her watch off and puts it on the table. Aashi is watched by Old Man who is at times, practised, playful, casual, wary, indifferent, and frightening.

AASHI *(using his first name in a familiar way)* Ah Sze, hemmeh? Ngai miang heh [my name is] Aashi.

Old Man watches Aashi.

OLD MAN Ngai diu mao ban fatt jor den khii [We could never stop it]
Mm bin khii liu [from overflowing, bah]
Fett jak hai coi pong ben liu choot loy
Haodoh bai ngai diu fong yit [So many times we put a]
kuai mook, sak gu, hai [piece of wood, stone, shoe]
makgai dou hao, jiu fong lok geh hang khii [whatever, and put it in the drain]
Yit taio seh seh geh hang khii, dou mang heh tiau [Small, shallow drain, not even a longkang[33]]
dou mang heh tiao longkang. Set lok he [Stuff it inside there]
gin fong dong see choy dang gao [keep putting things on top]
khon ha set det lok mau [see whether can make it all fit]
jiu mm bin sui liu chut loy [so that the water will stop]
dan heh yit yong hiao lok sui [but still the rains came]
[Of course when the rain stops, steaming fresh smell like *ketiak lepas mandi*[34] can stop the water. But it will somehow find a way over the top or underneath... so much blood.]

AASHI I am happy to meet you, sir... Henry Gurney school. What was it like?

OLD MAN *(cheerfully, in Japanese)* Hidari, migi, hidari, migi [Left, right] Hidari, migi, hidari, migi.

33. Monsoon drain
34. Armpits, freshly bathed

(In Hakka) Ngai miang heh [My name is...] Sze Sze/Sze Sze/Sze Sze.

AASHI Henry Gurney School, sir. What was it like?

OLD MAN Resurgam!

Aashi and the Old Man sit opposite one another.

AASHI Have you lived forever?

Old Man chuckles. Then he walks as if to feed the fish where his tank would be. There is no tank.

OLD MAN I think it would be nice to swim underwater *(He points to the bottom of the tank)*
I like the little fingers and toes underneath
Can build islands from it but
cannot mark how to go around
Because the sea can move it
Unless got birds on it, it will move.

AASHI What can you remember, Ah Sze?

OLD MAN *(barks)* Hey are you here for what
last time you asked me to go and eat bread
and for what I eat bread, for so many days

AASHI I'm here to find out what happened to you.

OLD MAN But I have one hundred heads
And you cannot come
and visit me for three days
and take pictures
and then go away
unless I can say...
I live with only a few things
because here will take care of me and I
will take care of myself, and as long as
I take care what do you care stupid fella

AASHI Stupid fella.

OLD MAN I shit in the leaves and I mandi in the water
and I eat the maggots from the floor
to clean my ears; you think I am simple

and I am *(whispers)* but he thinks I am stupid.

AASHI Maggots on the floor?

OLD MAN *(as if to genuinely share information)*
Gua tahu mana cara itu berumbung
Kasi hilang itu kuning dari luka
Gua tahu cari itu cendawan kasi tolong perempuan
Gua boleh makan, goa boleh simpan kasi anak bini

[I know where the berumbong lives
To stop the yellow from wound
I know where the mushroom is that
Helps a woman
I can eat and keep
For my family]

(His tone changes) Or you can come out and fight me
men on the bicycles, come out
here with my knife, no, not...
one man, he gave me one cap,
with a flap at the back, like a tongue
he lined up like the rest of them
to do monkey on monkey,
but then he cried and he ran away
and lived in the forest and nobody
found him until after the war, he
was living, not by
himself he was looked after
he would have died by himself
some of them tried to survive
we found one body once, with the stomach out
so we gave it to the pigs. His soul had gone.

AASHI Your friend in the forest?

OLD MAN *(darker then frightening)* If I
had an army I would come after
you tell me
when you dream at night
what you dream do you have no fear
that this will come back to you

you can move like the crab but all
crabs need a place to stay and I will come
and get you there, if you move like wet
I will wait for you, and then when
you lick salt and I see blood on your coat
I cannot eat you; meat of the tapir
will give me fever

AASHI All the things I promised but failed, that I want for myself, that I know I cannot get; so much effort, so little result.

OLD MAN *(lightly, smiling)* Get up, Get up!
I want to talk to him,
you may talk to my wives
and you may walk
with my children
but if you harm them
I will charm you
Tell me to pray
But don't tell me what time of day

AASHI Where are we now? (*Old Man looks at her)* People say I look like my mother. How, Ah Sze?

OLD MAN *(with the meaning and manner of a psychiatrist to his patient)* That's alright you can she is not part
of our bargain, she gave birth to you
but she is not responsible for what you
have done, no she is not...
I can give you sound of water but
you must leave me and mine for they have been
long before you and they will be long after
they might be asleep but they are there

AASHI I don't know the water,
Once I knew the wind, it flew around me
Could feel it cool on my face, in the hot sun
Then one day, it disappeared. Left me
So now I whistle.

Aashi whistles.

OLD MAN *(as if reciting the Rukun Negara, but mocking)*

Learn the power of the pineapple because this is
pineapple kingdom and we must know how
to cut so that there is no wastage from
left to right or from right to left,
come on children, all I want to know
and their children's children or if I have no children

AASHI *(holds up her hand)* I have no children.

Old Man looks at Aashi then takes her to see his tank. There is no tank but Aashi is attentive and follows his pointing to fish.

OLD MAN *(seriously, clearly)* Why do you put the man
who stole the banana from the orang utan
with the bear who has claws and teeth and fur
with lice and worms that if you eat them
you will die for the stomach falling out again

AASHI It wasn't me.

OLD MAN *(stares at her for a time then shouts)* If not you, then who?

AASHI Old man, I may have maligned a few buggers here and there. But just the ones that fucked over the country in plain view! Just the ones who think nobody is watching what they're doing. *(Softer)* You have my word it wasn't me. My word. It's a firefly, so easy to miss, flick off, close one eye, as if it isn't what it is... I've spent so much time in despair. Scabs like thugs on my back, but eyes still on the prize. What prize? This place, my place, to stand and look across the straits and say welcome. Or piss off... I'm talking about a square patch, you'd think I was talking about the planet. I know where the land lies but there is no land. Not for me. I've made room in my house, in my gut, here, for a hundred guests and their thousand desires, day after day after day. But still the landlord wants more! 'Like it or leave it'. Like it or leave it? They've forgotten their promise. And so it burns.

OLD MAN *(sympathising)*
They went to find the sunshine
who doesn't want
you cannot do anything for them
there is the rhinoceros beetle with pincers

it looks so kingdom beautiful
but it can be/crushed under the foot
or the rain falls/and it will scatter
it doesn't have the strength to stay
in the wind, but if it uses
its feet to move to other places

AASHI So bring me the wind, old man.

OLD MAN *(storyteller again, smiling now – he uses sign language as he speaks; they go on a sailing trip together, it is fun)* Resurgam!
I am a Bangladeshi I come from the bay
of Bengal and sail to the east with my
knees on the ground and my head to the
ground. Resurgam!

Ngai heh hakkah ngin [I am a Hakka-ngin I sailed]
Ngai hang sohndao nam ben ngai geh tiew hiong ten [To the south with my head to the altar]
Ngai geh giok hiong tee [And my feet on the ground]
Ngai geh ha yim mai choy nyion nyion geh nai di boy
nee soh ngai choy diboy [I came and my cock (*winks*) is inside this]
Bin ngai yit jak hao ma [Warm clay you lock me in here, give me the code]
Bin ngai mau hoi wee loy! [Give me
I have nothing to begin with!]

Old Man seems to awake and walk back to his tank; looking for it, making out its shape, but he realizes it isn't there.

OLD MAN *(tired now)* Fed up now because so hot
And tired so leave me alone
you know what I mean
I think it would be nice to swim underwater

AASHI I'm no Man from Atlantis! Indian ankles but no webbed feet.

OLD MAN I like finger and toes frozen underneath
can build islands from it but cannot mark
how to go around because the sea can move it

unless got birds on it, it will move...

Aashi goes to shake Old Man's hand but he takes Aashi's head and holds her to his chest for a moment.

Lights out.

SCENE 9

Editor's Office.

LEONG KIN I found an old caretaker who used to look after his Aunt. His mother was a comfort woman in the war. Afterwards, the villagers killed her, bound her up and left her in an old rubber estate. He found her after she'd been dead for days.

REGINA Jesus.

LEONG KIN I believe her.

REGINA I want to.

LEONG KIN He kept saying 'Resurgam'. Thought it was Tamil at first, but it's Latin... motto of Henry Gurney Schools... Resurgam: 'I will rise again'...

REGINA It's a good one.

LEONG KIN Must get it out before the parachute-set get it! *(laughs)* What's worse than a foreign correspondent in Asia? An Asian foreign correspondent in Asia... I'm going to see Aashi off at the airport.

REGINA *(loaded)* Oh, help her with her baggage?

Leong Kin starts to pack up.

LEONG KIN So when will it run?

REGINA They're talking about rotating the Chief Minister's position now. Rotate until it lands on the right choice and then somehow rotation will be dropped.

LEONG KIN But you will look at it.

REGINA Of course I will. Later.

Leong Kin pauses.

REGINA What?

LEONG KIN I thought you said if we got the interview, then we have the story.

REGINA Yes...

LEONG KIN But?

REGINA Until we can prove he has been stuck there that long, we can't use it. And you won't be able to prove it because you can't get access to the records, even if they exist.

LEONG KIN You sound relieved...

REGINA Oh come on.

LEONG KIN Yes you do.

REGINA Don't put words in my mouth.

LEONG KIN Freedom of expression means I have to tolerate nonsense that I disagree with. Some days, I just want to hear what I like to hear, you know?

REGINA Say what you need to say, Leong Kin.

LEONG KIN When the paper was suspended, at first it was fine. All this talk about the need to stand tall – well, we did. And we had so much public support! But then I realized, the people next door didn't give ten sen. Not really. They dropped money in the bucket to 'help the poor journalists' who were suddenly out of work. Not for freedom of speech, expression, so forth. Because we were their neighbours. I was out of work for months. Three children and a wife who doesn't work. So what to do? But there comes a time...

REGINA And luckily, we have that now.

LEONG KIN When you remember you can swim.

REGINA Swim, Leong Kin?

LEONG KIN Alright then, scull...

REGINA What are you talking about?

LEONG KIN I resign. You'll have my letter in the morning.

REGINA Leong Kin! Sleep on it. You're too good and too old to be threatening resignation letters.

LEONG KIN I'm serious.

REGINA So serious. Take a break.

LEONG KIN You need a holiday.

REGINA I need you to stay, Leong Kin.

LEONG KIN Maybe I'll teach. More colleges are opening up now.

REGINA Leong Kin, please. Take leave from today. Please go and help Aashi. *(Leong Kin is silent)* Rest and you will feel better.

LEONG KIN At Uni, in 3rd College, my girlfriend's hostel way back when...

REGINA *(has work to do)* Your girlfriends, now?

LEONG KIN She was my first real live bra-burning feminist. From Batu Pahat! She had a poster up on the wall. I've just remembered what it said.

Regina complies.

LEONG KIN 'Don't mistake my silence for compliance.'... I quit, Regina.

Leong Kin exits.

SCENE 10

Make-shift garden but no sign of Old Man. The fish tank is still there. Rudy comes in and takes a wad of envelopes from underneath the fish tank's cover. The coloured waves of light disappear.

SCENE 11

By the Sea. Aashi is wading with trousers folded up, out to sea. Skinny legs, looks odd, comic. Cornelia calls out to Aashi who cannot hear her. Cornelia wades up to her.

AASHI *(still hoarse)* Hey!

CORNELIA What happened to you?

AASHI What happened to you?

CORNELIA They dropped the charges.

AASHI How did you manage that?

CORNELIA Regina.

AASHI See, she is your mother.

CORNELIA But I'm suspended.

AASHI I agree! What were you trying to do? I heard about a very bad wig.

CORNELIA My mother's. *(Aashi laughs)* I got it for three hours. My father nearly hit me. But I knew Rudy was your route.

AASHI Regina reckons I put you up to it.

CORNELIA You saw him, I know you did. What was he like?

Aashi takes out a wad of envelopes.

AASHI This is for you.

CORNELIA What?

AASHI Letters. And drawings. By him.

CORNELIA What? How...?

AASHI The oldest is from nineteenth October, 1953 – look.

Cornelia accepts the papers and begins to look at one.

CORNELIA *(In Kadazan)* Noikot vinasi! [Very good.] Oh my God! So many. Just what we need. How did he keep them?

AASHI In a tube, up his backside I guess.

Cornelia treats the letters more gingerly...

CORNELIA Can you read Chinese?

AASHI *(in Hakka)* Ngai titdau sau sau, tanhe ngai mhiau tuk. [I can speak a bit of it but I can't read it.] *(Then)* ... Translators bah.

CORNELIA Look. A Queen Elizabeth stamp? British North Borneo!

AASHI I know.

CORNELIA Proof!

AASHI Not of what he did.

CORNELIA Proof he's been in there!

AASHI They're yours now.

CORNELIA Who will believe it?

AASHI Malaysians have never lacked the ability to suspend their disbelief.

CORNELIA I thought you said 'we' would finish it.

AASHI I'm tired, tired of banging my head on the wall, hearing my own voice. Nobody's interested, not the way I expect. All this second-guessing and reading in between the lines. So much seaweed that chokes! Maybe if I go away and come back, I'll feel differently.

CORNELIA Migrate?

AASHI No lah. Maybe take a course. Hotel management.

CORNELIA Hah.

AASHI Maybe run a small motel and tell earnest backpackers stories by a real native. Meanwhile there are reporters like you. With slightly more than a fingernail's grasp of what matters...

CORNELIA Leong Kin told me what Regina did.

AASHI He seems to be your source for everything.

CORNELIA He's resigned.

AASHI Resigned?

CORNELIA I just saw him... *(She looks at the letters)* These are fantastic bah!

AASHI *(about Leong Kin)* That's remarkable...

CORNELIA Big story stuff. *(Beat)* But...

AASHI What.

CORNELIA These are private.

AASHI Yes...

CORNELIA How much did you pay for them?

AASHI Not much.

CORNELIA You paid for them!

AASHI Yes.

CORNELIA But how could you!

AASHI How else to get them?

CORNELIA You just bribed somebody bah!

AASHI Girl, will you never learn? There is graft and there is corruption. And there is good corruption and bad.

CORNELIA Can you hear yourself?

AASHI *(happily)* Yes, I can hear fine. Not so giddy now either.

CORNELIA So much big talk about a journalist's calling.

AASHI You want them or not?

CORNELIA We need to put them back.

AASHI Don't be ridiculous! If you don't want them, I'll give them to someone else.

Aashi tries to take the package back. Cornelia fights for them.

CORNELIA They're not yours to give me, Aashi!

AASHI Yah, they belong in Arkib Negara!

CORNELIA Aashi, think! Where would he go?

AASHI That can be sorted out later.

CORNELIA No it can't. Immediate realities. If he were released, would he stay with you?

AASHI Of course not.

CORNELIA Then where?

AASHI The Ministry of Social Development...

CORNELIA No!

AASHI You want him to die in there?

CORNELIA Aashi. They're not yours. They're his.

AASHI OK fine...

CORNELIA 'OK fine'?

AASHI Put them in there *(the sea/audience)* for all I care.

Cornelia looks at the package, hesitates, then throws the package into the sea/audience scattering the letters. Aashi jumps up.

AASHI What are you doing!

Aashi tries to get the scattered letters. She shouts to Cornelia.

AASHI For God's sake, they're the originals not copies!

Cornelia tries to jump in to retrieve the letters too. They try to retrieve as much as they can.

AASHI You threw them into the sea!

CORNELIA They're not originals. I saw the photocopy receipt from Kedai Foto at RM24.

AASHI You did? You did? Where?

CORNELIA I saw it... it was inside!

AASHI Bloody hell...! Rudy! *(Beat)*

CORNELIA You mean–? Hah! You asked for that.

AASHI You'll have to talk to him again.

CORNELIA But we need Yew's permission.

AASHI Clever bastard... God, I really am getting too old for this.

CORNELIA We can get them translated. And verify the stamp.

AASHI I'm done, I told you. Off to the airport. Saved by a jet.

CORNELIA So soon?

AASHI Yah, how long do you think I can stay by the sea's edge? Makes me nervous.

CORNELIA ... I need to think for a minute.

AASHI OK, Rafflesia.

Aashi makes to leave; there is an awkward hug between them but Aashi signals Cornelia to stay on.

AASHI Be my guest.

Aashi walks back leaving Cornelia looking out with empty package in hand.

SCENE 12

Old Man near his aquarium. There is no light. He senses something is wrong. He quickly checks to see if his letters are still there; they are.

As he very carefully adds another drawing/letter and feeds the fish, the coloured lights return.

The end.

ANN LEE

Lee was born in Tawau, Malaysia. She is a playwright, writer, and currently a PhD student at the National University of Singapore, researching political satire in Southeast Asia. She began writing for theatre as a member of the Royal Court Young Activists theatre group, London, where she joined a writers' workshop with then writer-in-residence Hanif Kureishi. She holds a BA (Hons) in Applied Photography, Film and Television (Westminster) and an MSc in History of Science, Medicine and Technology (Oxon). She is also an Asia Leadership Fellow (ALFP, 2001), awarded by the Japan Foundation and International House of Japan, where she spent time in Tokyo with colleagues from China, India, Japan, Korea, the Philippines, and Thailand, and presented her research on 'the ghosts of Asian values'.

Lee was Artistic Director and co-founder of Kuali Works (1994–2011), an all-women theatre group in Malaysia that first produced her plays, including the critically acclaimed, *Kuala Lumpur Knock-Out* (1994), about a young factory worker who dreams of boxing Mike Tyson (which received a Director's Exchange Award from the Australian High Commission, Kuala Lumpur); *Hang Li Poh – Melakan Princess* (1998), a re-telling of the myth of the Emperor of China's daughter who married the Sultan of Malacca; and *From Table Mountain to Teluk Intan* (2001) by Shahimah Idris with Lee, Sue Ingleton and Jo Kukathas, based on the true story of a Cape Malay child in South Africa who leaves apartheid but ends up on the 'right side' of the tracks to face her most difficult trial.

The last play Lee directed was Eve Ensler's *The Vagina Monologues*, which was banned in Malaysia in 2000. Her last full-length play, *Tarap Man*, revised for this anthology, won 'Best Original Script' at the 2007 Boh Cameronian Arts Awards, Malaysia. She is working on a new full-length play, provisionally titled *Not Far Now*.

Lee's work for the stage has been performed at the Asian Monodrama Festival, Commonwealth Games Theatre Festival, Ubud Writers and Readers Festival, Sydney Writers Festival, and the New York International Fringe Festival.

DARK RACE

NGUYEN ĐĂNG CHUONG

Productions have been staged in Vietnam at The People's Police Theatre, Thai Binh Reformed Theatre, Nghe An Folk Theatre and the Center for Conservation and Promotion of Nghe Tinh Folk songs.

Characters

VÕ TRẦN TIÊN – Former Member of the Politburo, one of the chief organisers of the Revolution.

VÕ TRẦN TỔ – General Director of a Private Business Group, Võ Trần Tiên's son.

BÙI VIỆT THẮNG – Head of a Department under a Government Ministry.

DƯƠNG HƯƠNG LY – Bùi Việt Thắng's wife.

ĐINH VŨ BẠO – General Director of a Public Business Group.

NGUYỄN ĐÌNH MAI – Woman Deputy Head of Department of Human Resources Planning.

VŨ KIỀU LOAN – Woman General Director of a Private Business Group.

Time

Set in Hanoi in 2012.

SCENE 1

At Trần Tổ's house – a luxury villa in the most beautiful urban area in Hanoi. In the splendid living room, we see a white-haired old man who is Trần Tổ's father, Mr. Trần Tiên, sitting on a low couch near the door. The doorbell rings. Mr. Trần Tiên stands up slowly and walks towards the door. Việt Thắng and his wife, Hương Ly enter.

VIỆT THẮNG/HƯƠNG LY Hello, sir.

TRẦN TIÊN Hello, come in please. You have an appointment with my son, Tô?

HƯƠNG LY Yes, thank you, sir... You look so hale and hearty, Mr. Tô, you must be very blessed... are you 80?

TRẦN TỔ *(coming down the stairs)* He is celebrating his 90th soon. He was working even before the war... an esteemed veteran... very well-known...

VIỆT THẮNG Yeh... we know... it's hard to find anyone like him these days!

TRẦN TỔ Sit down, please... *(The old man sits down again while Trần Tổ makes tea)* He had a heart attack earlier this year *(smiles)* and hasn't totally recovered, still has to use the stick to get about...

HƯƠNG LY *(stares at the old man)* He looks well, so I don't think it will be long before he's better.

TRẦN TỔ OK, so... what's brought you two here? Tell me.

VIỆT THẮNG Well... *(looks at the old man, hesitating)*

TRẦN TỔ *(understanding Thắng's reluctance)* Feel free to speak. He's not listening... he just cares about reading his newspaper or watching the news on Vietnam TV.

HƯƠNG LY OK... we're here to ask you for a favour... to help Viet Thang.

TRẦN TỔ *(laughs)* Really? What kind of help do you want?

VIỆT THẮNG We heard that our Ministry is appointing a new Deputy Minister... and you are so close to the top... please help us... with all the other stuff, you know and we will show the necessary 'respect'...

TRẦN TỔ *(understanding)* Ah yes! It's true that your Ministry is appointing a new Deputy who will be up for promotion to the Central Committee next Congress. And being in the Central

Committee means you are not far off the Minister's chair. After the Congress, the Minister will retire and all the current Deputies are over the age limit, so that means they need a young Deputy Minister to train up for the job.

VIỆT THẮNG People say there are a lot of candidates, right?

TRẦN TỔ Of course! A title and power... if no one was interested in that, it would be strange... *(Stops and thinks)* But inside that Ministry, there are five candidates who are up for the Deputy post this time.

HƯƠNG LY And my husband, Thang, he's on that list, isn't he? *(Thắng glances at her)*

TRẦN TỔ Of course... *(Turning to Thắng)* According to the Institute, you are one of the leading candidates.

VIỆT THẮNG Thank you! So we'll leave it all with you then. With your backing, we can definitely win this. *(Thắng's phone rings)* Excuse me... *(Thắng goes out after answering his phone)*

HƯƠNG LY You've helped many people to get their promotions... please help my husband... we will show you respect until we die...

TRẦN TỔ If you insist... I won't say no.

HƯƠNG LY *(excited)* Fantastic! *(Pause)* Please kindly let us know how much we will have to find for this so we can start getting the money together.

TRẦN TỔ *(to Hương Ly)* You're his banker, eh?

HƯƠNG LY No, no, of course not... I wouldn't dream of it.

TRẦN TỔ It seems to me that beauty is the most valuable gift that nature can give to a woman, at any time...

HƯƠNG LY Yes, it may be so... *(Thắng walks back in, Tô now has a phone call)*

TRẦN TỔ Hello! Yes... *(Looks at his watch)* OK... in twenty minutes... *(Turns to Hương Ly and Việt Thắng)* I've noted your case and will try my best to help... for the rest of it, let's discuss that later...

VIỆT THẮNG Thank you! *(Winks at his wife)* So we won't disturb you any more... *(Hand in hand, Ly and Thắng look at the old man)* Good bye, sir. *(The old man doesn't respond. The husband and wife exit quickly)*

TRẦN TỔ *(to his father)* Today is my day off but I have some appointments with people at home, so please could you go in, Pa, and take a rest in your room?

TRẦN TIÊN *(stands up)* Mmm... an old man like me really needs peace and quiet, especially peace of mind...

The old man exits and then the doorbell rings again.

TRẦN TỔ Come in, please...

Vũ Bạo and Đình Mai both smartly-dressed, enter. Mai brings a suitcase with her.

VŨ BẠO Hi Bro'! *(Points at Đình Mai)* This is Đình Mai, my sis'. *(They shake hands)* I wanted to invite you somewhere nice and quiet to discuss this business...

TRẦN TỔ Take a seat... There is nowhere quiet these days... if you're on the phone you get overheard or if you go out you get filmed by someone's camera... even sitting in a meeting is recorded... talking in your own home is by far the safest.

VŨ BẠO Ah yes! Today I'm bringing supplies for the coming battle... No matter what it costs, just make it happen. Right, bro'?

TRẦN TỔ *(changing topic)* So... Đình Mai is on your side, is she?

VŨ BẠO Yes... Mai is the Deputy Head of the Operations and Planning Department. We're solid, just like you and me...

TRẦN TỔ Mmm... It's good to see family loyalty but... Bạo, since you first mentioned it, I've been thinking very carefully... and maybe you shouldn't be in this race.

VŨ BẠO Why not bro'?

The old man enters and stands in a corner listening to the conversation.

TRẦN TỔ Because whoever gets this position as Deputy will be lined up to join the Central Committee in the next Congress and then become the Minister. So, there's a bunch of contenders in the race for it. Not an easy win...

VŨ BẠO That's why I'm going after it and why I'm begging you to use your magic to do what you do best... if the job was just Deputy Minister, I'd rather stay where I am now as the Group General Director... I know there are four or five contenders up for it...

TRẦN TỔ How can there be four or five?

VŨ BẠO Easy, just count in the Ministry, Groups and Corporations.

TRẦN TỔ *(laughs)* Wow! That's a long line of Presidents and Provincial Heads standing on their tiptoes, fighting for your seat...

VŨ BẠO But I have you on my side! You know how to get them to drop out...

TRẦN TỔ You think they don't have any sponsors of their own?

VŨ BẠO Yes, but whoever they are, there's no comparison... you've never failed to get anyone in, so far...

TRẦN TỔ Well, it was easier in the past. Now it's becoming more and more difficult...

VŨ BẠO But if there are any problems, it's just a question of finding the right solution.

TRẦN TỔ Not that easy!

VŨ BẠO Why not, bro'?

TRẦN TỔ Since the application of Central Resolution Four, the top guys just keep quiet and are very cautious about doing anything...

VŨ BẠO *(becoming worried)* Is it so difficult that you have to back off completely? *(Trần Tổ is silent)*

VŨ BẠO You're a magician... you must know a way to fix it for me!

TRẦN TỔ *(stares directly at Vũ Bạo)* Look! What if there is a ninety-nine percent chance of success but there's also a one percent risk of failure?

VŨ BẠO Such a difficult question!

TRẦN TỔ To be frank, I just want to make you aware of all the circumstances. Anything may happen – who knows?

VŨ BẠO *(anxious)* So much stress! All right, if that's the way it is, God help me, I'll take the risk.

TRẦN TỔ Just so you know what might occur.

VŨ BẠO *(puts the suitcase on the table)* Please take this for me.

TRẦN TỔ You keep it for now. I'll let you know when it's needed.

VŨ BẠO No, please... I brought it here already, and I'm going home now.

TRẦN TỔ *(shakes hands)* Don't get so worried that you can't sleep!

VŨ BẠO No way bro'! This is Vũ Bạo, you know.

Vũ Bạo waves good bye. Vũ Bạo and Đình Mai start to exit.

TRẦN TỔ *(calls after him)* Bạo! You must be careful with that guy. He looks disloyal, he might sell you out...

VŨ BẠO Don't worry! I've just given him some money to buy his own seat of Deputy Head so he's praying for me to be successful in this venture... he wants to become Head in the next few years...

Vũ Bạo and Đình Mai exit.

Tô shuts the door and stands watching his father.

TRẦN TIÊN Son, can I ask you...?

TRẦN TỔ Yes, Pa, what's your question?

TRẦN TIÊN Is it true that people have to buy their promotions nowadays?

TRẦN TỔ *(laughs)* It's been going on for years, Pa, it's nothing new.

TRẦN TIÊN When I was in power, this never happened. Buying and selling seats only happened in the old days.

TRẦN TỔ Oh Pa... in your day it was the subsidy system which is very different from the free market. Everything is now based on the law of supply and demand. So buying a position is a common practice everywhere, from the centre, right out to the provinces nationwide. *(Pause)* You even have to pay for the post of head of the village let alone leader of the ward, the district, the province, the city or central ministries.

TRẦN TIÊN And it's happening in this house as well, isn't it? And you're involved in it, aren't you?

TRẦN TỔ Pa! Wha–?

TRẦN TIÊN Tell me, are you in a need of money?

TRẦN TỔ You're acting weird today, Pa! The whole country knows me and how much I'm worth.

TRẦN TIÊN Exactly! You have far too much money already... so why are you getting involved in all of these deals? How much do you make from each one?

TRẦN TỔ I just like to help people... even invest my own money for some–

TRẦN TIÊN Huh?! I'm your father and I've never seen you giving anyone anything for free...

TRẦN TỔ You're right! I help those who want to buy a promotion, but at the same time, it's a long-term investment for me with lots of potential benefits.

TRẦN TIÊN I don't get it.

TRẦN TỔ First we help them to get their job, then we ask them to come in as an investor on big projects... and of course, then we must be their strategic partner too. So what I am doing is totally legal, reasonable and beneficial...

TRẦN TIÊN I see... but it also means you are destroying this country. TT

TRẦN TỔ Why do you think that?

TRẦN TIÊN Because if those guys get into power, their only interest will be getting rich without any consideration for the people or this country... and then guys like you will manipulate them...

and together it's a totally corrupt system to drain people's blood and *(getting angry)* that's how you are destroying the country.

TRẦN TỔ You may be right. *(Pacifying him)* But Pa… there are hundreds of guys out of eighty million people in this country who are doing it… it's a rule of development that when someone builds something then someone else has to get knocked down. Buying and selling government jobs is a socially acceptable practice. If I don't do it, some other guys will. So why not take the chance when it comes? It's a wasted opportunity otherwise. *(Whispers)* As a matter of fact… all this deal-making helps me to get even closer to the top guys!

TRẦN TIÊN I've always known that you used my good name, which I devoted my whole life to achieving, to create political relationships… but I never dreamt that you'd use it for this dirty business… it's awful… really awful!

TRẦN TỔ It's not so bad. You know, these types of business deals are like a race in the dark… And no one can see in the dark, Pa.

TRẦN TIÊN No, what I'm telling you is – it's an awful future… Those who play these games are dangerous, reckless people. Power in the hands of such a guy will be like the force of a demon – he'll harm or kill all those who are weaker than him. Including all the good ones.

TRẦN TỔ *(sincerely)* Well, Pa, you are 90, you shouldn't worry too much about politics, just focus on exercising and keeping well… remember, if you have another heart attack, you can't be resuscitated.

TRẦN TỔ *(looking away, ignoring this)* In the old days, Uncle Ho always taught us "be hard-working, save, be genuine, honest, fair and clear…" but now, nobody listens to that. He paid attention to things like personal ethics, personal responsibility and to individual abilities whenever he gave someone an important position. But now, it seems you can buy such a position with money… I really don't understand it.

TRẦN TỔ Things are different now, Pa! In the past, the whole Party and all the people, were for the liberty of the South and for the union of the nation. And now, both the party and the people are out to get rich. Different mission, different goals, so the idea of ethics, responsibility and ability has to be different too.

TRẦN TỔ *(insistent)* But whatever the difference, surely the final goal must be for the people, for the country's good? Then or now, whatever age it is, the country needs leaders who have work ethic, responsibility and capability... not these guys who simply buy into power like the ones who just came to see you!

TRẦN TỔ *(sadly)* Oh God... you're so old and out of touch, being at home all day reading newspapers and watching TV, you can't imagine how complicated life is nowadays. People only care about one thing – money. No one cares about ability, ethics or responsibility. The selection criteria these days are not the same anymore.

TRẦN TIÊN What are they then?

TRẦN TỔ First is descendants, second is relationship, third is money, fourth is supporters, and finally there's talent.

TRẦN TIÊN What does that mean? Explain it to me in detail.

TRẦN TỔ Yeh, well the first one – descendants – means that those who are the son or daughter or grandson or grand-daughter of a top leader get priority... just like me, being the son of a well-known Revolutionary Leader, and former member of the Politburo, I must have priority over others. The second is – relationship – which means you must have a wide network and close relationships, especially a relationship with top leaders, just like me. Number three is – money – which means you have got to have a lot of money to get the seat, like the two guys who just came to see me... Number four is – supporters – you need supporters but you probably know this one already. And after all that, the talented ones are next on the list to be considered...

TRẦN TIÊN That means the talented and ethical people are always at the end of the list?

TRẦN TỔ Of course! *(Turns back to look at his father)* Do you know why? Because those who are both talented and ethical are always proud and they often challenge things. And challenging the boss is stupid... in this system, the boss is always right. What the boss says, you follow, even if he says something that everyone knows is wrong. You still have to smile and tell him that he is correct.

Trần Tiên is deeply shocked

TRẦN TỔ Why do you look so shocked? That's life... if you don't follow the rules, you have to sit out the games...

TRẦN TIÊN You have both the first and the second privilege so why don't you behave yourself instead of joining in the games?

TRẦN TỔ I am running a private business group. If it was a nationally-owned corporation, I'd behave very well at the very beginning.

TRẦN TỔ *(thinks for a while)* Tô...

TRẦN TỔ Yes, Pa?

TRẦN TIÊN However complicated things are, I'd prefer you not to be mixed up in this business... please stop it now so I can rest in peace.

TRẦN TỔ *(taken aback)* You what? Pa, please don't bother yourself with this. You just relax and enjoy the rest of your life... if you think too much and have another heart attack, no one can help... do you understand?

Lights fade.

SCENE 2

Morning. The house of Head of Department, Việt Thắng. Thắng is lying on the sofa, stretching his legs on the coffee table, listening to music and relaxing. Hương Ly enters in a luxury négligée. She walks behind her husband, unseen.

HƯƠNG LY *(looks at her husband for a while and smiles)* What are you dreaming about, dear? A hot girl or a fast car?

VIỆT THẮNG *(jumps)* A Deputy seat that several guys are fighting for... *(Sighs)* I don't really know what's gonna happen...

HƯƠNG LY Be confident, dear! Be determined!

VIỆT THẮNG But we don't have as much money as some of the General Directors of Business Corporations.

HƯƠNG LY If needed, we can sell this villa. That will bring in at least one and a half million US dollars.

VIỆT THẮNG *(surprised)* Sell this house? Then where will we live?

HƯƠNG LY Rent somewhere. As long as you get the job. When you're in that position, it will be easy to get back another villa like this.

VIỆT THẮNG Are you counting your chickens before they hatch? It's more and more difficult day by day. I'm afraid we won't make it back if we spend that much money.

HƯƠNG LY Don't worry... we can make it back, why else are there so many people in the running for this job? They're all stupid? *(Việt Thắng is silent)* Don't give up! We must stay focused, we have to win at any price. *(The doorbell rings)*

VIỆT THẮNG Come in, please... *(Đình Mai enters)*

ĐÌNH MAI For God's sake, how can you be so calm?

VIỆT THẮNG Why? What's going on?

ĐÌNH MAI According to the grapevine, there are now seven contenders for this Deputy Minister position.

VIỆT THẮNG Seven of them?

ĐÌNH MAI Yes, that's right. It's time to move. We can't wait anymore.

HƯƠNG LY We're considering what's best.

ĐÌNH MAI What are you considering? Đinh Vũ Bạo has already given a Samsonite suitcase to Mr. Trần Tô.

HƯƠNG LY What? Is that true?

ĐÌNH MAI I was there with him... *(Việt Thắng and Hương Ly look at each other worriedly)*

VIỆT THẮNG Did Trần Tô take it?

ĐÌNH MAI He did. He promised to do his best, solid as a rock.

HƯƠNG LY If they're so sure, why are you chasing us?

ĐÌNH MAI Come on! If he gives one million, you give two. In this race, the one who pays most, is the winner.

VIỆT THẮNG What about the other candidates?

ĐÌNH MAI They're doing their own thing... but most are going via Trần Tô. He hasn't lost a deal in this business for years...

HƯƠNG LY *(talks to himself)* Most are via Trần Tô? *(Comes back to check with Mai)* So, if it's the one who pays the most who wins, does the one who pays less, lose all?

ĐÌNH MAI Of course! Because this is a race, a big game... so the losers can go cry to God...

HƯƠNG LY Do I have to stand in line to cry to God as well?

ĐÌNH MAI You go and see Trần Tô and ask him directly... how much is enough and then pay him... once he takes your money, you just come home, sleep and wait for the decision with a red seal on it. *(Sees that Việt Thắng is still indecisive)* You nervous?

VIỆT THẮNG Of course! If we're not careful, we may lose everything...

ĐÌNH MAI *(shakes her head)* Let me tell you the truth... This is your one and only chance... if you don't take it, you will blame yourself for the rest of your life... you will be sick with regret... *(Pause)* I'm absolutely convinced of this. Unless you get it, I have no chance to move up either...

HƯƠNG LY We know!

VIỆT THẮNG *(to Đình Mai)* OK... Let me think...

ĐÌNH MAI Well, it's your decision, just don't think so much that your rival gets the job while you chase after his shadow... I'm off. *(Đình Mai exits quickly)*.

HƯƠNG LY I think Mai is talking a lot of sense. (*Việt Thắng ignores her. She looks at her husband, nervously)* Dear! What are you thinking?

VIỆT THẮNG *(hesistantly)* Ly...

HƯƠNG LY Yes...

VIỆT THẮNG *(looks into her eyes)* Do you really love me?

HƯƠNG LY *(surprised)* Why – are you being so weird? Why would I get married to you if I didn't really love you? *(A pause then more softly)* A beautiful young girl who had just graduated from Medical School agreeing to be the second wife of a man who is twenty-one years older than her... do you think she loved him or not? *(A bit annoyed)* But why are you asking me about this now?

VIỆT THẮNG *(quietly)* Just because I love you so much.

HƯƠNG LY What's going on in that mind of yours? Tell me the truth.

VIỆT THẮNG *(pause)* Actually... I have been thinking a lot these past few days... *(Pause)* But just forget it, just leave it be for a peaceful life.

HƯƠNG LY What is it? *(Direct to Việt Thắng)* What's going on? Tell me, tell me now.

VIỆT THẮNG *(uncertainly)* Well, I think Trần Tô likes you. A lot. The other day he looked at you as if he could devour you...

HƯƠNG LY *(laughs out loud)* Oh my God. I thought it was something serious... there are a lot of guys who'd do anything for your wife out there but that's their problem... you don't have to worry about that... it's pointless being jealous...

VIỆT THẮNG I'm not jealous. *(Feels it's too difficult to say)* This is different.

HƯƠNG LY What? Why are you being so mysterious? You're winding me up!

VIỆT THẮNG When I went off to make a call that day, Trần Tô asked you if you were my banker, right?

HƯƠNG LY Yes! *(Looks into Thắng's eyes)* No? You're not thinking what I think you're thinking? *(Việt Thắng puts his hand on Hương Ly's mouth)*

VIỆT THẮNG Stop, stop! Don't say it.

HƯƠNG LY *(takes Thắng's hand off)* No way! You're thinking of giving me to Trần Tô as part of the deal – to get the Deputy job? Is that right?

Việt Thắng is silent.

HƯƠNG LY *(holding back her anger)* Answer me... is that right?

VIỆT THẮNG *(closed eyes, face up to the ceiling)* Don't force me to answer...

HƯƠNG LY *(cold)* Right or wrong? Out with it. Speak up.

VIỆT THẮNG *(slightly nods)* Right! *(Hương Ly turns around and looks down. Both stand still like a post)*

HƯƠNG LY When that thought came into your mind, did you feel any pain?

VIỆT THẮNG Of course! But all the pain will be buried by the time we...

HƯƠNG LY Did you feel dishonored by it?

VIỆT THẮNG Of course! But the shame can be washed away...

HƯƠNG LY Do you realise that you are a complete shit?

VIỆT THẮNG Of course!!

HƯƠNG LY You admit it?

VIỆT THẮNG Yes, but there's the possibility for happiness later.

HƯƠNG LY *(turns back to Việt Thắng)* If we did this, can you imagine how painful it will be whenever I make love with him? It will be hell for you.

VIỆT THẮNG I know and I can see that hell very clearly. But I can cope. I'll just wrap it all up and throw it into the bin of what's past.

HƯƠNG LY So what about me when I am in that situation...?

VIỆT THẮNG You'll be strong enough to get over it once you're back with me.

HƯƠNG LY Aren't you scared of it going wrong?

VIỆT THẮNG How can it?

HƯƠNG LY You might lose me.

VIỆT THẮNG I won't lose you. Because you're always telling me how much you love me.

HƯƠNG LY But love is not forever! Anything can change...

VIỆT THẮNG Anything can change, yes, but you... I know you'll love me whatever happens... I trust you, whatever you do, as long as your heart is with me.

HƯƠNG LY That means you've decided!

VIỆT THẮNG *(beat)* Look at it this way... We don't have as much money as those guys... even if we sell this villa. What if there's another guy who pays with two villas? Then we lose everything and we'll not only be homeless but also humiliated... *(Pause)* If you do this... we can still keep the house and I can make it.

HƯƠNG LY Is everything as simple as you say?

VIỆT THẮNG Winning or losing depends on you, Ly. Just seeing Trần Tô's eyes on you, I know that he is dying for you... he couldn't keep his feelings hidden so he had to make a little joke about you being my banker.

HƯƠNG LY Those who are hungry are also dreamers... he might talk like that with any attractive young lady.

VIỆT THẮNG No! Among the big guys, Trần Tô is not that type. *(Pause)* You're the one who told me that we cannot give up, we have to be determined and I have to win at any cost.

HƯƠNG LY Yes! But the thing you want from me doesn't have a price. In other words, it's priceless. *(Looks at Việt Thắng)* Keeping trust and respect between husband and wife is precious, don't you see that?

VIỆT THẮNG Trust and respect in the modern world is secondary, baby. It's no longer as important. The most important thing is what we can do for each other to help the family move up in the world... how can you hold us back? Just see this as a sacrifice for your family, for your husband, and for our children, Ly.

HƯƠNG LY God, I'm tired! You go to bed first... I can't sleep yet. I'll stay up for a while and think about this carefully and I'll give you my answer in the morning.

Lights fade.

SCENE 3

The living room of Trần Tổ's villa, Mr. Trần Tiên is doing yoga exercises slowly with very soft music. The doorbell rings.

TRẦN TIÊN *(keeps going)* Come in, please.

Kiều Loan enters. She is dressed impeccably.

KIỀU LOAN Good morning, sir?

TRẦN TIÊN *(looks up)* Please take a seat. *(Mr. Tiên stops his exercise and offers Kiều Loan a chair and a glass of water)*

KIỀU LOAN I'm a friend of Trần Tô.

TRẦN TIÊN Do you have an appointment?

KIỀU LOAN Yes, I do. He's not at home, sir?

TRẦN TIÊN *(nods, points upstairs and presses the intercom button)* Please have a drink of water and wait for him for a while.

The old man takes his stick and exits.

Trần Tô comes downstairs.

TRẦN TỔ *(sees Kiều Loan)* Long time no see... Kiều Loan, you are as young and beautiful as ever. *(They shake hands)*

KIỀU LOAN Maybe... if you hadn't dumped me, I'd look even better.

TRẦN TỔ Please! It's been a long time, don't go over that! You're not exactly past it. You have everything going for you, now. You're one of the country's brightest and best.

KIỀU LOAN All right, let's not get into that.

TRẦN TỔ *(smiles and changes topic)* It must be something big that brings you here today?

KIỀU LOAN Small thing, nothing big, but it relates to you.

TRẦN TỔ Relates to me... mmm... a good project? A business partner? Or a miserable buddy who relates to me?

KIỀU LOAN No! It's about the executive recruitment at Ministry level. *(Looks at Trần Tô)* Are you arranging the Deputy Minister seat for Đinh Vũ Bạo in the coming Congress?

TRẦN TỔ *(smiles)* News travels fast!

KIỀU LOAN Can you answer my question?

TRẦN TỔ Well... *(glancing at Kiều Loan)* do you have a business relationship with Đinh Vũ Bạo?

KIỀU LOAN I did once, but now... we're at odds.

TRẦN TỔ *(confused)* Being at odds... why are you interested in what happens?

KIỀU LOAN I'm not interested in Đinh Vũ Bạo. *(Pauses)* Among the five contenders for the Deputy post this time, I'd love it if you could help Hoàng Quang Tất.

TRẦN TỔ How is Hoàng Quang Tất related to you?

KIỀU LOAN You shouldn't have asked that question.

TRẦN TỔ He's a Head of Department? Yes, Hoàng Quang Tất is an educated person, a professor, a doctor... but he is on his own.

KIỀU LOAN He's talented, honest, hard-working but doesn't like sucking up to people. That's why he is on his own. *(Pause)*. Please can you endorse Hoàng Quang Tất, I will take on all the costs.

TRẦN TỔ *(sighs)* You put me in a difficult position.

KIỀU LOAN If it's difficult, can you stay out of the race totally? Let me do the greasing of palms. But you have to be out of the game. *(Trần Tô walks around and thinks)*

Trần Tiên enters but goes directly into the back of the room.

TRẦN TỔ *(suddenly turns back to her)* What if I say no to you?

KIỀU LOAN That means I'll be up against you. We will be on opposite sides of the fire.

TRẦN TỔ You're still as strong as you used to be...

KIỀU LOAN I am stronger, smarter, and more powerful...

TRẦN TỔ OK, so now... you take charge of Hoàng Quang Tất's campaign. And I will run for Đinh Vũ Bạo. We're both in the same race, and the best man wins... so we'll both be happy.

KIỀU LOAN Are you kidding?

TRẦN TỔ *(cold)* No! Very serious!

KIỀU LOAN If you say so... then as we're both in the same race, we won't be seeing each other. *(Shakes hand)* Good bye!

TRẦN TỔ Let me see you off and chat a little.

KIỀU LOAN It's up to you!

The father comes forward when they both leave.

TRẦN TIÊN *(alone)* Another crazy scheme. If this carries on for a few more years, all the authority will be in the hands of ruthless capitalists. *(Pauses and feels miserable)* I have explained it all to Trần Tô but he doesn't listen... he is still jumping into this cesspool... why doesn't he understand that he is ruining the country, harming the people, and bringing on chaos. Future generations will have to pay for the mess. *(Pause)* I am old... *(Louder)* Old but not dead! Real communists cannot ignore it when bad things are happening. We have fought and sacrificed for the people's benefit, for the good of all. I'm sorry that I am too old... No! Even the old must be useful till the very last breath.

The doorbell rings.

TRẦN TIÊN Come in please...

Đinh Vũ Bạo and Đinh Mai enter.

VŨ BẠO Hello, sir.

TRẦN TIÊN *(looks at Vũ Bạo for a while)* I remember you two. You came to see Trần Tô, didn't you? Please have some water and wait for him a while. *(Offering water and talking)*. Next week is my 90th birthday, there will be some members of the Politburo who will come to say congratulations. *(Vũ Bạo gives Đình Mai a look)*. Trần Tô wanted to make it a big celebration but I didn't want that.

VŨ BẠO Oh, I hear you are still very influential, sir... as big as the shadow of a great tree... or as bright as the light from the sun... it's also thanks to your great influence that Mr. Tô now has such a big impact in the world of property development... if I could have a word from you, it would be very helpful...

TRẦN TIÊN How do you want me to help? Speak clearly...

VŨ BẠO Sir... *(Gives his business card to Mr. Trần Tiên)* This is my card... Please see me as your son or daughter. Please could you kindly talk to the Members of the Politburo about appointing me as the Deputy Minister...

ĐÌNH MAI Sir, Mr. Đinh Vũ Bạo is a leading candidate for the post already.

TRẦN TIÊN *(smiles)* I thought it was about another matter... this is too easy... *(Looks at Vũ Bạo)* But, why are you so worried if you are a leading candidate for the post, already?

ĐÌNH MAI Well, there are six or seven others like him who are also candidates for the post. So your voice is very important to us...

VŨ BẠO Sir, human resource management nowadays is very different from your time in the past. It's complicated and highly selective... they pay attention to differentials, ranking and market criteria but not actually to the candidate himself... how he performs or what he can do.

TRẦN TIÊN *(confused)* What do you mean by that?

VŨ BẠO Well, it means the strongest one wins. It's not important if you have any ability or knowledge to do the job... First is your family descent, second is your relationships, third is money, fourth is support, and finally comes talent.

TRẦN TIÊN *(understanding)* I see... so you are competing by using the second and the third of these.

ĐÌNH MAI Yes, that's why your word for Mr. Đinh Vũ Bạo with the members of the Politburo is so important...

TRẦN TIÊN OK, I will mention this.

VŨ BẠO It's much appreciated. Thank you, sir!

TRẦN TIÊN *(rubs his stomach)* I have a problem with my stomach since yesterday, so please just sit and wait for Tô. I have to leave for a while...

VŨ BẠO/ĐÌNH MAI Yes sir...

Trần Tiên exits.

ĐÌNH MAI *(laughs)* Whoa! You have the luck of the devil... if you don't get to be the Deputy, I will go down on my hands and knees.

VŨ BẠO This promotion game is just like martial arts. Having support and luck is one thing but you can still lose if you are too confident...

ĐÌNH MAI You're right! You should watch out for Bùi Việt Thắng. He and his wife are planning to sell their villa to invest to the maximum *(points up to the ceiling).*

VŨ BẠO What do you mean?

ĐÌNH MAI He will go to see the top people directly... he won't go through Trần Tô like you.

VŨ BẠO *(a bit nervous)* Where did you get that from?

ĐÌNH MAI His wife is the close friend of the son of a B.T.C. It's said that the B.T.C. has agreed to take him door by door...

VŨ BẠO *(annoyed)* Where did you get that info–?

ĐÌNH MAI Hương Ly, Bùi Việt Thắng's wife told me.

VŨ BẠO Why didn't you tell me before?

ĐÌNH MAI Because she just told me last night. She even borrowed five million from one of my friends in the Oil Corporation.

VŨ BẠO *(frustrated)* That's serious info... you have to tell me immediately if you hear this kind of news, all right? Send someone to follow them twenty-four hours a day!

ĐÌNH MAI Yes... OK.

Trần Tô enters.

TRẦN TỔ How long have you two been waiting?

VŨ BẠO We've just come...

TRẦN TỔ *(to Vũ Bạo)* You have one more competitor in the race, that's the Head of Department – Hoàng Quang Tất.

ĐÌNH MAI Hoàng Quang Tất? He is competent but poor. Hoàng Quang Tất doesn't dare to play the game, he may just stand by to observe and cheer us on.

TRẦN TỔ He is poor... right. But he has a big Asian backer investing in him.

VŨ BẠO So what do we have to do now, bro'?

TRẦN TỔ Admit it's a war... it's an open race to the top. If the enemy uses a CKC, we have to use an AK. If they use an AK, you have to get a machine-gun...

ĐÌNH MAI But if they have machine-guns already...

TRẦN TỔ Then we need a one-thirty-seven millimetre cannon to break through the fort.

VŨ BẠO I don't mind spending money. But how do we know the enemy's strategy and how much they have to spend? Not knowing, that's the problem...

TRẦN TỔ Right! What's most important now is to get the info on the other side...

ĐÌNH MAI It's no big deal for me.

TRẦN TỔ Not that easy!

ĐÌNH MAI Very easy.

TRẦN TỔ Tell me how?

ĐÌNH MAI I have some people working in information technology and telecoms – they can get all the info via phone calls and emails.

TRẦN TỔ Brilliant! If you can do that, the deal is ours.

VŨ BẠO *(as if he remembers something)* Bro'–?

TRẦN TỔ What's up?

VŨ BẠO Is next Sunday your dad's birthday?

TRẦN TỔ How do you know?

ĐÌNH MAI He just told me.

TRẦN TỔ *(laughs)* He's too old and senile... no one wants to come to his 90th birthday. *(Brusque)* I'll organise his birthday party. You don't have to come, you don't have to buy him a gift.

VŨ BẠO But I want to...

TRẦN TỔ *(cuts Vũ Bạo off)* I said, no.

Lights fade.

SCENE 4

The afternoon. A luxury apartment in the centre of Hanoi, Trần Tô walks into the living room in pyjamas. He lies on the sofa, pours some wine and drinks it then relaxes looking up at the ceiling, enjoying the soft music. Trần Tô suddenly sits up and looks toward the bathroom.

TRẦN TỔ Are you finished in there?

HƯƠNG LY I'm nearly done! *(Hương Ly looks glorious in a luxury négligée, entering from the bathroom and brushing her hair)* When did you buy this apartment?

TRẦN TỔ Over four years ago. Sometimes I come here, turn off the phone, forget the stress and enjoy a wonderful time right in the centre of Hanoi.

HƯƠNG LY And every time you come here... there's another beautiful woman too?

TRẦN TỔ Without beauty, it wouldn't be as wonderful... Let's not talk about that... today is a good day and I want to give you a small gift...

HƯƠNG LY What's that?

TRẦN TỔ Secret! Close your eyes and give me your hand. *(Hương Ly does as asked. Trần Tô puts the gift in Hương Ly's hand)* You have to hold it tight before you open your eyes...

HƯƠNG LY Can I now?

TRẦN TỔ Yes! But open your eyes before you open your hand...

HƯƠNG LY *(surprised)* Oh... A brand new Mercedes...

TRẦN TỔ Your favourite colour. Registered in your name and now parked in the basement of this building. *(Hương Ly jumps on him and they kiss deeply)*

HƯƠNG LY You are the best man in the world...

TRẦN TỔ And you're the best woman... *(Pause, then honestly)* I have been through quite a lot of women, you know. Yes, some were gorgeous, some were young and virginal... but I've never felt as alive as when I'm with you. It makes me forget everything else in life... You have the soul of an angel... and the most amazing body... you must have a hidden magnet inside you that attracts my whole being... I find myself feeling younger and stronger than ever before...

HƯƠNG LY Your youth and strength light me up. I feel like I'm floating in the clouds and flying high in the sky. I've never known such joy and it's unbelievably sweet...

TRẦN TỔ I have no interest in looking at other women since I've been with you... even all of them put together, they're nothing compared to you...

HƯƠNG LY And when I'm with you, I feel like I've blossomed. *(Pause suddenly shows a bit of sadness)* There's only one thing...

TRẦN TỔ What is it? Tell me! Is it because of my endless long parties with my business partners?

HƯƠNG LY No... I don't interfere in your business...

TRẦN TỔ So what is making you unhappy?

HƯƠNG LY *(looks away)* Whenever I'm with my husband, I have to close my eyes to imagine that I'm with you or I can't go through with making love to him.

TRẦN TỔ I'm so glad to hear that.

HƯƠNG LY You're glad that I'm miserable?

TRẦN TỔ Because it means... I'm in your heart. Do you know how much I love you? It's more than the love of all the men in this world added together. *(Looks at Hương Ly's eyes)* Hương Ly...

HƯƠNG LY Yes, honey?

TRẦN TỔ I want to have you completely...

HƯƠNG LY Don't, honey! We both have a family, even if it's not perfect... we should just make the most of this... being each other's private blue sky, which we can have whenever we want...

TRẦN TỔ You know, baby, you've woken up the love inside me... whenever I sleep alone, I always imagine that you and your husband are making love... and that thought is killing me...

HƯƠNG LY Sex between me and him is not great since we've been together... Actually, it feels like my duty recently and I get no satisfaction from that...

TRẦN TỔ So why don't we get rid of all those strings to be together for good?

HƯƠNG LY No my dear! Just let it be like this... I still have you and my family, you also still have me and your family... just leave it be like this for a peaceful life...

TRẦN TỔ *(insists)* Hương Ly...

HƯƠNG LY Yes honey! I'm still listening to you...

TRẦN TỔ I'm really miserable when I have to leave you... I'm really addicted to you... and this addiction is stronger than any other drug in the whole world...

HƯƠNG LY Don't be so dramatic, honey! Everything will be ok when you get back into the daily routine of your business, you'll see... *(Pause)* I also have a question for you now

TRẦN TỔ Go on.

HƯƠNG LY How much will it cost to take care of my husband's promotion? Please just tell me so I can arrange things...

TRẦN TỔ Don't, baby.

HƯƠNG LY Why not?

TRẦN TỔ Because you are my treasure... I can pay everything for him as long as I have you.

HƯƠNG LY It shouldn't be like that – I don't like it.

TRẦN TỔ But I like it! So please, please, please be happy too.

HƯƠNG LY One more thing *(feels hesitant)* but no... I won't...

TRẦN TỔ You can't half say it. Tell me... just tell me.

HƯƠNG LY *(hesitant)* People say that... you are campaigning on Đinh Vũ Bạo's behalf as well. Are you?

TRẦN TỔ *(laughs out loud)* That's right!

HƯƠNG LY So, what about Thắng?

TRẦN TỔ Thắng will be the winner, don't worry. *(Beat)* Look, this deal is like a race... if there's only your husband on the track, it would no longer be a race... this race has at least five people competing, but the important thing to remember is – which one will be first past the post? *(Turns to Hương Ly)* Have you heard about the so-called "red soldier and blue solider"?

Hương Ly shakes head slightly.

TRẦN TỔ Like when you have a cake and you want to sell it to one guy but you are still offering it to other guys... Those who have money and want the cake will come... And they have to pay for it.

HƯƠNG LY But who gets it at the end of the day?

TRẦN TỔ The one who has the most money.

HƯƠNG LY What's this got to do with the red and blue soldiers?

TRẦN TỔ At first I am the red one, but if others have more money, then I become a blue soldier... and when the blue soldiers get more money, then the others turn red again...

HƯƠNG LY It's too complicated!

TRẦN TỔ That's why it is a dark race... and because it's dark, no one can see the other's face even if he is in or out...

HƯƠNG LY So in that case, Đinh Vũ Bạo could lose it all...

TRẦN TỔ Of course... once you decide to be in, you have to accept the rules of the game. *(Remembers something)* Where is my mobile phone, do you know?

HƯƠNG LY In the bedroom.

TRẦN TỔ Can you please go find it for me?

Hương Ly exits to the bedroom, Trần Tô drinks some more wine. Hương Ly returns with phone.

HƯƠNG LY *(gives the phone to Trần Tô)* Here you go.

TRẦN TỔ It was turned off the whole day to be with you, there must be a lot of missed calls. *(Turns the phone on)* Wow... forty-five missed calls. *(Trần Tô is looking at the list of missed calls when the phone rings)* Hello! Trần Tô speaking.

Vũ Bạo is on the phone at the other end.

VŨ BẠO Bloody hell Tô... why did you turn off the phone all day?

TRẦN TỔ I had an important meeting. What's the problem?

VŨ BẠO I'm done, bro', I'm dying...

TRẦN TỔ Why are you dying? Calm down!

VŨ BẠO I received notice that the Government Auditor is coming to do a general audit of the whole of my group this morning.

TRẦN TỔ What? A general audit? Who signed it off? Who is the chief auditor?

Lights fade.

SCENE 5

The meeting room of the Business Group where Vũ Kiều Loan is the General Director. Only Võ Trần Tổ and Đinh Vũ Bạo are waiting. Đinh Vũ Bạo impatiently watches the clock, then stands up and paces around.

VŨ BẠO Why is this taking so long?

TRẦN TỔ Calm down. She's making us wait on purpose to annoy us. *(Gives Vũ Bạo a newspaper)* Read it to kill time. *(He reads. Vũ Kiều Loan enters)*

KIỀU LOAN Sorry for keeping you waiting for so long. I had an urgent meeting this morning.

TRẦN TỔ It's fine, waiting is to be expected. *(Points at Vũ Bạo)* You two know each other so no need for introductions.

KIỀU LOAN Yes, five years ago, Mr. Đinh Vũ Bạo was incredibly successful in winning our top project in this city. We lost about twenty billion on that deal.

VŨ BẠO It was a top down decision for awarding the project to our team on that occasion.

KIỀU LOAN *(to Vũ Bạo)* Win or lose it's the way of things in business. I just wanted to let Mr. Tô know a bit more about our business dealings.

TRẦN TỔ I've come to see you, Kiều Loan, for a very important reason...

KIỀU LOAN Very important? Hmm... go on, please...

TRẦN TỔ How do you explain the fact that the Government Audit team is investigating Đinh Vũ Bạo's corporation?

KIỀU LOAN Ah! I get your drift. If I say 'no idea', you won't believe me because you think I'm involved in this purely to stop Đinh Vũ Bạo from getting the promotion.

TRẦN TỔ Exactly! Because we are in the same race.

KIỀU LOAN You have a very low opinion of my business ethics. Can I just ask you – where did you get the idea that I could tell the Government Auditor what to do?

TRẦN TỔ No, not saying you do... but influence maybe...?

KIỀU LOAN *(serious)* I'll have to ask you to leave immediately if you continue to insult me in this way.

TRẦN TỔ *(being nice)* Please, don't take this the wrong way... *(Pause)* You do provide the documents to the Auditor, don't you?

KIỀU LOAN Yes, I do! The Government Auditor asked me to provide him with all the documents relating to the urban development project that Vũ Bạo led five years ago. I just give the Auditor the truth, nothing but the truth. We are working transparently and everything is by the book here so I don't have to pay back anyone any favours.

VŨ BẠO The city awarded your project to us in a top-down decision. It's as clear as daylight, nothing was hidden...

KIỀU LOAN There are still some shadows even walking in daylight, Mr. Bạo.

VŨ BẠO Can you clarify that?

KIỀU LOAN The Auditors have said that your corporation didn't have the appropriate license for investing and developing an urban area. People are saying that you invested in cross sector development, and are asking whether you invested in the wrong sector with nine thousand billion from the government budget.

TRẦN TỔ Oh, surely that's normal practice...

KIỀU LOAN I'm not saying it's abnormal. So, please don't bother about what I submit to the Government Auditor.

TRẦN TỔ Did the Auditor request those documents in writing?

KIỀU LOAN *(smiles)* Mr. Trần Tô, since when do you have so little faith in people? Are you suggesting that I deliberately informed the Auditor of Mr. Vũ Bạo's wrong-doing on that project? I never stooped to that level even when I was going through hell after being cheated on by you! *(Pause)* Excuse me for a moment. *(Kiều Loan walks out of the meeting room).*

VŨ BẠO *(to Trần Tô)* Such a bitch.

TRẦN TỔ *(pretends to ignore Vũ Bạo's comment)* What Kiều Loan just said is correct, right? You did invest in cross sector development with nine thousand billion from the government budget?

VŨ BẠO Well, yeh, I had to. When the project was nearly finished, I sent a proposal to get a new license but they rejected it.

TRẦN TỔ That's a big problem. You have broken the rules for the sake of your own business interests.

VŨ BẠO Can it be fixed?

TRẦN TỔ A problem can always be fixed. Even the crab-pot at Song Tranh Hydroelectric[1] was fixed. *(Looks at Vũ Bạo and speaks louder)* It can be fixed but... needs a lot of time and energy, understand?

Kiều Loan enters and gives Trần Tô a document to read.

KIỀU LOAN Read this...

TRẦN TỔ *(Reads it carefully and then gives it back to Kiều Loan)* Thank you! But I wasn't convinced you were involved in this anyway.

KIỀU LOAN *(smiles)* It doesn't matter what you believe about me... the problem now is how to blow away the big dark cloud hanging over Bao's head. If you can't blow it away, it might turn into a hurricane that will destroy Bao's chances of going anywhere.

TRẦN TỔ Should I consider this as sincere advice or a warning?

KIỀU LOAN Whatever you like! *(Offers a hand to shake)* Good luck!

TRẦN TỔ *(shakes hands with Kiều Loan)* Good bye! *(Pause)* I hope you'll still keep to our agreement as per our meeting the other day.

---

1. A hydroelectric dam which suffered several minor earthquakes and needs repeated repairs to stop it leaking

KIỀU LOAN We're both running in the same race. May the best man win, as they say.

TRẦN TỔ And neither one of us can see what the other is doing?

KIỀU LOAN You have my word. We never even catch sight of each other.

Lights fade.

SCENE 6

Evening in the living room of Bùi Việt Thắng's house. Việt Thắng is stretched out on the sofa, listening to music when the doorbell rings.

VIỆT THẮNG *(bored)* Come in... *(Đình Mai excitedly enters)*

ĐÌNH MAI Do you have any champagne?

VIỆT THẮNG What for?

ĐÌNH MAI To celebrate our success.

VIỆT THẮNG You've just won a big deal?

ĐÌNH MAI I don't have any deals to win or lose... You're the winner, Thắng! *(laughs happily).*

VIỆT THẮNG *(sits up immediately)* Why? I don't understand?

ĐÌNH MAI You don't have to waste any bullets on your biggest rival. He is out of the running completely... Đinh Vũ Bạo is finished, probably running away before they throw him in prison.

VIỆT THẮNG *(excited)* Really?

ĐÌNH MAI Bạo's corporation invested fifteen thousand billion in the wrong sector, then lost nearly three billion, so he's guilty of breaking the rules to the tune of several hundred billion. The report is being issued soon by the Government Auditor... He's likely to be arrested...

VIỆT THẮNG Let's drink to that! *(Takes out a bottle from under the table and pours it into two glasses)* Cheers! Any news about any of the other chaps?

ĐÌNH MAI The one to be most concerned about is that Head of Department Hoàng Quang Tất.

VIỆT THẮNG We don't care about him, do we? Capable but no money...

ĐÌNH MAI Don't be so sure... *(Looks at Thắng)* Have you heard about her ladyship Kiều Loan in Ho Chi Minh city?

VIỆT THẮNG She's one of the richest women, I know that.

ĐÌNH MAI *(serious)* She has enough power to storm any fortress and she is investing in Hoàng Quang Tất.

VIỆT THẮNG *(worried)* Hoàng Quang Tất is not as high up as Đinh Vũ Bạo.

ĐÌNH MAI That's right! You need to make that point to Trần Tô, and don't be afraid of spending money. But now you've mentioned Trần Tô, there is one thing... *(Pause)* But no... it's nothing...

VIỆT THẮNG Why do you do this? It's annoying.

ĐÌNH MAI OK, fine. I'll tell you... but don't take it the wrong way and don't blame me...

VIỆT THẮNG OK. Speak.

ĐÌNH MAI I've heard rumours that Hương Ly is in a relationship with Trần Tô.

VIỆT THẮNG What do you mean by that?

ĐÌNH MAI People are gossiping about it at the ministry.

VIỆT THẮNG *(calm)* Yeh, I heard about that as well. *(Pause)* Do you believe it?

ĐÌNH MAI *(hesitant)* I... I... don't know

VIỆT THẮNG They're just winding me up! They're saying it to get at me.

ĐÌNH MAI But I know there's some substance to it.

VIỆT THẮNG Really? How?

ĐÌNH MAI Lots of people... me too... have seen Hương Ly and Trần Tô walking hand-in-hand going to posh clubs and smart hotels around the city.

VIỆT THẮNG *(angry)* So you believe in the rumours? Not you too? You should have slapped all those idiots who tell you that bloody story.

ĐÌNH MAI You get so angry! I shouldn't have told you about this...

VIỆT THẮNG *(calms down)* If you hear it again, slap them in the face for me...

ĐÌNH MAI I did slap them. And I told them that if they keep making up lies, they'll go to hell...

VIỆT THẮNG Yeh? Who did you say that to then?

ĐÌNH MAI *(embarrassed)* Well, I told Đinh Vũ Bạo... and Hoàng Quang Tất, just yesterday.

VIỆT THẮNG Those two guys are in on this?

ĐÌNH MAI Those two are the authors of this rumour... they're even asking their people to spread it around... just to upset you... they want to stress you out.

VIỆT THẮNG Fine! I know how to deal with them.

ĐÌNH MAI No no no! Please don't over-react... the louder they talk, the more you need to keep quiet... that's what any smart guy would do... if you over-react, it will come back to bite you in the bum. *(Đình Mai's phone rings. Mai takes it out and looks at the phone number)* Huh! The lion is calling. *(Talks on phone)* I am coming back... it was urgent so I had to go see Mr. Thắng. Keep it down or Mr. Thắng will laugh at us! Yes! Just leave them, I will wash up.

Đình Mai says good bye to Thắng and leaves quickly. Thắng holds onto the glass of wine and walks around the room, deep in thought when Hương Ly enters.

HƯƠNG LY Not asleep yet?

VIỆT THẮNG *(angry)* I wish!

HƯƠNG LY What's up with you today?

VIỆT THẮNG *(frustrated)* People are talking about you and Trần Tô everywhere out there...

HƯƠNG LY Look at you... It's you who forced me to do it...

VIỆT THẮNG *(grumpy)* But you have to do it secretly... you want to humiliate me?

HƯƠNG LY Both of us are being humiliated, not just you!

VIỆT THẮNG *(surprised)* What do you mean?

HƯƠNG LY Because this affair is between me and him.

VIỆT THẮNG *(curls his lips)* You need to remember that this is only a deal, so you have to keep your distance... just give into him little by little...

HƯƠNG LY Oh yeh, sitting here and giving orders is easy as you are on the outside... but I am inside this mess, and it's difficult to get out. Having an affair puts you into a spin, it can sweep you off your feet...

VIỆT THẮNG Well, it was the only option. If you hadn't quit your job as a doctor to become Assistant to the General Director for Trần Tô, who would know about this?

HƯƠNG LY The salary of a doctor is just six million dongs a month, whereas the salary for the G.D. Assistant job is four thousand US dollars... and you said that it was up to me to decide... and now you are annoyed with me. *(Both keep silent for a while)*

VIỆT THẮNG Since you started the relationship with Trần Tô, you've been like a block of wood when we're together...

HƯƠNG LY What about you? You think making love with your wife is just a duty now? You think you're being tortured... why? Because all your love and strength is going to Van, the single girl at work who is the deputy manager of the Planning department.

VIỆT THẮNG What? What are you saying?

HƯƠNG LY Are you denying it? *(Pause)* Don't even try! *(Becoming emotional)* I have it here with me – hundreds of your messages to and from her which describe your love, the dates, the sex and even details of each time you slept with her.

VIỆT THẮNG Any man who has to imagine that his wife is in the arms of another has the right to do something to forget the pain and shame of it all.

HƯƠNG LY Huh? *(Smiles)* If I hadn't confronted you with this, you'd go on pretending you were a decent husband!

VIỆT THẮNG *(pacifying)* Please Ly, I just do it to get away from the hurt and feeling so jealous, thinking about you lying in Trần Tô's arms.

HƯƠNG LY Maybe we... should just close our eyes and try to ignore all of the bad things we've done... leave it be...

VIỆT THẮNG No! We have to try and bring our family back to normal... for our own sakes.

HƯƠNG LY It's not that easy!

VIỆT THẮNG So what else do we do? Carry on arguing and bitching all the time? Breaking up this family day by day?

HƯƠNG LY *(breathes deeply to stay calm)* I think... it's time for us to break up. Full stop.

VIỆT THẮNG *(shocked)* What? What did you say? Break up?

HƯƠNG LY Yes! Just so we're released from this mess... or more exactly, to be free from this living hell...

VIỆT THẮNG Has Trần Tô taken over your mind and soul so much that you are a complete zombie when you come back home?

HƯƠNG LY *(very calm)* Look, I should tell you the truth... *(Pause)*

VIỆT THẮNG OK, tell me! What is it now.

HƯƠNG LY I haven't been in love with you for a long time. I love Tô.

VIỆT THẮNG *(stops)* What the–? You must be crazy! Are you crazy??

HƯƠNG LY I'm perfectly sane, Thắng... Since I've been with Tô, I've felt that I'm really living my life... seeing myself flying free in blue skies, surrounded by love in a wonderful world.

VIỆT THẮNG Yes and it tastes like money money money, right?

HƯƠNG LY No! Real love tastes wonderful, intense, free... I see my life with you like being a seed that was withering in the desert but now that I'm with Tô, I can grow in good earth, and bloom.

VIỆT THẮNG *(cries)* How can you say that?! You whore, you bloody bitch!

HƯƠNG LY *(still stays calm)* Carry on swearing, more and louder if it helps you feel better... *(Suddenly depressed)* Yes, most men marry whores... but you, you force your wife to be a whore... *(Cries)* It's rare for a man to ask his wife to sleep with other men to get himself promoted! *(Both stay silent)* It made me realize that you don't love me... you've never loved anyone except yourself... you're a very selfish person, wanting everyone around you to sacrifice themselves for you...

VIỆT THẮNG Yes, I do love myself. I want people to love me. But what's it all for? It's just for this family... for the children we were going to have one day...

HƯƠNG LY Lucky that I haven't had any then...

VIỆT THẮNG You're going too far... I never said that I'd divorce you.

HƯƠNG LY Not to me, but you have to Van. I'm keeping that message you sent to her...

VIỆT THẮNG It's just what every man having an affair says to his lover...

HƯƠNG LY *(interrupts)* No! What you say to people counts. Life is one big drama full of ups and downs... *(Takes a piece of paper from her bag)* This is a divorce letter. I wrote it already, you just need to sign it.

VIỆT THẮNG No! Never! I'll never sign it! I'm not so crazy to get rid of both my assets and the profits!

HƯƠNG LY Sign it... I guarantee that you will get that Deputy seat anyway.

VIỆT THẮNG Huh! Wait and see! Who knows?

HƯƠNG LY If you don't, that's fine... I will submit this letter to the courts to have a one-sided divorce.

VIỆT THẮNG If you push me too far I'll bloody kill you!

Việt Thắng threatens Hương Ly. Trần Tổ appears.

TRẦN TỔ Stop it! Calm down! Don't get so worked up! *(Directly to Thắng)* I had a bad feeling, so I came over. *(Pacifying)* Thắng... you know, for happiness you need to have love on both sides... and love always follows the heart which no one can control... you should think about how you can win from this... *(Pause)* About your promotion... I promise you, on my word, that you will get it... I'll pay off everyone, you don't need to spend a penny. *(Hương Ly feels uncomfortable and looks sick)*

VIỆT THẮNG Hương Ly! Are you OK!

TRẦN TỔ She has morning sickness!

VIỆT THẮNG *(surprised)* Morning sickness! You're pregnant?

HƯƠNG LY Yes, but it's not yours! Not your child, understand?

Lights fade.

SCENE 7

The living room of Trần Tổ's villa. Trần Tổ is pacing up and down, highly stressed. Vũ Bạo and Đình Mai are sitting on the sofa and worriedly watching Trần Tổ. Trần Tổ suddenly stops. Both Vũ Bạo and Đình Mai start to stand up but then sit down to wait for something.

TRẦN TỔ News still leaks out fast even when we've tried to keep it quiet.

VŨ BẠO *(miserable)* You know many of the top guys, can't you find a way out?

TRẦN TỔ The police have jumped on this even before the Auditor's released his report... that makes it doubly difficult...

ĐÌNH MAI I think it's time to trade off something or someone to save Mr. Đinh Vũ Bạo.

TRẦN TỔ The situation is beyond that, no point doing a deal at a lower level.

ĐÌNH MAI Me and Bao were discussing it this morning... *(Bạo gives a stop signal to Đình Mai)*

TRẦN TỔ Discussing what? *(No one answers)* Why the silence?

VŨ BẠO Well, Đình Mai has advised me to go abroad...

TRẦN TỔ Going abroad is the very last option.

VŨ BẠO That means there's still a way out? It all depends on you now whether I live or die.

TRẦN TỔ Go home. Vũ Bạo, you have to stay off the phone... I'll contact Đình Mai for any updates.

Vũ Bạo and Đình Mai go out, Trần Tổ thinks for a while and looks on his phone to find the right contact. Then Kiều Loan comes in.

KIỀU LOAN *(boldly)* Today I'm back with my claws out...

TRẦN TỔ *(looks up)* Whoa! What a coincidence! I was looking for your number just now.

KIỀU LOAN Really? That means there's an issue... good or bad?

TRẦN TỔ Let's talk plainly.

KIỀU LOAN OK!

TRẦN TỔ The Police have started looking into Đinh Vũ Bạo's corporation. I'm asking for your help with this, as you're very close to the Deputy Commander...

KIỀU LOAN *(surprised)* You're very close to him as well...

TRẦN TỔ But I can't move on this.

KIỀU LOAN Why not?

TRẦN TỔ There's another issue in the background that I can't tell you about now... *(They both stay silent for a bit)*

KIỀU LOAN I see... well, I can't promise anything but I'll try and sort out this mess for you, on one condition.

TRẦN TỔ And that's why you've come today, right?

KIỀU LOAN Of course! You think I come to see you just for fun? It's only on a special occasion now.

TRẦN TỔ Tell me! What's your condition?

KIỀU LOAN You need to stop pissing about and get behind the campaign for Hoàng Quang Tất.

TRẦN TỔ You're as direct as you've always been.

KIỀU LOAN Don't dismiss the idea out of hand! *(Pause)* We had a deal before... we're in the same race and we were blind to each other's manoevres... but I can see you now... you're blocking Hoàng Quang Tất to clear the way for Đinh Vũ Bạo.

Trần Tổ stays silent.

KIỀU LOAN Đinh Vũ Bạo is going to fall down all by himself and is in serious trouble... his top priority now is to avoid going to prison.

TRẦN TỔ You're right! But I'm not the one doing it.

KIỀU LOAN *(smiles)* It's time to move on. What you have to do now is to run for Hoàng Quang Tất. *(Sees the stress on Trần Tổ's face)* Don't get so stressed out... There's no reason for you now not to get behind Hoàng Quang Tất, is there?

TRẦN TỔ But what if I fail?

KIỀU LOAN Huh! You've never failed any case ever before.

TRẦN TỔ But this might be the first. Human Resources is becoming very complicated and unpredictable... who knows what might happen?

KIỀU LOAN We both know you can make it happen. The only issue is whether you want to do it or not.

TRẦN TỔ You talk as if everything is in my pocket!

KIỀU LOAN It may not be in your pocket but it's easy for you to swing it... because you walk in and out of the top office as if there's a free place for you there. *(Đình Mai runs in)*

ĐÌNH MAI *(breathless)* Mr. Trần Tô! It's over.

TRẦN TỔ What's over? Tell me quick!

ĐÌNH MAI On his way back from here... Vũ Bạo was stopped by the police and arrested. They're turning over his house and his office.

TRẦN TỔ *(sighs)* Poor bastard... it's the end of the line.

ĐÌNH MAI If he'd agreed to fly to Canada last month, he wouldn't be in this mess. But, he was still determined to get the seat of Deputy and become a member of the Central Congress...

TRẦN TỔ *(shouts)* Stop it! Don't blame this on me.

KIỀU LOAN *(to Trần Tổ)* So my part in this is all over now?

TRẦN TỔ Look, don't ask me to run for Hoàng Quang Tất... Do you know why? Because the seat is already filled.

KIỀU LOAN That means it was never going to Đinh Vũ Bạo?

TRẦN TỔ It was going to Đinh Vũ Bạo at first, but then it moved to another candidate later.

ĐÌNH MAI You mean Bùi Việt Thắng?

TRẦN TỔ *(angry)* Don't talk about what you don't know! Just keep quiet. *(Mai moves away quickly. Trần Tổ looks to the door and sees Việt Thắng coming in)* Oh! Thắng! Why are you here?

VIỆT THẮNG I couldn't get through by phone so had to come in person.

TRẦN TỔ *(looks at his phone)* Oh, shit! I forgot to turn on the phone.

VIỆT THẮNG Mr. Tô... The decision on the position of Deputy Minister is being announced tomorrow morning.

TRẦN TỔ What? They're announcing it tomorrow morning? Why did no one tell me about this?

VIỆT THẮNG But I already know it's not me.

TRẦN TỔ *(stunned)* So who is it? Who...?

VIỆT THẮNG It's gone to some guy who is the Deputy Chair of a Province in the country who is just 45 years old...

TRẦN TỔ That can't be true. *(Takes the phone and presses a number... the operator says that the number dialled is not available... Tô presses another number)* Hello! Hello! Fuck it... the phone is ringing but nobody's fucking answering... *(Hương Ly walks in, clearly pregnant)* Hương Ly, You need to rest... Why are you here?

HƯƠNG LY Thắng called to tell me the news, so I came to see what's going on...

TRẦN TỔ I'm as surprised as you are. Just called some guys, some not available, some didn't pick up... *(Talks to himself)* What the hell is going on? It's not possible... no.

Mr. Trần Tiên enters.

TRẦN TIÊN It's very easy to understand... because what the Party needs is somebody who is honest and capable, not these silly buggers who just use their money to buy a seat...

TRẦN TỔ Look, Pa, you don't know anything about this... please sit down and have a rest...

TRẦN TIÊN Huh, you think I'm an old fool? I know exactly what you're up to. It's me who wrote a letter to the leaders of the Party to ask them to get rid of all the people buying and selling seats in the government.

TRẦN TỔ What? *(Laughs out loud)* Oh my God... you think, that you're still a powerful member of the Politburo? No... you are done... you are now just an ordinary citizen... when you retired, you had about as much power as a group of country farmers... you are out of date, old man... do you think that they are listening to an old veteran like you, sir? They might pretend to listen and nod their heads... but your words go in one ear, and out the other... you understand?

TRẦN TIÊN You're wrong! The Party listens and acts for the good of the people... *(To Đình Mai)* You! Read this letter out loud so everyone can hear...

ĐÌNH MAI Yes, sir... *(Takes the letter from Mr. Trần Tiên and reads. Mr. Trần Tiên's voice is also heard off-stage)* To the leaders of the Party. I am Võ Trần Tiên, former member of the Politburo, Management Board of the Communist Party of Vietnam. I am writing, in good faith, to make some comments about the current management team of the Party. In the past, our Party and Uncle Ho always chose people on merit. We appointed people who were ethical, talented, hard-working, patient, open, honest and fair to the important positions. All these criteria nowadays seem to be less important, leading to a system of trading for the top positions everywhere. If you don't eliminate these activities from the system, I think our country will be put in the hands of those incapable of good management and those who are lacking in ability and integrity. And if this occurs, it will be very easy to bring this Party down. Considering the current trade in top positions, I wonder who, among you, is accepting the money for this? Is it all of you? No, I don't believe that is the truth. But there is no way of knowing where the money is going. The practice of buying a position, buying power, buying grades, buying a place at a school, buying a project and buying many things in our society is creating a big problem in the whole of our country these days... I would like to attach herewith evidence I have recorded of all the conversations, discussions, and agreements of a deal for a government position to prove what I have mentioned above. This is enough evidence for you to eliminate certain individuals who are trying to use their money to buy promotion and power. How many other people in this country are buying their positions now not only here in the centre but right down to the local level? I would also be willing to accept any punishment from the Party and from the people for not educating my son properly, although I am old. In fact, my son has been a leading dealer in the corrupt system of people paying bribes for government positions for many years. Wishing you all the best!

VIỆT THẮNG *(upset)* It's absolutely fucking clear as daylight! Why the fuck did I risk losing my wife, my reputation and my career?

TRẦN TIÊN Your own fault. You're to blame, not anyone else!

TRẦN TỔ *(to Trần Tiên)* Pa! I can't believe that you could do such a bloody awful thing... What do you gain from that? *(Distressed)* You killed me! You've just destroyed me and a lot of other people... do you understand what you've done?

TRẦN TIÊN *(contented)* You have destroyed yourself and the others, Tô. I feel at peace with myself for doing a good thing.

TRẦN TỔ *(pained)* You're feeling at peace?! *(Charges at his father and shouts)* There's no peace until you're buried six feet under! But no... you'll never find peace even then, when you're stone cold dead.

Mr. Trần Tiên suddenly stops still and falls over. Đình Mai and Kiều Loan try to catch the old man.

ĐÌNH MAI Mr. Trần Tô! *(Pause)* He seems to have passed away...

KIỀU LOAN *(frightened)* Put him on the sofa and pump his chest... *(To Việt Thắng)* Call the ambulance! *(Thắng gets on the phone)*

All of them surround the old man, and Trần Tổ listens for a heartbeat, but after a while Mr. Trần Tiên comes to again and sits up.

TRẦN TIÊN How can I die! When you're all still here, how can I leave...? I don't dare to join my ancestors or my comrades... not yet, anyway!

Blackout.

The end.

NGUYEN ĐĂNG CHUONG

Nguyen was born on May 25, 1964 in Khanh Trung commune, Yen Khanh district, Ninh Binh province Vietnam. He has gained a Bachelor of Arts, a Master of Cultural Studies and is currently a graduate student at the Institute of Art and Culture, Vietnam.

He is well-known for his plays. From 1998 to date, Nguyen Đăng Chuong has written more than twenty works for the theatre, and has recieved thirty prestigious awards in the categories of plays, screenplays and TV drama, as well as the top awards from the Vietnamese ministries and Literary Arts Society.

Dark Race was awarded the Gold Medal for plays in the Professional Dramatics National Contest of Tuong, Folk and Drama 2013 and the Gold Medal for plays and Best Writer in Professional Dramatics National Contest 2015. He was awarded Prize A for Best Play in 2013, and Prize of Best Drama Script in 2012 from Vietnam Stage Artists Association.

While exploring philosophical issues through his drama, Đăng examines characters whose actions often contradict their purported good intentions.

He is currently director of the Department of Performing Arts, Ministry of Culture, Sports and Tourism and a Member of the Executive Committee Stage Artists Association Vietnam, terms VI, VII and VIII (from 2005 to date).

Playwright's Note

Frangipani (*Phka Champei*) was developed as part of a workshop facilitated by playwright Catherine Filloux.

Catherine Filloux is a participant in the New Generations – Future Collaborations programme, funded by Andrew W. Mellon Foundation and administered by Theatre Communications Group, the national organization for American Theatre.

Catherine Filloux and John Daggett also provided private funding for the development and workshop of Frangipani, which took place at AMRITA in October, 2009.

www.catherinefilloux.com

I'd also like to thank my translator Suon Bunrith and Sokhorn Yon at Cambodian Living Arts.

www.cambodianlivingarts.org

FRANGIPANI

CHHON SINA

Translated from Khmer
by Suon Bunrith

Characters *(Actors can double roles)*

NAPHAN – age 18, daughter of Noeun and Han, a sex worker who was raped at 13 by her father.

SAMNANG – age 16, picks up trash for money, daughter of Tha and Lang.

NY – age 20, sex worker and a victim of sex trafficking. Sold by her parents, came from a province and is living in the slum area with Naphan, her good friend.

DUONG – 20, female high school student.

Ka – 19, female high school student; daughter of Auntie Srouy.

CHHAY – 21, male high school student; boyfriend of Duong and Ka.

PAMESANN – male, 25, a nightclub manager.

SRAS – age 25, a student at a university, who works at a nightclub.

VANN – age 27, a student at a university, who works at a nightclub with Sras.

PAPA – age 53, a government official.

BODYGUARDS – two men who accompany the government official.

NOEUN – age 43, mother of Naphan. She was raped at age 16 by her husband before they were married.

HAN – age 65, cremator at a pagoda, Naphan's father and Noeun's husband.

THA – age 39, motorbike taxi driver who lives in the slum area.

LANG – age 32, wife of Tha.

SROUY – age 45, a neighbour in the slum area, mother of Ka.

MONTHA – age 46, living in the provinces; sent her daughter, Sras, to university in Phnom Penh.

Time

Present day.

Place

Phnom Penh, Cambodia.

PROLOGUE

A small pond. Naphan, 18, wearing a mini-skirt and light pink, flowered blouse, sits throwing white frangipani flowers into the water. Another girl, 16, Samnang is a trash-picker, wearing shorts that go below her knee and a dirty white shirt. She holds a bag in one hand and a hook for picking up trash in the other. She stands watching Naphan throwing flowers into the water. Naphan raises her head and looks at Samnang.

Blackout.

SCENE 1

At a nightclub. Naphan, Ny, Duong, Ka, and Chhay are enjoying themselves, dancing to foreign rock music. The male manager [Pamesann is his nickname], is 25.

CHHAY Hi Pamesann! Please get me some drinks, Pa!

MANAGER How many of you?

CHHAY Three, or four – give me a strong one, and make it easy to drink.

The manager puts drugs in the drinks under the table. The manager gives Chhay glasses of an orange soft drink, and Chhay passes them out.

KA I don't drink. I'm afraid I won't be able to go to school in the morning.

CHHAY Drink, Ka! I diluted the medicine. Hey, Duong, drink this!

DUONG I never drink! *(Chhay forces Duong to drink)*

CHHAY You'll take to it like a duck to water! Drink and you'll see. *(Shouting offstage)* DJ, turn it up!

They all drink and dance.

CHHAY *(approaching the manager)* Hey Bro,' I'm smashed – I want to eat a child.

MANAGER Which one you want?

CHHAY *(points to Naphan)* That girl, Naphan! *(Gives $20 to the manager)*

MANAGER Don't worry – I'll call her over for you!

The manager walks to Naphan; gives a signal that Chhay needs her now, and he keeps the $20 for himself.

NAPHAN *(to please her boss; to Chhay)* You need me, honey?

CHHAY That's right! Here, drink!

NAPHAN *(accepting the drink)* Thanks, darling.

They dance as the drug takes effect on Naphan.

DUONG Look at Chhay, he invites us to come here, but then he dances with another girl.

KA I hate that guy.

Sras, the nightclub supervisor, and Vann, a male prostitute, enter in school uniforms with an old man (Papa), who wears a batik shirt, and is with bodyguards.

SRAS *(welcoming Papa to a seat)* Papa, please come in! *(Calling to Ny)* Ny, please serve Papa!

Naphan leaves Chhay, who carries on dancing alone.

NY Yes, sister. *(Going to get some wine and drinks)*

SRAS Pa, I'm going to go change my clothes quickly.

PAPA Okay!

NY *(pouring a drink for him)* Pa, I want to toast you!

PAPA Yes! Why not?

Ny and Papa drink. Sras comes out in a sexy dress and Vann wears jeans and a white t-shirt. They walk towards Papa.

SRAS *(going to the old man and telling Ny)* Ny, go serve another guest now.

NY *(going back to dance with the others)* Okay, sister.

SRAS Pa, don't you want to try anything else?

PAPA *(pointing to Naphan)* I want a taster... that girl who is dancing over there!

Sras motions for the manager to come over. Ka refers to Vann.

KA Chhay, who's that man?

CHHAY Want to try him?

KA Mmm, maybe. *(She considers)*

CHHAY But he charges a lot.

KA No, problem.

The manager approaches Chhay, who gives him a signal.

CHHAY Hey bro', my friend needs the boy wearing the white jeans.

The manager gives a signal to Vann to come over. Ka gives $20 to the manager and $50 to Vann.

CHHAY *(holding Naphan's hand)* Let's go have some fun!

Naphan and Chhay start to walk away.

MANAGER Hold on a second!

CHHAY What's up?

MANAGER Someone else wants her.

CHHAY *(angry)* But I paid for her in full!

MANAGER *(coaxing)* Yeh, I know but – come on help me out, Chhay!

CHHAY *(dragging Naphan off)* No.

PAPA Stop!

CHHAY What right do you have to stop me?

PAPA *(standing up)* My money talks! That's why.

CHHAY Money doesn't mean you can get everything you want!

PAPA *(walking toward him)* Hey!

SRAS *(intervening)* Papa, please don't do that, I can take care of you.

PAPA *(angrily)* I don't want anyone to insult me!

CHHAY I don't want anyone to insult me either!

VANN *(trying to stop Chhay)* Bro', please stop, don't make a major scene here!

CHHAY I don't want to play games with this old man!

PAPA *(furious, assaulting Chhay)* What did you say? You want trouble?

SRAS *(interrupting)* Pa!

CHHAY You're the one making trouble in the first place!

PAPA Give me the girl now!

CHHAY No. What are you going to do about it?

Papa breaks his wine bottle and tries to attack with the sharp edge.

PAPA You want to die? Come on...!

KA/DUONG *(panicking and dragging Chhay away)* Chhay, let's go home now!

Chhay runs out of the club with Naphan. Papa chases them outside, brandishing the broken wine bottle.

Samnang, picking up trash, sees Naphan. Chhay, Ny, Duong and Ka run away. Papa slaps Naphan, as Samnang quickly hides behind a trashcan. Papa tips Naphan and walks away.

Lights fade.

SCENE 2

We are in a slum area at midnight. Samnang, with her trash bag and hook, is sitting in front of her house. Tired, she lies down on a bamboo bed outside the house. We hear a car engine and see headlights on Samnang, who dozes. Chhay drags Ny, who is drunk, to her house, and Naphan follows after them. Chhay goes offstage to the car and leaves. Samnang slaps a mosquito and Naphan notices her. Naphan covers up Samnang with a scarf and starts to go.

SAMNANG Hey there, Naphan.

NAPHAN Why are you sleeping outside the house?

(Samnang doesn't answer)

NAPHAN Uncle and Auntie fighting again?

SAMNANG I'm used to it – I don't care. Why are you back so late?

NAPHAN Tonight, I had too many clients.

SAMNANG *(looking at a bruise on Naphan's face)* What happened to your face?

NAPHAN *(turning away)* Nothing, I wasn't paying attention, I hit myself on a table.

SAMNANG I'll go find something to put on it. It must hurt a lot.

NAPHAN Not as much as it hurts in here. *(Taking a deep breath, leaving)* I'm exhausted. I want to go to bed now. *(Turning back)* Tonight you don't have to pick up trash. Take this money and give it to Uncle and Auntie!

SAMNANG No, I don't want it.

NAPHAN You were happy to take my money before.

SAMNANG *(pushing the money back)* I took it before but I don't want it now.

NAPHAN Why? You hate me now?

SAMNANG No. Who dropped you off here?

NAPHAN You know me – I'll let anyone bring me home. Samnang, don't be so suspicious. Take the money – a client just gave it to me.

SAMNANG It's also because of you I'm not taking your money.

NAPHAN Samnang, you're acting weird. What are you talking about? I don't get it.

SAMNANG I know all about you. I don't have what you have.

NAPHAN Are you making fun of me? You're wrong, Samnang. *(Taking a deep breath, sitting down next to her)* You really think I want to do this? Every day – I force myself to go through with it. These sexy clothes – they're just to make me feel good for the night. Being pretty is a curse. I may smell nice, but the perfume hides the way I stink. It hurts to be treated like a dog.

SAMNANG Why do you look down on yourself like that?

NAPHAN Look, me and a dog – what's the difference? When a dog's hungry, it rushes to catch its prey, the same as me.

SAMNANG You know, I've been picking up trash since I was 7, now I'm 16. Didn't go to school very often. But what I experience out on the street from one day to the next is my lesson for life. This job doesn't mean anything to other people; you can't get any cheaper than this bag and hook. But if you use this *(referring to her bag and hook)* honestly, you'll get some good karma!

NAPHAN You don't think I live from one day to the next, like you?

SAMNANG But what do all those days add up to? Does it make you happy? No.

NAPHAN Samnang, don't ever copy me. Never do what I do. *(Yawns)* Sorry I have to go to bed now. *(Entering her house)*

SAMNANG Won't anything change your mind?

Naphan looks at Samnang then goes inside.

SCENE 3

It is dawn in the slum area at Auntie Lang's house and we hear the sound of breaking plates. Tha throws down utensils and the rice pot; Samnang picks them up. Rice has fallen out of the pot and Samnang picks up the rice. Naphan hears the noise of the dishes breaking and comes to have a look, then goes back in her house. Tha shouts furiously because there is no rice left in the pot.

THA Why the hell is it that every time I want to eat something the pot is always empty? Why isn't there anything left? *(Banging the pot)*

LANG Hey! How many million do you bring home each day?

THA Whatever, never enough!

LANG You're so selfish! You earn 10 – you spend 20!

THA What about Samnang?

LANG I already told you she didn't earn anything today, didn't you hear me?

THA Wo! Don't you raise your voice to me. Okay, then I'll stop earning money too. I don't care who gets fed or not!

LANG Of course you don't care! All you care about is having fun. When you do earn a little money, you go get drunk – that's all you do!

THA If you carry on nagging me like this, I swear, I won't come back home at all!

LANG Don't blame me for this. *(Throwing plates)* You're the one who brings all the problems home – so no use blaming me.

THA *(furiously, throwing the pot, then walking out)* Wah, so boring!

LANG *(chasing him)* Where are you rushing off to? We need to talk! *(She angrily pulls his shirt, then sees a bite mark on his shoulder)* What's this? You let some woman bite you now?

THA *(pushing his wife's hand away)* Let go of me – don't be stupid!

LANG You still deny it? *(Turning)* Samnang, why haven't you left to go pick up trash?

SAMNANG I'm about to go out, but you're fighting!

LANG It's none of your business! Clear out!

Samnang starts to go and Naphan comes out.

NAPHAN Samnang, take this money and give it to your mother!

LANG I don't need anybody's charity.

NAPHAN Auntie! This is me...

LANG *(cutting her off)* Enough! *(Pushing Samnang out)* Why are you still standing there? Why don't you get going?

Samnang leaves. Naphan starts to go and stops at her house door, listening to Lang.

LANG *(to herself, glancing at Naphan)* Pretending to be generous, huh!

Tha stares at Naphan too.

LANG Hey, what? Never seen a woman before? Why you staring at her?

THA *(angrily)* What's up with you today, you seen a ghost?

LANG I have my reasons! Take off that shirt, I want to see what happened.

THA *(surprised, looking at the bite mark)* Wah, I didn't realize it was that bad.

Lang is furious. Naphan walks in.

LANG *(to Tha)* Look, there's no smoke without fire, no woman that isn't jealous!

THA I had to see a friend I hadn't seen in a long time. If I hadn't gone, I'd have been rude.

LANG You spent all our money! *(Moving away, hurt)* Last month when my dad passed away and I needed some for the funeral, you said "we have no money!"

THA Eh, that's an old story – yet you still bring it up, over and over again?

LANG I can't forget it. You only die once.

THA You're always nagging, I can't take it. *(Sitting on the bed)*

LANG Ah, go to the karaoke bar. Having fun with young girls is all that matters to you! *(Walking to her husband)* If a girl calls you "honey" then you'll give her all the money in your pocket.

THA I work hard to earn my money – why can't I spend it? A woman like you does a man's head in, always arguing.

LANG It's because you're always cheating your wife and child.

THA And you women don't have a bag of tricks?

LANG You men are worse!

THA You women are!

LANG Men!

THA I can't take any more of this!

He starts to hit her.

LANG *(daring him)* You want to hurt me, come on then!

THA You're asking for it!

LANG You know there are laws to protect me. You can't touch me.

THA You wanna find out?

LANG Yes. Go on.

THA *(raises his hand, ready to hit her)* Hmmm, huh!

LANG *(shouting)* Help! Domestic violence! Human Rights! Please help me!

THA Look at you, I didn't even do anything yet and you shout for help like crazy?

Ny shouts, rushing from the house, as Naphan follows.

NY Oh, you're always so noisy! From the second you open your eyes, you open your mouth. Don't you two ever stop fighting? Don't you ever get tired of it? Don't you have any shame?

LANG If it's noisy, block up your ears. You have a scarf, don't you?

NY *(mumbling)* It's a strange way to live.

LANG No one's better than anyone else here! Nobody can afford to do more than buy rice one day at a time, can they?

NY But we sweat for it just the same! Can't you behave yourself for once, Auntie?

LANG *(pretending to laugh)* Huh, you act like you're so high and mighty but you're really living in shit, like the rest of us. *(Mumbling and walking away)* You just pretend to be better!

NY Just stop all the trouble, Auntie!

NAPHAN *(intervening)* Ny, give it a rest, let's go back inside.

Naphan pulls Ny, but Ny resists.

NY Don't stop me – I'm not finished. Where are you hurrying off to, Auntie?

LANG *(shouting)* Hey, Ny, you just said "it was too noisy"!

NY I don't want to stick my nose into your family business but...

LANG But what? You want to lecture me? *(Turning to Tha)* Husband, you hear this? You're not helping me out here?

THA Eh, you're so good at making trouble – go ahead and deal with it on your own!

LANG *(angry)* So you prefer to take her side, huh?

NAPHAN Auntie, think about it for a second. We all know that Samnang gets up at the crack of dawn to go and pick up rubbish just to earn some cash for you but when she comes home, she doesn't even get a mouthful of rice.

LANG Eh, what the hell are you talking about? It's my family – none of your business!

NAPHAN I've lived here with you a long time. I've seen it all with my own eyes, heard it with my own ears – you forced Samnang to go out picking up trash from the age of seven. Now she's grown up. What happens if some day she picks up somebody's valuable stuff by mistake, and the owner hits her or puts her in jail – what will you do for her?

LANG Eh, Ny, my daughter will never have "a bad hand", like you say.

NY Samnang is such a good kid – a thoughtful girl. You know, Uncle, Auntie, there are lots of bad guys around out there. What happens if she gets raped, kidnapped, or sold into a brothel? Don't you ever stop to think of her future?

LANG *(angry)* Ny, why don't you mind your own business?

NY Auntie, my parents sold me like an animal. I don't want to see Samnang go the same way!

NAPHAN Uncle, Auntie, please help Samnang to walk on the right path.

Tha is staring at Ny.

LANG *(turning to her husband)* Ey, are you thinking or just looking?

THA *(coming to)* Hmm... I'm thinking.

Ny and Naphan look at each other – then go back into their house. Tha picks up his scarf and exits.

LANG Eh, where are you really going?

THA To make some money, why are you so suspicious?

LANG Because you always lie, you old rogue – that's why!

THA Oh, there's no pleasing you, is there? *(Walking out)*

Samnang runs in, bumping into Tha. Shocked, she stands in front of her father.

THA Why are you back so early?

LANG What's happened to you? Your eyes look like a boiled fish.

SAMNANG They're trying to stab each other.

THA Who's fighting who?

SAMNANG *(frightened)* It's those girls – Duong and Ka.

LANG *(shouting and angry at Samnang)* What are you so worried about? They only fight for one reason.

SAMNANG I don't know why but they're hitting each other like crazy, running all over the street!

We hear Ka and Duong fighting. They enter from the audience and Ka has a black eye.

KA *(angry)* Hey, Duong, you hit me – then you run away like that?

DUONG *(trying to escape)* What do you want, Ka?

KA *(catching her hand)* Come on then, this isn't over.

DUONG *(turning, sarcastic)* Ooh, I'm so scared of you – I'm trembling! *(Laughing)* One black eye isn't enough?

Walking away.

KA *(pointing to Duong's face, furiously)* I swear you'd better keep your dirty mouth shut instead of gossiping about others.

DUONG *(laughing)* And you're the queen bitch. Your bite is so vicious you need a muzzle on it!

KA *(angry)* You're the one who's out of order. I'm not done with you about last night.

DUONG So what? You're jealous?

KA That's right. You should know who belongs to who.

DUONG *(laughing)* Nothing's fair in love, and the stronger one wins!

KA *(angry)* But one mountain can't afford two tigers.

DUONG Right, so why don't you clear off then?

KA No. You're the one who has to leave!

DUONG *(taking out a pocket-knife)* Come on then, if you're so brave!

Ka takes out a razor.

KA You think I'm afraid of you?

THA *(intervening)* Enough! Stop this fighting!

LANG *(grabbing Tha)* Tha, stay out of it!

THA Let go of me! Can't you see they're fighting, huh?

Auntie Srouy, mother of Ka, comes in with Chhay.

SROUY Stop this! What's the problem here? Why are you going mad like this, huh?

DUONG Your daughter started it!

KA You did!

SROUY *(to Duong)* Enough! Has my daughter been hitting you? Why does she have a black eye?

KA It's Duong's fault, she stole my boyfriend!

DUONG Nobody stole anybody from you. Chhay came looking for me all by himself!

SROUY Ooh, Duong, if you weren't out to hook him, you couldn't reel him in!

DUONG Auntie Srouy, that's not fair, you only take your daughter's side.

SROUY I'm not taking any sides? *(Looking at Ka)* You hurt my daughter – you gave her a black eye. I didn't say anything yet. Chhay, who started this brawl?

CHHAY It's really hard to tell, Auntie. These two never get tired of fighting!

KA Eh, you, jerk. It's never your fault. *(Approaching him)* I'm not like a ball for you to kick whenever you want!

CHHAY Look, Ka, I never said which one of you I like best.

KA *(shouting)* What an arsehole!

CHHAY *(taking Duong's hand)* Duong, come back home with me.

DUONG *(shouting as she goes)* Okay, Ka, this isn't over.

Duong walks away.

KA I'll be waiting for you to set a date for it!

SROUY *(hitting her daughter)* Want to cause a scandal, do you? Are you from the kind of family who knife each other? Open your mouth – and the first word out is "fight". Can't you see that boy cheated on you? Don't you have any self-respect? To fight on the street because of a boy?

KA I told you she started it.

SROUY You can't clap with one hand! You say you're going to school but instead you're going to learn to behave... *(Suddenly staring at her a moment)* Oh, my God! What kind of clothes are you wearing? Highlighted hair... like a wild animal. How can you go to school like that?

KA Everyone's dressed like this, Ma.

SROUY You want to roll in the gutter because everyone does?

KA You don't give me any freedom.

SROUY Because you disobey me, and you're out of control on the street. We can't tell who is the student and who isn't!

KA You're just old fashioned, Ma!

SROUY You think old people are out of date? But the old ways are the best. We had rules and we had manners. No wonder the men say, "The girls today don't wear enough clothes, they show off their bodies..."

KA What is it with you, Ma? If you want to lecture me – let's go home.

SROUY *(raising her voice)* A person like you doesn't have any secrets. If you don't want people gossiping about you, behave like a Khmer girl.

KA When you're mad at me, I'm always wrong. *(Walking away)*

SROUY See, when there's talk about good manners, and good discipline you pretend to be deaf – it's too boring – but you're very good at acting silly.

KA Well, you always win. I don't need to talk to you anymore – I'm leaving!

SROUY Where?

KA Home. *(Walking out)*

SROUY Make sure you do go home!

KA Boring! Too many sermons.

SROUY *(taking a deep breath, looking at her daughter. Then turning back to the others)* I'm really sorry for all this trouble. Thank you so much for helping to stop them fighting!

LANG *(pretending to smile at Srouy)* Lucky I don't send my daughter to school!

SROUY Maybe lucky – maybe not. It's easy to cheat those who can't read or write. You should let her do some studies. Picking up trash forever won't do her any good! I have to go now. Goodbye! *(Walking away)* Do you know where I can find an auto rickshaw? Everyone's gone – so quiet!

THA *(taking his scarf and approaching)* I'm a driver.

SROUY Oh, that's good.

LANG *(to Tha)* Where are you going?

THA *(going)* Don't you see I have a customer?

LANG *(jealous)* Is that an answer?

(Naphan and Ny look at each other and go back in their house. Samnang picks up her bag, wanting to go)

LANG *(shouting to Samnang)* Stop right there! *(Checking bag)* What were you hiding? Why's there nothing in it? *(Throwing the bag to Samnang, who picks it up)*

SAMNANG I did make a start but on the way their fighting scared me so I called for help.

LANG No excuses. *(Pushing her head)* Today – nothing to eat. *(Samnang wants to leave but her mother stops her again)* What will you get at this hour? *(Giving her a small bill and a piece of paper)* Hurry – go play the numbers.

SAMNANG *(annoyed)* Mother! No.

LANG Take these numbers. I've tried them for a long time. Today I'm sure I'll win!

SAMNANG It's too late now.

LANG Not yet, hurry up! *(Samnang leaves, going the wrong way)* Eh, where are you going? Go that way, over there!

SAMNANG *(looking at mother)* Yes. Alright.

She changes direction, as Auntie Montha, Sras's mother, arrives. She is from the provinces. She walks straight to Sras's house, bumping into Samnang, who drops her bag. Montha picks it up and gives it to Samnang.

MONTHA Sorry!

Samnang leaves. Montha unlocks Sras's door. Samnang returns, because she has never seen Montha before and wonders who is breaking into Sras's house. Montha goes into the house and lights some clothes on fire. Samnang looks inside the house and screams.

SAMNANG Help! Please, she's setting the house on fire!

Lang, Naphan and Ny come running.

LANG *(alarmed)* Fire? Where?!

SAMNANG In there, Ma.

NAPHAN It's Sras's house.

NY Oh, yes, let's go help.

They get some water. As they start to run inside, Montha comes out with a big pot, in which she has set a lot of clothes on fire.

MONTHA I'm burning all of them. Destroying the whole thing! I don't care how much they cost, I'm setting them on fire.

Everyone is speechless as they watch her. Sras and Vann run in.

SRAS *(rushing to Montha)* Mother, what are you doing?

MONTHA *(staring at her daughter, angrily)* Huh, a dead elephant can't hide behind a small basket.

SRAS *(astonished)* What are you talking about? I don't understand.

MONTHA You're good at pretending! Where did you just come from?

SRAS Don't you see, I just got back from school?

MONTHA A university student, right?

SRAS Mother, you can see me. Why these weird questions? I...?

MONTHA I... what? No answer?

SRAS *(looking at the clothes on fire)* You have no reason at all to do that!

MONTHA You're blaming me?

Montha takes Sras's handbag. She finds condoms and make-up inside.

MONTHA Is this your reason? Is this what you're worth? *(Showing her the items)* Look!

SRAS *(trying to stop her mother)* Please, Mom, that's enough. I beg you.

MONTHA *(furious)* Before you did this, didn't you think–? Aren't you ashamed? Why? Where did you get all this cheap fucking crap? You didn't think about saving face for me, did you? *(Starting to strangle her)* I want to kill you.

VANN *(intervening)* Auntie, please don't do that. Stop it.

MONTHA Don't touch me. Who is this man?

SRAS He's my friend.

MONTHA There is a guy to accompany you home every day, right? *(To Vann)* Are you the one who ruined my daughter and forced her into this?

SRAS It's not his fault.

MONTHA You're on the same team – so obviously you'll take the same side. *(Turning to Sras)* Tell me the truth – you're involved in selling your body for money?

SRAS *(dragging her mother inside)* Come in the house first, before you say anything else.

MONTHA Just answer my question.

SRAS *(walking away from her mother)* You don't know what I need, Ma.

MONTHA Oh, now your story's coming out. Why do you need this rubbish? Did you ever think of what you're doing? I bought a house for you but you sold it without a word. I sent you money every month, always on time. How can you say I don't take care of you? And you pay me back with this – trashing our family name.

SRAS You have your reasons, and so do I. You let me live by myself – did you know what happened to me?

MONTHA I can't believe you lied to me for so long. Such a cold heart!

SRAS You can't put all the blame on me. If you want to blame something, blame the world. That's what turned me into this.

MONTHA Okay, if this is your choice, why blame others? Go pack your stuff – I'm taking you back home with me.

SRAS I won't go with you.

MONTHA *(showing her the condoms, make-up, jewellery)* Is it all this crap that makes you not know right from wrong? If you want to walk alone, you should watch your way carefully. I'll stop you from going to university.

SRAS You threatening me?

MONTHA You're not afraid, right? I'm really disgusted to know my daughter sells flesh and blood for a living. Most decent people hate this business.

SRAS Mother, you don't know where my pain comes from.

MONTHA I sent you to the city for an education, not this cheap job. Don't you have any conscience? You're from the swan family not the duck!

SRAS That's just your opinion. I'll make a duck fly around the world!

MONTHA I don't have any other way to guide you. You're choosing this all by yourself. Later on, don't say it's my fault.

Montha starts to go.

SRAS *(asking her mother)* Are you disowning me?

MONTHA You know the answer!

NAPHAN I don't believe you could cut off your own flesh and blood.

MONTHA *(turns to Naphan)* She wants to do this – she'll find out it leaves a bitter taste. I'm just sorry that I raised an ungrateful daughter. *(To Naphan, Samnang and Ny)* You all need to stop taking this dead-end road. You will ruin your lives with it.

Walking out.

NAPHAN/NY Auntie/Auntie!

SRAS Mother!

Vann starts to go.

SRAS Where are you going?

VANN I don't think I'm needed here.

SRAS What did you say? Can't you stay to comfort me a little?

VANN Sras, you know that's not part of the deal.

SRAS You were never going to stick by me, were you?

VANN Nothing lasts.

SRAS Huh, see me in trouble – then push the boat away?

VANN I can't help you with anything now, Sras.

He starts to leave.

SRAS *(catching his hand)* My mother disowns me. You walk out on me? *(Holding his hand)*

VANN *(trying to release her hand)* Sorry, Sras, stop dreaming.

SRAS Dirty man, black heart.

She goes into the house. The others go to her door.

ALL Sras/Open the door/Please/Sras!

SRAS *(calling from inside)* Go away! Don't worry about me.

Naphan and Samnang stand together in silence at Sras's door. Naphan looks at Samnang and holds out her hand.

NAPHAN Come with me. I want to tell you something...

Naphan takes Samnang's hand, as lights and scene shift to the countryside, to the thatched cottage where Naphan grew up. We hear flute music, as Naphan goes to a small pond, sits and throws in white frangipani flowers. Samnang sits next to her.

Naphan's mother, Noeun arrives taking Naphan, who is now 13 years old, towards the cottage, where the father, Han, is waiting. As the lights dim, Samnang watches.

NAPHAN Mother, I'm afraid – I'm scared.

NOEUN Hold my hand, baby, don't be afraid!

HAN *(to Noeun)* Where did you just bring her from?

NOEUN The hospital.

HAN What did they say?

NOEUN You answer your own question!

HAN Are you looking for trouble? Want a smack?

NOEUN My skin is used to it.

NAPHAN Mum, I don't want to stay here, I'm scared.

NOEUN Mother will take away your fear, darling.

HAN Where do you want to take her?

NEOUN Far away from any dirty peasants.

HAN I warn you, if you tell anyone, I'll kill you both!

NOEUN You're heartless, cruel.

HAN Tell people that she fell from a tree!

NOEUN I wish I'd never met you.

HAN Aren't you the one who asked me to be your husband?

NOEUN I was so ashamed of what happened that I had to hide it by marrying.

HAN Because you were such a stupid girl!

NOEUN Your daughter's a human being made of flesh and blood. She has a heart and feelings. Not an animal who doesn't know who is the parent and who is the child. But you're an animal with no conscience. I can't believe there's a father like you on this earth. One who could do something so terrible to his own daughter? You ruined her future.

HAN Let it go! Let bygones be bygones. Taking revenge won't make it better.

NAPHAN Mom, mom.

NOEUN *(going to hold her daughter, talking to Han)* You are a man who doesn't know how a woman hurts. This karma, one day, will take you to hell.

HAN Both of you are like objects I pick up to use, so I can throw you away whenever I choose.

NOEUN Why do men use women like this? Your mind is twisted. I always served you as a wife even though you abused me. I still looked at you with goodness. I should have known better and walked out of this foolish life with you.

HAN Go ahead – taste a life without a husband. Will it be comfortable?

NOEUN Sometimes I feel so lonely. I'm bursting from your brutality. I should spend my life with my daughter – I don't need to depend on a man like you.

NAPHAN Mum, I don't want to live with him. I want to be with you.

HAN You have to live with your father.

NOEUN You're not a father. Every father devotes his life to saving his child. And you, what did you do for her? Not even a little love or care. For twenty years, I've been an idiot. I'm sick of repeating my mistake over and over. Nothing ever changes.

HAN You can't win. Bring her back inside the house!

NOEUN You could stop my body but you can't stop my mind. Besides swigging from the alcohol bottle, you're incapable of anything.

HAN You dare to look down on me, huh?

NOEUN What should I be afraid of? You're just an old undertaker who fucks virgins.

HAN *(laughing)* Starting with you.

NOEUN Yes, over thirty years ago, do you remember? There was a girl who begged you to cremate her mother because she didn't even have a penny, and you didn't give her any pity but raped her for the payment instead. Why did the world create a foul man like you?

Lights shift to Naphan and Samnang sitting near the small pond, now back in present day. Naphan throws white frangipani flowers into the pond. She has come back home and brought Samnang with her.

NAPHAN Why did I come here? Who am I? I know everything there is to know. I can go home without ever arriving. Whatever was lost is lost. I don't regret it – I don't need to hide.

Naphan begins washing her hands in the pond angrily.

SAMNANG I don't believe it. I can't believe you have such an awful past.

NAPHAN Samnang – that means lucky. You're lucky like your name. You don't have a bad past like me. I'm the kind of girl the world doesn't need. A girl everyone despises.

SAMNANG I don't care what they think. We have to struggle through life, and avoid the wrong road. I'm proud of you.

Noeun, who has been living in the house these past five years, now enters. She looks older. Daughter and mother look at each other. Naphan turns and goes on washing her hands, angrily.

NOEUN Naphan, after that bad start where did you go?

Naphan does not answer.

NOEUN I searched everywhere – I almost went mad. No mother on earth doesn't love her child.

NAPHAN I've met so many more bad stories. They cheated me, sold me from one brothel to another. I was forced to sleep with five to ten clients a day. When I was exhausted, they tortured me, beating me so hard. It was hell. A very dirty place. I hated life over there. I remembered your words, telling me to do good deeds. It was all my fault because I left you.

NOEUN It's my fault. Over my whole life, I wanted you to know what was in my heart. My words and tears can't be held back. Both are mixed up. A woman tries to live her life, even without wanting her life, a life so full of damage. When I think about the past, it hurts me. Naphan, you're back. I don't question anything you've done.

Noeun takes water in her hands from the pond and tenderly puts the water on Naphan's head, as if bathing her small child. She touches Naphan's head with love and compassion. She embraces her daughter.

NOEUN Please let me do something for you. I don't want to lose this precious time. From now on, it is your mother alone who will untie the knot in your mind. When the truth comes I hope you will forgive me.

NAPHAN Father should be tried under the law.

NOEUN He received his due in this life, no need to wait for the next. He died at the crematorium. He left a bottle of wine. Because Buddha could be a bridge to pardon his sin.

Naphan looks at her mother. Naphan puts her hands in prayer position, and closes her eyes.

NAPHAN May Buddha give him a chance to cleanse his karma. In the next life may you be my good father. *(Pause)* I forgive you, father.

Noeun hugs her daughter.

NAPHAN Mother, all humans are animals. They have to be born and they have to die.

SAMNANG *(speaking to audience)* I'm 16 years old. Am I lucky like my name?

Lights down.

The end.

CHHON SINA

Chhon is a playwright, actress and teacher. She pursued her studies in directing Modern Theatre at the Faculty of Choreographic Arts, Phnom Penh, where she obtained her Bachelor of Arts. She has been involved in educational theatre and film projects on drug abuse, domestic violence and other serious themes.

She collaborated with Singaporean artist William Teo on his Cambodian play *Year Zero* in 1995. She is currently a Modern Theatre Teacher at the National School of Fine Arts, Phnom Penh.

She and other Cambodian artists were sponsored by the Theatre and Visual Arts Deprtment, Fordham University at the Lincoln Center, to visit the USA and present their work there in 2010. She is a survivor of the Khmer Rouge regime, which saw the killing of up to ninety percent of artists from this time.

SUON BUNRITH (TRANSLATOR)

Suon is an advisor to the Cambodian Ministry of Culture and Fine Arts, developing a performance programme at the Chaktomuk theatre. He is a former Director of Phare Ponleu Selpak, a local non-profit organization which uses the arts in human development projects. Prior to this post, he worked as Country Director for Amrita Performing Arts, a US non-profit and a pioneer in promoting creativity in Cambodian music, dance and theatre. He was also Head of Production of Cambodian Living Arts, overseeing the performance series at the National Museum, Phnom Penh.

The first Cambodian to win an award from the Asian Scholarship Foundation, he conducted a research project on arts management in Indonesia in 2003. He also attended the Kennedy Center Arts Management Institution's Summer International Fellowship Program (2010).

In 2014, Norodom Sihamoni, the King of Cambodia, awarded him the Gold Medal of the Royal Order, for his contribution to the restoration, preservation and development of the Cambodian performing arts.

Previously, he worked for UNESCO's Phnom Penh Office as an Intangible Cultural Heritage Specialist and assisted the Royal University of Fine Arts and other arts organizations with numerous projects.

Playwright's Note

Bali is a place to see many beautiful things. Bali is the place for 'picnics'. Hilmar, Sobirin and Wid have come to Bali to be happy and to bear witness to all that beauty, for different reasons.

Hilmar wants to see Tanah Lot with a pretty woman leaning on his arm, like the cigarette ad he saw on a billboard.

Wid wants to cure the pain of never having visited any beautiful places in his whole life.

Meanwhile Sobirin has come to Bali because if his friend Hilmar is happy, he will be happy too.

The desire to 'picnic', to have a fun trip, has landed them in Bali, and caused them to end up as attendants in a toilet in the lobby of a luxury hotel, where they have to clean up waste.

During this extended 'picnic', from which they still plan to go home, they each try to find what they are looking for, while having little picnics where they can.

All the airline timetables mentioned were checked with the schedule of flights in the international arrivals terminal at Ngurai Rai airport, Bali in May, 2010.

PIKNIK

JONED SURYATMOKO

Translated from Indonesian
by Barbara Hatley

for Yogie Wirasta Pamungkas

This play has been given staged readings in Yogyakarta (Indonesia) 2011, in Melbourne (Australia) for the Asia Playwrights Meeting in 2011 and in New York (USA) for the PEN Festival, 2015.

Characters

WID – a young man of about 20 from Solo, Central Java. Attendant at a toilet in the lobby of a luxury hotel in Bali.

SOBIRIN – a man in his early 30s, from Banten (West Java), who looks after plumbing in the maintenance section of the hotel where Wid also works.

HILMAR – a man of same age as Sobirin, also from Banten, a tour guide and owner of a travel agency in Bali.

HOTEL GUEST 1 – a man of about 40.

HOTEL GUEST 2 – a man of about 30.

All the characters are migrants/tourists in Bali.

Setting

The events take place in a male toilet in the lobby of a 4 star hotel in Bali. Generally the toilet looks wide, clean and luxurious, in the style of a classy hotel. The doorway into the toilet is on stage right. From this door in the offstage direction (stage right wing) the actors can see a corridor leading towards the main lobby of the hotel. This corridor ends at the door of the women's toilet. At the back of the stage right, there are two wash basins with automatic soap dispensers alongside each tap. There is also a pot-plant for decoration at the end of the console. There is a big mirror on the back wall. When the actors wash their hands or look in the mirror, they have their backs to the audience but their reflections can be seen in the mirror.

On the right wall next to the basins there is a paper tissue dispenser. Underneath it is a rubbish bin for waste paper. The washbasin area has to be quite extensive like a toilet in a hotel lobby that can accommodate a lot of people taking turns washing their hands and looking into the mirror.

To the left of the washbasin are four toilet cubicles. None of the toilet doors are open wide, all are closed or open only 5cm. Apart from the cubicle on the far left which is wide open so that the audience can see inside a white pedestal toilet and a plastic bucket.

(Note for the artistic director: the wall of the cubicle has to seem wide even though it is actually narrow so that the audience members in front of the stage on the right hand can see this toilet. Likewise the viewers at the front of the stage on the left can see the actors who are washing their hands or looking at themselves in the mirror.)

Meanwhile on the fourth, imaginary wall, at the front, from the left, there is an installation of five waist-high urinals. When an actor uses a urinal to pee he faces the audience with only his penis and thighs covered by the urinals. There are no separations between the urinals. All the installations on the fourth wall are as light and minimal as possible so that they are more like a foreground and don't obscure the stage.

Time

About 1am at the start of the long holidays.

SCENE 1

The audience can hear the sound of the instruments of the Balinese gamelan playing softly throughout the performance as often heard in hotels in Bali. (This music may also be heard playing loudly at first as introductory music indicating that this is taking place in Bali. Or the director may choose not to use the gamelan in order to explore the possibilities of a different form of illustrative music.)

Sobirin, a plumbing technician in his uniform is seen passing the time looking in the mirror. His actions have no clear aim, only sometimes he moves his head in order to be able to see his reflection in the mirror.

A guest at the hotel, Hotel Guest 1, dressed in jeans and a T-shirt with a collar is seen undoing his belt in order to pee in the second urinal from the left. He presses the flushing knob but it doesn't work. He presses it again and it still doesn't work, no water comes out. With his belt still undone he moves to the urinal first from the left and checks that the flushing knob works properly. He opens the front of his trousers and pees there. Not long after he finishes, presses the flushing knob and is seen washing the end of his penis. He does up his pants, then goes to the wash basin and washes his hands, takes a tissue and dries his hands. Then he throws away the tissue without looking at Sobirin who is also at the washbasin. His mobile phone rings.

HOTEL GUEST 1 *(talking into his mobile phone)* Yes, I've just arrived at the hotel. *(Pause)* Not yet, I haven't got into the room yet, he asked me to wait in the lobby. *(Pause)* You're already in the lobby. OK, just a minute, I'm in the toilet. *(Pause)* No, I'm in the toilet in the lobby. Not the toilet in the room. I already said he told me to wait in the lobby. *(Pause)* Yes, yes, I'm coming to the lobby now. Are you by yourself? *(Pause)* Who else?

Hotel Guest 1 keeps talking as he leaves the toilet pulling along the suitcase which he has left near the doorway. He encounters Hilmar who enters wearing casual but expensive clothes and carrying a paper shopping bag from a well-known mall in Bali. Hotel Guest 1 lets Hilmar enter first, then goes out.

Hilmar is going to put his bag down near the wash basin but decides not to when he realises who is looking in the mirror. At the same time Sobirin sees in the mirror Hilmar coming in and looks at him slowly, without expectation. Hilmar takes his bag to the urinal second from the left (the broken one) and gets ready to pee.

HILMAR *(while starting to urinate)* How are things?

Sobirin just stays silent. Hilmar also pees in silence while looking at an imaginary wall in front of him. Sometimes he looks at his penis. From time to time he glances at Sobirin. Sobirin looks at Hilmar for a moment but then leans against the wall near the tissue dispenser as if waiting for something.

Hilmar finishes urinating, then does up his trousers again without washing the tip of his penis. He presses the flushing button but no water comes out. He tries again but still no water. He leaves it as is without flushing. He goes to the wash basin to wash his hands.

He is held up for a moment because Sobirin is standing near the tissue dispenser. Sobirin moves aside lazily and stands leaning on the wall facing him, next to the cubicle. Hillmar then dries his hands with a tissue. He wants to start up a conversation but hesitates, merely looking in Sobirin's direction. At that moment Wid, the toilet attendant, wearing a uniform like Sobirin's, comes in carrying a sign saying 'Out of order'.

From the right hand pocket of Wid's overalls a small cloth dangles.

WID *(talking to Sobirin as he passes and putting the sign up in front of the second urinal on the left)* At last I found this sign. There should be a few of them in the store room. Yesterday they were still there. *(Pausing, realising that the out-of-order urinal smells badly)* What, although they knew it was out of order someone still peed here?

Hilmar who has finished drying his hands, turns towards Sobirin and Wid.

HILMAR *(looking at Wid)* A new recruit. How long has he been here?

WID *(taking a few steps forward, in Sobirin's direction)* Who is he?

SOBIRIN *(not taking his eyes of Hilmar pretending to take no interest)* Don't know.

HILMAR *(with a strange laugh)* Work hard! *(To Sobirin)* I need to talk to you later, when I come back.

Hilmar gets ready to leave and goes out without looking back. Sobirin then heads towards the urinal second from the left that has the out of order sign placed in front of it. Wid is still waiting for explanation of the strange interchange that has just taken place but seeing that Sobirin seems to be paying no attention to it he doesn't ask.

Wid then stands in front of the toilet door. He pokes his head out to make sure that Hilmar has left.

SOBIRIN You should flush the out-of-order urinal. The person who just left peed in there so of course it smells.

WID *(while taking water in a plastic dipper from the bucket in the toilet cubicle)* I've had this bucket and dipper ready since this afternoon. I was sure someone would pee there.

SOBIRIN Next time, don't wait before putting up the out of order sign. How are people to know that it is not working if you don't put up a sign?

WID *(putting the dipper back in the cubicle)* Yeah, how am I to know to put up a sign straight away if I'm not instructed to do so?

Sobirin just shakes his head, indicating that he doesn't understand Wid's attitude. Once the urinal is cleaned Sobirin tries repeatedly to press the flushing knob with a frowning expression. He bends over to inspect the knob. For comparison he presses the flushing knob in the urinal on the left. The sound of running water is heard, like someone flushing away urine.

SOBIRIN *(while inspecting and taking hold of the knob in the urinal that's not working)* This is not just loose, but will need to be replaced. It can't be left like this with the holidays coming up. *(To Wid)* There's no-one else coming in?

WID *(sticking his head out the door)* Seems not. *(As if talking to himself)* Hopefully there won't be any more checking in.

SOBIRIN In an hour's time there certainly will be. The long queue of guests you saw out front just now had just got in from Korea They landed at twelve midnight.

WID So many of them?

SOBIRIN Because some came on Korean Airlines and the rest on Garuda. All from Korea. Don't you like it if there are lots of guests? What time is it now?

WID One o'clock!

SOBIRIN That means the two airlines were on time. I saw on the schedule that they were both due to land at five past twelve. Garuda is getting better organised these days. Aren't you proud that your own country's airline is well organised?

Wid takes no notice of Sobirin. He walks up to the urinal which Sobirin just looked at.

WID *(coming up to Sobirin, then pressing the knob that is not working)* So it really has to be replaced?

SOBIRIN Better to do it now. The long holidays are coming up, with lots of guests.

WID Now? Changed now?

SOBIRIN I mean this morning. In an hour there will be guests checking in from Taipei. China Airlines. Maybe they will want to pee here or at least wash their hands while they are waiting to register like the Koreans just now.

WID How do you know they travelled China Airways?

SOBIRIN From Asri and her friends. The last plane to land at the airport gets in at twenty minutes past one if it is not delayed. Then there aren't any more until half past eight. After the guests from Taipei check in I'll replace this broken button. Maybe in an hour. Get it done by daybreak at the latest.

WID *(a bit jealous)* Asri! Ah, how come you're pally with all the receptionists?

SOBIRIN Later when you've been here a long time you'll surely be able to get to know them too. If you only finished training a month ago of course you don't know anyone. When you're friends with them you'll be able to ask about the guest arrivals too.

WID I just want to get to know them. Not to ask about guest arrivals, let alone flight schedules.

SOBIRIN Ah, when will you learn to take an interest in things outside your work?

WID But what connection is there between a toilet attendant like me whose job is to clean toilets and the schedule of planes from China?

SOBIRIN Certainly there's no connection. But Mr. Jatmiko likes clever employees, who know a few things.

WID So if we're smart, Jatmiko and his people in the personnel department will give us a raise?

SOBIRIN *(silent for a moment, looking at Wid)* What work do you think Asri did before she became a receptionist?

Wid doesn't say anything.

SOBIRIN *(while washing his hands)* When she left high school she often helped her mother who worked as a bamboo-cutter in the garden next to the garage. She got to memorise all the flight schedules because she liked chatting with and questioning the drivers of the pick up vehicles. Mr. Jatmiko was impressed and suggested that the hotel give Asri a scholarship to go to school. The condition was that she work here after she graduated from the tourism academy. Then she became a receptionist although she still often had to work night shift. And this hotel began a program of scholarships for local residents or children of employees. All because of Asri's cleverness.

WID Oh, that's what you mean about memorising flight schedules.

SOBIRIN *(rather annoyed)* Studying, that's what I mean! Look at Asri! Absorb everything you can from the place where you are working, even though your job is looking after the toilets in the hotel lobby.

WID *(lightly)* I didn't come to Bali to work as a toilet attendant in a hotel lobby.

SOBIRIN Well then! You often say that but why don't you do something about it?

Wid silently takes out the rag which is hanging from his pocket. Slowly he wipes the basin which got wet when Sobirin washed his hands just now. Sobirin just looks at him.

When he finishes wiping, Wid looks at his face in the mirror. Sobirin gropes around in his pocket, takes out a sweet from its packet and eats it.

WID *(lamenting his fate)* Working here you see only piss and shit and don't get any time out, not even to have a smoke.

SOBIRIN *(offering the sweet packet to Wid)* In time you'll get used to entertaining yourself with little sweets like this and forget about smoking.

WID You seem to be used to it.

SOBIRIN I've been here ten years. For the first three years I worked as a toilet attendant like you.

WID *(as if wearying of hearing the story)* Then in the fourth year you moved to the maintenance section.

SOBIRIN Didn't move, got moved. Here your boss has the power to decide where you get placed.

WID Yes, it's clear we can't organise our own lives.

SOBIRIN But don't forget, other people organise our lives for a reason. And that's what we've got to do.

WID What do you mean?

SOBIRIN Do you think I could have got out of this toilet and moved to the maintenance section if I couldn't do anything?

Wid just holds his head on one side, waiting.

SOBIRIN Wid, I'm not a graduate of technical school like you. But in the three years I worked here in this toilet I learned from the maintenance staff who repaired the toilets.

WID Ah, I understand now. *(Sobirin looks happier)* It looks as if Asri copied your way of studying rather than you following her like you said just now.

Sobirin is not happy.

SOBIRIN Up to you, Wid. I'd better go. You can stay here by yourself and think over what I just said.

WID Where are you going? Are you going to leave me here all alone?

SOBIRIN Aren't you used to being here alone? The more often you sit alone the better for you.

WID There's no-one to talk to! Usually I don't have to be on duty here in the middle of the night.

SOBIRIN *(getting fed up)* Ah, you're complaining again like an old pensioner. It's not every day that you have to guard an out-of-order urinal like this. In less than an hour I'll come back and we'll fix that flushing knob. Don't go away, a guest might come and pee in it again *(pointing to the out-of-order urinal).*

Without looking back Sobirin goes out. Wid appears rather dejected at being left alone. At first he doesn't know what to do, then he looks in the mirror and wets the ends of his hair with water. But after that he doesn't know what else to do. He walks to the urinal on the far left. He pushes all the flushing knobs one by one in each of the urinals, then does it gain starting from the right.

Wid then comes back to the wash basin. He looks at himself again in the mirror. Then he turns his back to the wash basin and leans his bottom against the edge of the console. He looks up at the toilet ceiling. At that moment Hilmar enters carrying his shopping bag as before.

HILMAR Hey, where is Sobirin?

WID *(rather startled)* He's gone. But he'll come back again later.

HILMAR Oh, I've been in the lobby for a while but I didn't see him come out.

WID *(trying to smile)* Maybe you just didn't happen to see him. Do you want to leave a message for him?

Hilmar just raises his eyebrows.

WID Or do you want me to call him?

HILMAR No need. I'll see him later.

WID Just wait for him here. He'll be back later. There is something that needs fixing *(looking at the out-of-order urinal).*

HILMAR Wait? Here? What will people say if they see us waiting in the toilet?

Wid looks a bit embarrassed. Because he was feeling lonely it seems he has come up with an inappropriate suggestion.

HILMAR I'll wait in the lobby. But if I get too tired I'll go home.

Hilmar goes out. Wid looks lonely. He is still leaning on the wash basin. But he looks down. He doesn't notice when Hilmar comes in again quietly and leans against the toilet door.

HILMAR You're new eh?

WID *(startled, looking up)* Oh... yes! You decided not to wait in the lobby?

HILMAR Since we're both alone, I think it's better to wait together. *(With a little laugh)* Even though it's in a toilet we've got a friend.

WID *(starting to be brave enough to make a teasing remark)* You're not afraid someone might see you?

HILMAR *(walking to the edge of the wash basin and parking his bottom there like Wid)* Why would anyone come to the lobby toilet in the early morning hours like this? They are surely all in their own rooms. *(Then realising that Wid is there in the early morning hours)* Why are you yourself minding the lobby toilet at this time?

WID Waiting for Sobirin too. I said just now that there was something broken. We have to replace the flushing knob before daybreak.

HILMAR Ah... I didn't know that the knob was stuck. I just peed there. I saw that you got angry just now because I'd peed there.

WID Oh, were you the one who peed there just now? Sorry! Indeed there was no sign.

HILMAR What's your name? I'm Hilmar.

WID I'm Wid!

HILMAR Wid who? Just Wid? Short for Widodo?

WID Widadi.

HILMAR Widadi? Is there such a name? You're from Java aren't you?

WID Solo.

HILMAR Ah, that's why you call me 'Mas' rather than 'Bang'. Or 'Bli' like people do here. Oh, so there is a name Widadi. *(Pause)* What does it mean?

WID Maybe that I should Dadi – become something or someone. Dadi in Javanese means the same as Jadi in Indonesian, to become. Yeah, maybe my parents intended that in future I should become someone.

Hilmar doesn't comment, only looks at Wid's toilet attendant's uniform. Wid looks ashamed that his parents' hopes are not reflected in his uniform.

HILMAR *(breaking the silence, looking around)* There's no chair in here?

WID No there's not.

HILMAR Yes, I know this isn't the lobby where people sit around. It's a toilet. But in the hallway there is a chair where I could wait.

WID Yes, an ordinary plastic chair.

HILMAR It would be OK if you brought it in. You can't sit on it either outside. Just bring it in. In the past Sobirin often moved the chair in here. He sat here. In the corridor there's nothing to see he said.

Wid goes out. He comes back with a plastic chair. He gives it to Hilmar.

HILMAR *(taking the chair and placing it near the paper tissue dispenser, then sitting in it. He leaves his bag on the edge of the wash-basin)* Seems like you don't yet know how to amuse yourself here. Do you sometimes get the chair for yourself?

WID I don't dare.

HILMAR Yes, I know, Sobirin and I were like that too.

Wid looks at Hilmar.

WID You used to work here?

Hilmat nods. Wid looks at Hilmar's fine, clean clothes. He doesn't believe him.

HILMAR *(not paying attention to Wid)* Sobirin was bold enough to go into the women's toilet opposite just for something to do. *(Points with his chin in the direction of the women's toilets)* They are not very different and they're empty anyway.

WID Women's toilets? Isn't there an attendant there?

HILMAR Yes, certainly, That's one reason Sobirin went there. To chat with Menuk who worked there. Is she still around?

WID I've never heard of anyone called Menuk.

HILMAR Ah, she must have moved. Or left. Or got pregnant! What do I care? *(Silent for a moment)* Yes, that's how it was. Sobirin would go to the women's toilets to have a chat to Menuk. But often Sobirin went there even though there was no-one on duty there.

WID What for?

HILMAR For no particular reason. Just because he was bored being on duty here so he went over there. Even though he didn't do anything there. Just sat on the edge of the wash basin in the women's toilets. Like you are doing now.

WID Was that all right? In a women's toilet?

HILMAR Oh, how many people go to the toilet in the lobby? The guests who are staying here surely use the toilet in their room. If there is an event in the hall on the second floor they use the toilet there. At the most one or two guests, or more if lots of people check in at the same time as happened earlier. Otherwise, yeah, like this.

WID Sobirin never told me.

HILMAR Never told you what? That the toilets are deserted or that he often went to the women's toilet?

WID That he went to the women's toilet.

HILMAR *(laughing for a moment)* Maybe he was embarrassed. Because when he told me I laughed at him. *(Imitating his questioning of Sobirin)* "What did you do there 'Rin?" It was a crazy thing to do I said. But one time he invited me to go there for a 'picnic'.

WID A picnic?

HILMAR Yes, Sobirin called it a picnic.

WID You were a toilet attendant? And cleaned the toilets too?

HILMAR Yes, I was here too in the past. Sat minding this toilet. Cleaned it. Taking turns with Sobirin. *(Trying to recall how long ago)* Hmm... maybe nine or ten years ago.

WID So why did Sobirin act like he didn't know you earlier?

HILMAR *(laughing hesitantly)* Seems like Sobirin hasn't told you much. Ask him! But at least you know that we were together here in the past.

WID You must have been quite close. Because he invited you to the women's toilet too.

HILMAR To go picnic in the women's toilet you mean? That's what Sobirin called our visits to the women's toilet, right? And I just copied the term.

Wid nods.

HILMAR Yes, we were certainly close. Sobirin even told me everything he did when he went there.

WID He didn't just sit there?

HILMAR At first he just sat. But every time he went there he discovered something new.

WID For example?

HILMAR The women's toilet doesn't just smell like a toilet, I mean smell of toilet deodorant like this one. There it is more fragrant because women using the lobby toilet often spray on perfume before meeting someone in the lobby. Sobirin liked to sniff the remains of that perfume. *(Imitates sniffing)* Then while he was sitting there he would imagine what type of woman had used that perfume.

WID The scent was still clear?

HILMAR *(laughing)* No. of course it wasn't. It got mixed with the smell of the toilet deodorant. It wasn't distinct any longer. But Sobirin insisted that he could imagine what kind of woman had used that perfume. I didn't argue with him because he had his own imaginings.

Wid joins in laughing, as if pleased to hear about Sobirin's stupidity.

HILMAR If a woman guest entered the toilet he would act as if he was cleaning the wash basin then he would leave immediately. Sometimes he didn't mind but sometimes he would feel that his 'picnic' had been disturbed. He would wait for the guest from behind this door *(points to the door of the men's toilet, walks up to it and tries to open it a bit)*. When he saw the guest who had used the toilet leave *(imitates someone spying)* he went back again.

WID The attendants there didn't mind?

HILMAR *(coming back to his usual place)* Menuk? You don't think she had her own 'picnic'. She was happy if Sobirin joined in looking after and cleaning the women's toilet. Menuk's work was reduced. She could go for a 'picnic' in the kitchen and watch TV. She watched telemovies there.

WID Menuk called it a 'picnic' too?

HIMAR Yes, imitating Sobirin. We all called it that, including Wanti, the other girl attendant who rotated with Menuk. When they strolled past we would ask them "Where are you going?" On a picnic they'd say. Ha, ha, ha... *(Laughing)*

WID *(laughing also)* So you would have time out together.

HILMAR No! *(Standing next to the door)* Sobirin and I would go on a picnic to the women's toilets. *(Indicating the door of the women's toilet through the door)* Menuk and her friends would 'picnic' in the kitchen, watching TV. We were by ourselves.

WID Yes, that's what I meant.

HILMAR *(still standing)* Once Sobirin's 'picnic' was disturbed. While he was sitting there a woman guest came in. As usual he waited here for her to leave. But when one guest was finished more came, one after another. Sobirin couldn't go there. He could only look at the door of the women's toilet from here. And regret the fate of his 'picnic'. All that day Sobirin was grumbling and angry. Ha... ha... ha! *(Laughs till he chokes)*

Hilmar walks to the urinal to spit but he sees that the door of the cubicle on the far left is open. He goes in there. He can be heard clearing saliva from his throat, then spitting it out. Wid just waits, sunk in thought.

HILMAR *(standing in front of the cubicle on the right)* What?

WID *(half asking himself, half directing the question to Hilmar)* Now that Sobirin is in maintenance, does that mean when he comes here he is on a picnic?

HILMAR *(shaking his head, while leaning his right shoulder against the door frame of the far right cubicle)* Sobirin isn't doing that. For three years he worked in this toilet every day. It's not possible for him to come here to picnic.

WID But he often comes here. Maybe he has his own term for it?

HILMAR No, he doesn't. I've never heard him talk about it.

WID But he often keeps silent, and looks around him. Like at the picnics that you described just now.

HILMAR Eh, I think that would be better described as *(thinks for a moment)* going home! Going back to his roots! *(Laughs again, chokes again, then goes to the far left cubicle to spit out the saliva as before)*

Wid laughs, happy that Hilmar has found a new term.

WID *(laughing)* Ha, ha, ha. Maybe that's it When he comes here he's coming home.

Hilmar takes his shopping bag. Gestures to Wid to move to the right to the end of the console. He looks in the mirror for a moment. Then he opens his shopping bag. He takes out a can of drink, opens and drinks it to wash away the remains of the saliva. He looks up and gargles the liquid in his throat.

WID Is your throat sore?

HILMAR *(shaking his head)* Just choked up. But it was sore yesterday. The weather is unclear at tbe moment. Bali is sometimes hot, then sometimes rains. There's no pattern. You can get sick if you don't look after your body.

Wid looks at Hilmar's can of drink. Then he looks away when he sees Hilmar looking at him. Hilmar then also perches on the edge of the wash basin. He takes out another can of drink for Wid. Then he takes out, one by one, biscuits and snacks.

WID *(taking the can of drink)* Did you bring all of this food? *(Hilmar nods)* What for? *(Hilmar smiles. As if he has suddenly understood)* Are you having a picnic here? Or a visit home?

Hilmar and Wid laugh together.

HILMAR I'm not crazy like Sobirin. Yes, I often went to the women's toilet in the past to picnic. But that was because Sobirin asked me to. And I had no choice.

Wid doesn't believe him. As he drinks from the can he looks at Hilmar.

HILMAR I don't need to explain to you why I brought food here. Just eat it if you like. *(Opening a packet of biscuits and offering it to Wid)*

Wid takes one and chews it. He glances casually into the bag to see what else is in it.

WID *(surpised)* Wow, there are apples and oranges too. This is really like a picni–

Wid doesn't continue as Hilmar is looking at him sourly. Wid falls silent. They are both silent for a while, just eating biscuits and drinking from their cans. Wid then moves to sit on the plastic chair.

HILMAR How do you come to be here? How long since you came?

WID It's a long story!

HILMAR Oh, so you'd rather we just keep silent? You don't want to tell me? All right!

Wid doesn't say anything. Hilmar is silent but his eyes look over at Wid from time to time. His fingers drum on the drink can.

WID *(finally)* Sobirin invited me here.

HILMAR Sobirin invited you to Bali? How did that happen?

WID *(cutting him off)* No, Sobirin brought me to work at this hotel. Coming to Bali was my own choice.

Wid looks at Hilmar for a moment while Hilmar doesn't make any response apart from waiting for the story to continue.

WID *(silent for a moment, then as if giving up)* It's such a long story I don't know where to start.

HILMAR *(turning his head)* You give up very quickly. *(Drinks from his can)*

WID You do the talking. I'll just listen.

HILMAR I don't like that. Up till now I've talked about this and that and you've just laughed. I like to listen to people's stories too. But don't feel forced into it if you don't want to.

Wid is still silent. Then he takes out his wallet and takes out a small photo the size of a section of the wallet. He shows it to Hilmar.

HILMAR *(looking in surprise at the photo)* What's with this photo? Is this you when you were small? Where was it taken? Not in Bali I think.

WID It's a photo of me when I was small, still in fifth grade primary school. *(Pointing to the photo)* This is my mother. We are at Prambanan.[1]

HILMAR Prambanan temple?

WID Not Prambanan temple because I didn't go into the temple.

HILMAR So?

WID This is my photo taken from outside the temple. At the bus terminal in front of the temple.

HILMAR But it looks as if you are at the temple?

1. Extensive Hindu ruin near Yogyakarta

WID That's why I kept the photo. The fence around the temple is not visible so it looks as if we're in the temple. Whereas in fact we're outside.

HILMAR Why didn't you go in?

WID We went to Prambanan with a group of my mother's friends who were attending a funeral of an acquaintance in Prambanan. We didn't take our own car as no-one had one. We took the bus from Solo. Going home from the funeral we waited for the bus again at the terminal in front of the temple. While we were waiting my mother asked her friend to take our photo with the temple in the background.

HILMAR Why didn't you go in?

WID It didn't feel right. Because we were going home from a funeral it wasn't good to call in like that. That's what my mother said.

HILMAR You could have whimpered and complained. Since you were still a kid in fifth grade primary school your mother would have understood.

WID I did that. I kicked up, but this photo was all we got. We still didn't go in. It wasn't till I got home that I found out why we didn't go in.

HILMAR Why?

WID My mother had only enough money for the bus fare home.

HILMAR As far as I know it doesn't cost much to go into the temple.

WID I don't know. But with the little momey we had we didn't dare to do much. Even to ask the cost of a ticket to enter the Prambanan temple.

Hilmar nods.

WID Ah, the story is too long and it's going all over the place, you see?

Wid tries to take the photo from Hilmar's hand but...

HILMAR *(dodging out of the way)* That doesn't matter. The important thing is that we're not waiting here in silence for Sobirin to come back. Go on!

WID *(after hesitating for a moment)* Yes, that was it. We didn't go into the Prambanan temple.

Wid stops again. Hilmar waits for his story to continue as if asking wordlessly 'And then?'

WID Then there was another incident. When I was in year two in Junior High School my school made a study tour to Bali. They went at the end of the school year but it was announced at the beginning of the year. The idea was so that people could start saving the cost of the study tour from the beginning of the year.

HILMAR And your mother couldn't pay although it was announced at the beginning of the year.

WID *(nodding)* And it happened again when I was in grade six in Primary School and the school had a farewell picnic.

HILMAR Ah, that's why you didn't want to tell your story. It would make us feel sad.

Wid just smiles, signaling his agreement.

HILMAR Sorry if I don't look as if I'm sharing your sadness.

Wid looks at Hilmar in surprise.

HILMAR That was years ago. You should forget about it.

WID I have forgotten. But I always remember if someone asks me.

HILMAR So you took your revenge by coming to Bali by yourself.

WID I wasn't taking revenge.

HILMAR Ah. just now you were sad. Now you say that you weren't avenging yourself. What was it then?

Wid smiles, embarrassed.

WID I was bored working in the printery.

HILMAR What printery?

WID Just a printery, in Solo. After I graduated from technical high school I worked in a printery in Solo. Its owner was a neighbour, although a rather distant neighbour.

HILMAR Good that you got work, wasn't it?

WID How could it be good if what we did each day was to print invitations to other people's weddings? While we ourselves would probably never have a fine wedding invitation like that.

HILMAR Ah. now you are being envious of other people's fortunes. You never feel gratitude!

WID Maybe not. But maybe I was bored! So then I left Solo.

HILMAR Then you came to Bali?

WID On the ferry I met Sobirin.

HILMAR Where was Sobirin coming from? He never goes far from Bali.

WID From seeing his wife and child in Madiun, he said.

Hilmar nods.

WID On the ferry Mas Sobirin offered me work here. A vacancy had just come up, he said.

HILMAR You didn't like looking after other people's wedding invitations and now you're looking after other people's body waste.

Wid just smiles bitterly.

Hotel Guest 2 comes in, wearing casual but expensive clothes. He is rather startled to see there are two people in the toilet but he keeps going and pees in the urinal at the far left because he feels uncomfortable in front of Wid and Hilmar. Wid feels embarrassed and signals to Hilmar to clear away the biscuits on the wash basin.

HILMAR It doesn't matter. No need to clear them away. Just put them to one side. *(Goes to leave)*

WID Where are you going?

HILMAR To picnic!

WID Picnic?

Hilmar then points to the women's toilet and goes out. Wid smiles when he understands and pushes the biscuits and drink to the side of the wash basin. Hotel Guest 2 is still peeing.

Wid then sticks his head out the door looking for Hilmar. But he can't see his new acquaintance. After hesitating for a moment he follows Hilmar on his visit to the women's toilet. Hotel Guest 2 is left alone to finish peeing. At that moment Sobirin enters and is somewhat shocked to find that Wid is not there. He approaches the scattered biscuits and cans of drink rather angrily. Hotel Guest 2 finishes peeing, then washes the end of his penis and presses the flushing knob. He then heads to the wash basin. He takes off his watch and places it on the edge of the wash basin near the indoor plant. He washes his hands and splashes his face. Meanwhile Sobirin looks into the far left toilet cubicle, the door of which is open. Wid is not here. He looks at the doors of the other cubicles, wondering if Wid is there.

SOBIRIN *(calling out in front of the doors of the cubicles)* Wid... Wid!

As there is no answer Sobirin leaves. Hotel Guest 2 then takes a tissue and wipes his hands. He looks at the mirror for a moment. Then he goes out and meets head on with Hilmar and Wid who are coming back from their picnic. Hotel Guest 2 gives way and backs off a bit to let them pass. Only Hilmar goes ahead. Wid instead waits for Hotel Guest 2 to go first.

HILMAR *(coughing up phlegm and getting ready to spit it out in the far left toilet cubicle)* What did you think of your first 'picnic' to the women's toilet?

Wid does not answer immediately, letting Hotel Guest 2 pass by first.

WID *(with a little laugh)* Nothing special. I don't know what was so good about it. We just sat there silently.

Wid then leans against the wash basin again and starts to pick up the biscuits and drink.

HILMAR *(still coughing up phlegm)* That's because you don't easily feel grateful *(laughs scornfully, still coughing).*

WID What do I have to feel grateful about in going to the women's toilet?

HILMAR *(not answering)* I know why you didn't feel the enjoyment of 'picnicking' there. Because you have a friend here. Me! We've been talking all along, so you didn't feel bored.

WID Maybe.

HILMAR Imagine if you were alone here. No friend. Only guests peeing who regarded you as if you didn't exist. You'd certainly long for a different space, and the women's toilet could be heaven! *(Laughing to himself because he realises he is exaggerating)* Try it another time if you don't believe me.

WID Try it once and it will become a habit.

HILMAR *(laughing, grabbing a tissue and sitting on the plastic chair)* Oh, good. That means you've understood the enjoyment of picnicking there.

WID Or I will ask Sobirin sometime to take me there.

HILMAR Yes, just ask Sobirin! Who knows, he may be better at showing you the pleasures of picnicking in the women's toilet.

WID I've known all along that Sobirin has lots of ideas. Including the idea of going there.

HILMAR You don't think it's stupid any longer?

WID I never said it was a stupid idea.

HILMAR But you laughed at it. You thought it was stupid, didn't you?

WID Maybe!

HILMAR Not maybe! Certainly! Because I laughed the first time Sobirin invited me there. Finally I realised it was a great idea ha... ha... ha.

WID Sobirin is always like that it seems.

HILMAR Like what?

WID Has lots of ideas! Likes studying!

HILMAR Does he tell you to be like that too?

WID Like that in what way?

HILMAR To like studying.

WID Sobirin tells me to study whatever I can pick up. If people from maintenance are working here, fixing something that's broken, he says I should watch them carefully. Study what they're doing.

HILMAR *(choosing another biscuit, making a guess)* So that later on you'll be like Asri?

WID How do you know? Yes, Sobirin did say that earlier.

HILMAR How many times has he spoken like that to you?

WID I've only heard it once. Exactly like that. Asri studied hard memorising the flight schedules, yeah?

Hilmar nods.

WID *(repeating the question, even more curious to know)* How did you know?

HILMAR Sobirin is really proud of Asri. I'm not surprised he should tell you to follow Asri's example, to absorb all the knowledge around you. *(Smiles mockingly)*

WID What do you mean?

HILMAR It doesn't matter. I agree with Sobirin telling us to study like that. But he is too naïve. He thinks that Asri got her scholarship from Mr. Jatmiko because she was clever at studying, good at picking up the knowledge around her?

Wid nods.

HILMAR Sobirin is too simple so that he doesn't know whether Asri got her scholarship because she picked up knowledge or because she sucked up Mr. Jatmiko. *(Putting the stress on 'sucked up'),*

Wid just looks at Hilmar doubtfully.

HILMAR You don't believe it?

Wid just keeps silent. Hilmar is silent too.

WID I guessed it. I had that thought too.

HILMAR How is possible that a hotel would be generous enough to give scholarships to the children of employees just because they were smart? Even when hotel guests forget to pay for peanuts and chocolate from the minibar they chase them up. Isn't that how they make their profit? So would they want to redistribute it again to pay for the schooling of the children of employees?

WID Sobirin never mentioned that.

Hilmar suddenly gets up and heads for the out-of-order urinal. He presses the broken knob.

HILMAR Things like this. *(Still pressing)* Sobirin immediately knows what is broken even though he has only seen it from outside.

Wid nods.

HILMAR But with the deceit of his superiors he just doesn't catch on.

WID But is it true what you said about Asri?

HILMAR What do I care whether it is true or not when I sense it so strongly? They're not going to confess, are they? *(A pause. Hilmar sees that Wid is quieter now)* Hey, what is making you sadder now, Asri or Sobirin?

Wid smiles but keeps silent.

HILMAR Ah, you like Asri don't you? She turns you on?

WID She's pretty.

HILMAR About Sobirin you don't feel sad?

WID Sobirin never told me weird stories like that.

HILMAR Ah, now you call my stories weird. Before when you heard them you were rapt.

WID *(correcting the picture)* No, it's not like that! But Sobirin only tells me stories that...

HILMAR That make you want to study harder?

WID Yes!

HILMAR Sobirin is a good employee. He was happy to guard this toilet enthusiastically in line with what Mr. Jatmiko always says. *(Imitating Mr. Jatmiko)* "Regard this hotel as your home. Look after it and clean it like your home. Take care of the guests as if they had come to visit you." *(To Wid)* Like that, eh?

Wid smiles again

HILMAR Sobirin never realizes that his wages haven't gone up for years even though the number of guests at the hotel has increased, maybe because he loves his work.

WID Was that what made you leave here?

HILMAR I didn't come to Bali to be an attendant in a toilet in a hotel lobby.

Wid is silent, remembering his own words. Silence falls again. Wid takes a biscuit and eats it slowly.

HILMAR I'm sorry, I didn't mean to undermine your respect for Sobirin.

WID You don't seem to like Sobirin?

HILMAR I don't like his naiveté. But as friends I always think of him as a friend.

Wid looks at Hilmar

HILMAR Sobirin and I have been friends since our childhood in Banten. We were very close. But I always felt that Sobirin looked too positively at bad things.

WID But isn't it good to be like that?

HILMAR *(laughing briefly, looking at Wid, exhaling)* Once there was an Independence Day competition in our village. There was a pole-climbing competition. Lots of prizes were hung up. There were pans, a fan, a mini radio, baby clothes, a child's school bag, all kinds of things. Including a watch with the famous Casio brand. We all knew that the Casio watch was a fake one that cost about the same as a fan or a pan. But Sobirin wouldn't listen.

WID Sobirin chose the Casio watch?

HILMAR Yes, because he was the smallest at that time our team chose him to be at the top. Meaning he would take down the prizes if we could get him up there. I said to him *(imitating what he said to Sobirin)* "Don't worry about the Casio watch, 'Rin. It's surely a fake."

WID What did Sobirin say?

HILMAR How could it be fake, that's what he said.

WID So he insisted on taking the fake watch?

HILMAR At first the whole team agreed that Sobirin could take the watch for himself once he had knocked down the other prizes which we thought were better. I myself ordered a little radio which was hanging up there.

WID Did you get the radio?

HILMAR That's Sobirin. The pole was very slippery. We couldn't grip it very long. Because time was so short Sobirin was tempted to go for the fake Casio watch. He got it, along with the little radio for me. But he wasn't able to knock down the other prizes for the others.

WID I remember Sobirin saying that he had once had a Casio watch. But he didn't say anything about the pole-climbing competition.

HILMAR Yes, that's Sobirin. Even when after six months his fake watch was broken, dead, couldn't be used any more, he still believed it was a real one.

WID Poor Sobirin.

HILMAR At first I felt sorry for him but then I saw that that was what Sobirin was like. He thought the Casio watch was a real one, whereas it was a fake. He thinks this hotel cares about its employees while in fact they look on us as shit which is a bit useful since it's willing to clean up the guests' shit.

WID *(continuing Hilmar's line)* He thinks that Asri is clever and keen to study whereas maybe she is just taking advantage of her opportunities.

HILMAR You're getting sharper and sharper.

WID But everyone here seems to like Sobirin.

HILMAR Don't be naïve like Sobirin. No-one here thinks well of his workmates. Especially if you are only a toilet attendant.

WID Sobirin once spoke about that. He said...

HILMAR No need to worry about their attitudes towards us. What matters is how we work. *(Wid nods)* Poor Sobirin, thinking like that for years.

WID It's odd.

HILMAR What's odd?

WID I've known Sobirin for some time, he was indeed the first person I got to know here, but why don't I know much about him. And now I'm getting to know him through another person.

HILMAR For you I may be an 'other'. But Sobirin and I are not 'others'. If I hadn't known Sobirin well I would never have come here to Bali with him.

WID Did you bring Sobirin to Bali?

HILMAR I didn't bring him. Sobirin wanted to come to Bali for his own reasons. I had my reasons too. I happened to be bolder about leaving home. Sobirin worried too much at that time but eventually he said he was willing to leave with me.

WID Why did you go to Bali?

HILMAR *(silent for a moment)* I remember clearly when I was small on the main road near our village there was a great big bill board. It had a cigarette advertisement showing a man holding a cigarette. There was a woman leaning against his shoulder, maybe his girlfriend. Behind them there was a scene of the setting sun. When I got older I found out that it was the view of Tanah Lot temple. In Bali.

WID Oh yes, I can imagine that picture. It's often used on postcards in Bali.

HILMAR Not only in Bali. Postcards of the Tanah Lot temple are found everywhere. I even saw the picture on a calendar in a restaurant in Surabaya.

Wid nods. But he's clearly waiting to hear more of Hilmar's story.

HILMAR Every day when we were going home from school I'd ask Sobirin to go past that billboard. I'd ask him to sit at the side of the road looking at that picture. I said to Sobirin *(Imitating what he said)* "We'll feel really happy 'Rin, if we could see that view. With a pretty woman beside us. We'd look like real men."

WID So you liked to fantasise when you were little.

HILMAR What little kid doesn't like to fantasise?

Wid laughs.

HILMAR Apparently Sobirin wasn't particularly interested in that picture. Because I asked him along, he would sit at the edge of the road looking at that picture but he didn't seem to admire it the way I did.

WID So what did he do?

HILMAR Yeah, he just kept me company. He was always good to me. Although he didn't realise it one day he said something to me that I remember most of all.

WID What was it?

HILMAR Sobirin said that he had seen that billboard at night. And that the lights shining on it made it stand out brightly in the darkness. *(Imitating Sobirin)* "You can see it more clearly, 'Mar." *(Smiling)* That's what he said to me.

WID Seems like Sobirin paid attention to it also.

HILMAR Yes, he paid attention to it. But it wasn't the billboard he was interested in. What he cared about was whether I was happy that the billboard looked beautiful. I remember how Sobirin always tried to please me then.

WID Did you go to see the billboard at night too?

HILMAR Yes! After evening prayers Sobirin invited me to look at the board. It was certainly lit up well. The man with the cigarette looked more handsome. The girl was prettier. The picture of Tanah Lot could be seen more clearly. Imagine that great billboard shining out on the main road near our quiet village.

WID So from then on you started looking at the billboard at night because it looked more stunning.

HILMAR *(laughing)* Ha... ha... ha. Yes. Every evening after prayer time Sobirin and I would sit on the edge of the road watching day turn into night. Seeing that billboard get clearer and clearer day by day.

WID Sobirin is really good.

HILMAR That's Sobirin. He really knew how to please his friends. And as far as I can remember it was from the time Sobirin showed me the billboard at night that I started to promise myself. When I grew up I had to be as handsome and strong as the man on the billboard. The woman beside me had to be as pretty as that woman. And I had to travel to Bali to see Tanah Lot with my own eyes. Not in a picture in a cigarette advertisement.

WID You've been determined to do that for a long time.

HILMAR Yes, as long as Sobirin stuck with me in dreaming of 'picnicking' to Bali.

WID Just as you said, what child doesn't fantasise? What person doesn't dream?

HILMAR It took a long time to come about, didn't it? When I left high school I went to Jakarta. I worked at all kinds of things there. A waiter in a Padang restaurant, cleaning people's houses, a builder's labourer. But I never forgot my desire to go to Bali.

WID Sobirin has never told me that he went to Jakarta.

HILMAR Sobirin didn't come with me to Jakarta. He stayed home in the village. After I had been in Jakarta I came home. I told Sobirin that I wanted to 'picnic' to Bali.

WID Did he want to go immediately?

HILMAR I forget what Sobirin said at that time. But he invited me to look at the billboard on the edge of the road near our village.

WID Ha, ha, ha... was it still there?

HILMAR The billboard was still there. But the picture had changed. There was no handsome man with a cigarette or pretty woman. There was no picture of Tanah Lot.

WID The advertisement had changed. It had happened some time before.

HILMAR Yes, it had been replaced by an advertisement for cooking oil. I saw that again there was a pretty woman, wearing an apron after cooking. She was carrying a big plate with fried chicken on it. Beside her was a handsome man. And there was a little child. They were like a family. Smiling happily, although all they were doing was eating fried chicken.

WID Ah yes, an advertisement for cooking oil like you find in the papers and magazines.

HILMAR Sobirin pointed to that billboard. He said *(Imitating Sobirin)* "Look at that billboard 'Mar. It's much bigger than the one with the cigarette advertisement that we had looked at earlier. And the picture is different. But you still hold to your dream of going to Bali?"

WID What did you answer?

HILMAR I didn't reply to him. Sobirin knew that I still wanted to go to Bali. So he took me at night to see the billboard with the cooking oil advertisement. Who knows I might be tempted by it and forget my dream of going to Bali.

WID Ah, he was doing the same thing as when he tried to please you in the past.

HILMAR Yes! But I felt just the same. I couldn't understand why the man was smiling happily just because the woman had made fried chicken for him.

WID I understand. Sobirin must have wanted to be like that man. He had a pretty wife who was a good cook, they had a nice house with a clean kitchen and a healthy child.

HILMAR Don't think I'm stupid. I knew that Sobirin wanted to have a family like that. But I couldn't understand why such small things would make someone happy.

Wid looks at Hilmar, trying to take in what kind of person this is in front of him.

WID You don't want to get married? Don't want to have a family?

Hilmar doesn't answer. He holds his head up straight as if he has heard something.

WID What is it?

HILMAR Do you hear that voice?

WID What voice?

HILMAR *(putting his index finger to his lips)* Sshh... just listen!

Wid tries to listen but he can't hear anything.

WID There's no voice...

Wid doesn't continue. The faint sound of a woman's voice can be heard, talking on a mobile phone, along with the sound of high heels on the floor outside, heading for the women's toilet. Wid looks as if he is still trying to take in what is happening.

HILMAR Quick, she is going into the women's toilet.

Wid immediately hurries out.

Hilmar coughs up phlegm again and spits it out in the farthermost cubicle where the door is open.

Wid comes in again, looking rather confused.

HILMAR What's she like?

WID I was almost too late but I got to see her back.

HILMAR Do you think she's pretty?

WID Umm... judging from her clothes perhaps she's pretty.

HILMAR Pretty women don't need to dress up. Only women who want to be pretty dress up.

WID Yeah, that's just my guess. But what would a woman like that be doing in the women's toilet in the lobby in the early hours of the morning?

HILMAR You ask too many questions when God gives you blessing. Just enjoy it! Just look at the pretty woman rather than being bored here.

WID Yes, I'm not used to minding the toilet in the early morning. So naturally I've got lots of questions.

HILMAR In a few minutes she will come out of the women's toilet. If you want to try a 'picnic' like Sobirin's we can go there. I'll show you how the scent of the woman's perfume blends with the toilet deodorant.

WID Yes, let's do that!

They are quiet. Waiting.

HILMAR She is peeing even though she didn't really need to.

WID *(as if asking Hilmar to repeat what he said)* What?

HILMAR The woman went to the toilet in the lobby so that when she enters the hotel room she won't need to pee.

WID How do you know?

HILMAR *(laughing)* Later when you grow up you'll find out too.

Wid laughs too.

HILMAR *(explaining slowly)* Some women never like to pee in front of their man As soon as they enter the room they should be ready for bed. Every part of their body should be fragrant. The woman you saw just now was like that. She wanted to pee first before she went to the room of whoever had called her. As soon as she entered the room she would be ready. Her crotch would no longer smell of pee. She would have perfumed it again in the lobby toilet.

WID She was a call girl? A bad woman?

HILMAR *(with a little laugh)* They're not bad, they bring pleasuure. Our people call them late at night like this. Western tourists usually engage them for a long stay, not changing every night like us. Watch *Pretty Woman*. Julia Roberts stays with Richard Gere for a long time. Sleeps with him, eats with him, talks to him.

WID So the person calling that woman just now was a local tourist?

HILMAR Maybe. Ah, let's see, maybe that woman has come out already.

Wid intends to go out the door ahead of Hilmar. But before they reach the door Sobirin opens it and appears carrying a box of tools. All of them, including Sobirin, are startled. Wid remains where he is for a moment. Hilmar immediately backs off and leans against the washbasin.

SOBIRIN *(to Wid, without looking at him)* I came here earlier. I wanted to see you, to find out if you needed someone to keep you company. But there was no one here. And the edge of the washbasin was dirty.

WID Um... just now we...

SOBIRIN *(now looking at Wid, cutting him off)* went to the women's toilet. I knew! I left you alone. I didn't want to spoil your enjoyment. You haven't yet been here three months and all you've done is to go in and out of the women's toilet. *(Looking at Hilmar)* And I see you've now got a friend with the same tastes.

HILMAR *(to Wid, amazed to discover that Wid, too, is used to 'picnicking' in the women's toilet)* So before this you've often gone in and out of the women's toilet by yourself?

Wid doesn't nod but the expression on his face indicates 'yes'. Hilmar is shocked but covers up by laughing.

HILMAR You, you *(intending to say 'You've often picnicked in the women's toilets but you pretended to be innocent and naïve' but not getting it out because he is still startled)* Aha...ha... ha *(To Sobirin)* Where did you get this kid from?

SOBIRIN *(cutting him off)* You'd better go straight away, 'Mar. Asri has told me what you did to her just now.

HILMAR So she's told you. Seems like she still likes reporting things!!

SOBIRIN What harm has that girl done to you? She told me that you grabbed her cheek, that you tried to grab her breast. She's disgusted by your behavior. *(Hilmar tries to answer but has a coughing spasm. He gathers his phlegm, walks past Sobirin then spits out the phlegm in the cubicle on the far left. Wid seems not to be involved any longer, he sits on the plastic chair)* If you do it again we'll expel you from here like we did when you made Menuk pregnant.

Hilmar is fairly calm now.

HILMAR *(holding the door frame of the left most cubicle, half in and half out of the cubicle)* Before you could expel me, 'Rin! But now I have many Korean guests and later lots of Chinese guests will stay at the hotel. And remember they only want to stay here because I have been their guide in the past. Because my travel agency and I organise their visits.

Sobirin keeps silent. He realises that what Hilmar is saying is true.

HILMAR If I were you I would be more careful dealing with a travel agent who sends many of his clients to stay in this hotel. Like I do!

SOBIRIN *(looking at Hilmar)* What has Asri done to you, 'Mar? So that you want to ruin her future as you did with Menuk when you made her pregnant, then dumped her.

HILMAR I gave her money to have an abortion. You must know that.

SOBIRIN You're a monster, 'Mar. You make Menuk pregnant, then you tell her to kill her own child.

HILMAR Well, what else was there to do?

SOBIRIN Indeed that's all you have in your head since you are always using it to find opportunities to go in and out of the women's toilet. Chasing the scent of their perfume. What was it that you used to call it, a 'picnic'?

Wid who has been following this conversation starts with surprise. He stands up and looks at Hilmar.

WID *(between Hilmar and Sobirin)* So it was you, Hilmar, who liked to 'picnic' in the women's toilet?

SOBIRIN Why are you surprised? You can see from his face that he's a sleaze, can't you?

WID *(to Sobirin)* He said it was you who invited him to picnic in the women's toilet.

Sobirin only laughs cynically and turns his back. He faces the mirror near the potplant on the edge of the washbasin. He lets Wid sort out his confusion with Hilmar.

WID *(to Hilmar)* Which one is right?

HILMAR Ah, why do you suddenly care which of my stories is correct and which is wrong? You yourself lied.

WID I didn't lie. I didn't say that I had never hung out in the women's toilet.

HILMAR Same thing!

WID You also said that you didn't know where Menuk had gone. Whereas in fact you had made her pregnant.

Hilmar is silent.

Wid is silent. Then he remembers something, the case of Asri. Wid approaches Sobirin.

WID Sobirin...

Sobirin turns around. His right hand is in the pocket of his pants.

WID *(pointing to Hilmar)* That guy...

HILMAR Ah now you call me 'that guy'!

WID *(ignoring Hilmar)* That guy said that Asri got her scholarship not because she's clever, not because she soaked up lots of knowledge but because she 'sucked up' Mr. Jatmiko. *(Wid stresses the word 'sucked up' in the same way that Hilmar did earlier)*

SOBIRIN You believed him?

Wid keeps silent. He didn't expect Sobirin's reply, and tries to continue his questioning.

WID Is it right that Asri said that that guy *(indicating Hilmar)* had rubbed her cheek and tried to touch her breast?

SOBIRIN *(annoyed by Wid's sudden fussy attention to detail)* What do you want Wid? Do you want to try to be a hero too?

Wid turns bright red. Still standing at the door of the left-most toilet, Hilmar laughs. Phlegm comes into his throat again, he coughs it up and spits it out.

Wid sits down again. Sobirin moves forward from the place where he's been leaning in order to see Hilmar more clearly.

SOBIRIN It would be better if you left, 'Mar. We want to work.

HILMAR You can't drive me away, 'Rin. I know you're fond of me. We're friends.

SOBIRIN In the past we were friends. But not any more.

HILMAR You're lying, 'Rin. If you hated me you wouldn't have married Menuk. You wouldn't have looked after my child in Menuk's belly.

Sobirin is silent, very shocked. Wid is also shocked, but can only guess the focus of their conversation.

SOBIRIN *(softly, very softly)* How did you find out that I married Menuk?

HILMAR Just now! Less than a week ago. I heard from an employee here, no need to mention the name. People here have been very good in keeping it a secret from me for years, and they did it just for you.

SOBIRIN *(cold, threatening)* 'Mar, keep away from us! Don't disturb us any further.

HILMAR How could I disturb you? Menuk is not in Bali any more, you've sent her home to live with her parents in Madiun haven't you?

SOBIRIN *(even more startled)* How do you know that Menuk is in Madiun? *(Suspicious)* Have you been trying to contact her again?

HILMAR *(pointing to Wid)* That kid told me. He said he met you on the ferry, coming back from visiting your wife and child in Madiun. At that moment I knew that you had told Menuk to live in Madiun, to go home to her parents' house.

Sobirin looks at Wid. He seems angry. Wid looks confused.

WID *(his voice getting louder, panicking because he has offended Sobirin)* I only told him how we met. I didn't know that your going back to Madiun was a secret.

HILMAR *(to Wid who is making too much noise)* Shshh! *(to Sobirin)* 'Rin, I didn't come here to disturb you. When I heard that you had married Menuk and you were looking after my child I only wanted to say thank you. And to ask how they are.

SOBIRIN There's no need to make a big fuss. It's not your child! Your child has died. You told Menuk to kill it. *(Sarcastically)* You didn't want to have a family, did you? You didn't want children. Why do you suddenly care now?

HILMAR Even though I gave her the money I was sure that Menuk wouldn't kill it. I know it's my child, 'Rin. *(Pausing. Coughing up phlegm into his throat, then spitting it out in the toilet. Calming down again)* Is the child big now, L'Rin? Maybe six or seven. *(Trying to remember his own calculations)* He must be already at school.

Sobirin is silent. Hilmar leans forward but he doesn't dare to come up close to Sobirin.

HILMAR Tell me, 'Rin, does the boy look like me?

Sobirin says nothing. Wid looks at Sobirin as if he is waiting too.

HILMAR 'Rin, does he look like me?

Hilmar comes out of the cubicle. But he still doesn't dare to get close. Sobirin doesn't return Hilmar's gaze.

HILMAR 'Rin?

SOBIRIN *(softening, letting out breath)* He likes to listen to the radio like you did when you were little. I bought him a little radio like the one you had, that we got from the pole climbing competition back then.

HILMAR *(his voice trembling a bit, smiling)* Does he sing along with the songs on the radio, 'Rin, like I did back then?

SOBIRIN *(sinking into thoughts of the child)* Yes, like you did. He memorises the songs on the radio. He keeps his mother company cooking while listening to the radio. He takes his afternoon bath while listening to the radio. He takes it everywhere, he takes the radio to bed with him. He hugs it, then he goes to sleep smiling to himself. Just like you did in the past.

HILMAR He must be really cute. Can I see him sometime 'Rin?

SOBIRIN Why would you want to see the child that you thought was dead?

HILMAR I just want to see him, 'Rin!

SOBIRIN I already said, don't disturb us, 'Mar! Don't go near the child. I'm taking care of him as if he were my own child. I love him as I once loved you.

HILMAR Are you still fond of me, 'Rin?

Sobirin is silent.

HILMAR Are you growing to hate me, 'Rin?

Sobirin is still silent.

Hilmar approaches and touches Sobirin's shoulder.

HILMAR *(gently, companionably)* Do you remember the fake Casio watch that you got from the pinang pole competition back then? Would you like me to get you a real one, 'Rin? Next month I'm going to Japan. I'll buy a real one for you. That doesn't stop working after only six months. A real Casio watch will surely last. You can keep on and on using it.

Sobirin moves away. He approaches the broken urinal. Hilmar glances at Wid for a moment then ignores him. He looks at Sobirin again.

HILMAR Do you want to come with me to Japan, 'Rin? Look on it as an expression of thanks for looking after my child. We can picnic, we can walk around. You don't get around much do you, 'Rin, even though we've been in Bali for a long time?

SOBIRIN No. I'm happy here. Didn't you want to live in Bali before?

HILMAR You're wrong, 'Rin. You've always had it wrong. I only wanted to 'picnic' in Bali. Now after ten years here I still regard it as a picnic. I don't want to live here, I sometimes feel I'd like to go back to our village. To grow old there. To sit on the edge of the road as before. I don't want to stay here. We came to Bali to picnic, to have fun. I don't want to live here. Nor to look after toilets in a hotel lobby. You feel the same way don't you?

Sobirin looks at Hilmar, as if agreeing. Then he looks at Wid who has been listening for some time.

SOBIRIN Better for you to go, 'Mar. Or to wait in the lobby. Or to help your assistants who are waiting at the airport for the guests from Taipei. China Airlines has certainly landed now also. Your guests will be heading to the hotel.

HILMAR *(smiling)* You still remember the schedule of arrivals and departures eh, 'Rin.

Sobirin is silent. His expression is very different from the angry look he had when he first arrived.

HILMAR Will you let me know when you would like to visit Japan?

Sobirin is silent.

HILMAR Will you let me know?

Before Sobirin has a chance to reply Hotel Guest 2 arrives. His right hand is clutching his left wrist.

HOTEL GUEST 2 *(to Wid and Sobirin because they are wearing uniforms)* Excuse me, I left my watch here just now.

Everyone looks at each other. Wid gets up from the plastic chair. Hilmar stands so that he doesn't prevent Hotel Guest 2 from checking the surrounds of the wash basin. Sobirin is still near the broken urinal but he doesn't move.

Hotel Guest 2 examines the washbasin area. Wid helps by picking up the packets of biscuits and canned drink. Hotel Guest 2 doesn't find his watch.

WID Are you sure that you placed your watch here?

HOTEL GUEST 2 Yes, I washed my face, washed my hands and took off my watch. I put it here *(indicates the corner of the area around the washbasin).*

HILMAR Hopefully no-one picked it up. What kind of watch was it?

HOTEL GUEST 2 Digital.

WID Was it a Casio?

Hilmar and Sobirin both look at Wid, trying to work out his intention in asking that question. Wid himself realizes only afterwards that his question may have offended Sobirin.

HOTEL GUEST 2 No! Why?

WID *(covering up his gaffe)* Oh it doesn't matter. Just that knowing the brand will make it easier to look for it.

HOTEL GUEST 2 It wasn't a Casio. It was an Alba.

Wid looks at Sobirin as if apologizing for the presumption of his question.

HILMAR It's not here. There is no Casio, no Alba. We've been here all along and no watch has been left here.

HOTEL GUEST 2 I put it a bit to the side so that it wouldn't get wet when I was washing my face.

SOBIRIN *(still standing near the out-of-order urinal)* An expensive watch like that surely wouldn't damaged by water. Why take it off?

Hotel Guest 2 looks at Sobirin, amazed that he is suddenly being blamed because he has taken the watch off.

HOTEL GUEST 2 *(to thaw the tension)* Just from habit. Oh, all right. Maybe I left it somewhere else even though I'm actually convinced that I put it down here just now. If anyone finds it later please let me know. I'll still be in the lobby.

Hotel Guest 2 leaves, disappointed.

There is silence for a moment. Everyone seems to have forgotten what they were talking about earlier.

HILMAR *(restoring the equilibrium)* I think I'll go out to the lobby too, 'Rin. I'll wait for my guests there. And I've told you why I was looking for you earlier. *(Pauses, as if he wants to continue but not knowing how).* I'll wait to hear whether you want to come with me to Japan.

Hilmar wants to go past but...

WID Wait a moment, what about this watch?

HILMAR What do you mean?

WID The guest's watch was left in the toilet and disappeared. If he makes a complaint I'll be the one who gets into trouble.

Hilmar is still silent, holding his head on one side, trying to work out what Wid is getting at.

HILMAR So?

WID I didn't take it. Sobirin came in when we were already here. You were the only one here. Didn't I leave you here alone earlier?

Sobirin looks at Hilmar, waiting for his answer. Hilmar looks at Sobirin and Wid. Then Hilmar comes up to Wid.

HILMAR One day when I was picnicking in the women's toilet I encountered a Japanese woman at the toilet door. She was quite old, but a widow and very rich. She was waiting for her friend in the lobby. As soon as I saw that Japanese widow I was convinced I had to wait for her to come out of the toilet.

Wid looks confused as to why Hilmar is talking in this way.

SOBIRIN *(interrupting, to Wid)* Then they got to know one another. The Japanese widow asked Hilmar out. And so it went each time she came on a trip to Bali. Until eventually the Japanese widow gave Hilmar the money to open a travel agency with her here so that he didn't have to look after the lobby toilet any more. *(To Hilmar, sneering)* I've helped you tell the story of how you became a gigolo and got money from the Japanese widow, now go. We've got work to do.

Hilmar only smiles at the sneer.

WID What's all that got to do with the missing watch?

SOBIRIN *(rather tensely, annoyed)* Ah, you still want to string out the story further. He only wants to say that with all his money and his travel agent business, what reason would he have to take the watch, Wid!

HILMAR *(smiling again)* Ah, I should have continued the story myself just now, 'Rin. You didn't need to help me. *(Pointing at Wid)* Then the kid would have understood better.

WID *(ignoring the story)* But it's clear that only Hilmar was here by himself earlier.

SOBIRIN You also had the chance to take the watch, Wid. You need money. You just sold your mobile phone in order to eat. You need money! There is enough reason to accuse you, isn't there?

WID But I didn't...

SOBIRIN But I am not accusing you. So that's enough, maybe the watch was left somewhere else, not here.

There is a pause. Wid looks at Hilmar and Sobirin in turn.

HILMAR Can I go now?

Sobirin waves his hand slowly, signaling that Hilmar can leave. Wid wants to stop him but doesn't. Sobirin takes the tool box near the urinal and places it front of the toilet cubicle on the far left.

WID *(softly, calmly)* Sorry about that just now.

SOBIRIN *(indifferently)* What?

WID Yeah, everything. Telling Hilmar that you were coming back from Madiun.

SOBIRIN But you didn't do it on purpose you said?

WID No, I didn't mean to tell him. I didn't even know the story about Menuk.

SOBIRIN That's enough, no need to go on about it.

WID Sorry also that I believed Hilmar's stories about you. I thought it was you who liked to 'picnic' in the women's toilet.

SOBIRIN *(laughing)* Hilmar really wanted to change his fate just by coming to Bali. The Japanese widow isn't the first woman who has given him money. Don't be surprised that he's been able to improve his status from a toilet attendant like you to the owner of a travel agency with lots of guests here.

WID Don't you want to be like that?

SOBIRIN Why? It seems you want to be like Hilmar?

WID Just now I wanted to say to him that if I could I'd like to work for him in the travel agency.

SOBIRIN Why didn't you tell him?

WID I don't know, I was still unsure.

SOBIRIN *(giving advice, in a light-hearted way)* To make a living in a strange environment we have to be very good at looking after ourselves. Don't act immorally! Hilmar has asked me to prostitute myself like he does. A few times, but of course I didn't accept. Even after he was already a success and turned up from time to time at the hotel with his guests.

WID So when he came the first time just now he wanted to invite you again?

SOBIRIN Maybe! But maybe he wanted to meet me to talk about Menuk. *(To himself)* At last he knows about Menuk. *(To Wid)* It's an old story. And nothing to do with you. What time is it now?

WID *(not answering, walking to the toolbox in front of the far left cubicle)* Should we dismantle it now?

SOBIRIN No need to rush. We've still got time. The guests have probably just landed, they'll need time to get out of the airport and come here.

WID It'll be quite a while.

SOBIRIN Go outside and have a smoke! *(Pointing to the remains of the food on the sides of the washbasin)* And clean up Hilmar's food first!

WID *(while cleaning up the food scraps on the washbasin)* This is the first time I've seen someone bring food into a toilet.

SOBIRIN That's Hilmar. He likes sitting around and brings snacks along when he 'comes home' to this toilet.

WID *(as if he's heard the word before)* Comes home?

SOBIRIN Yes, Hilmar calls it that. When he goes to the women's toilet he calls it a picnic, when he goes to the men's it's coming home. Coming back to home ground. *(With a little laugh)* Makes sense doesn't it?

Wid smiles uncertainly.

SOBIRIN What's up? Did Hilmar tell you that earlier?

Wid doesn't respond. He throws some rubbish in the bin beside him.

Wid then walks out.

SOBIRIN Where are you going?

WID *(pointing to the women's toilet)* On a picnic!

SOBIRIN Don't you want to go out to smoke?

WID *(laughing)* I was joking. I'll go outside and have a cigarette.

Sobirin looks relieved. He waves his left hand, signaling to Wid to go outside.

Sobirin remains alone in the toilet. He looks at himself in the mirror as he did earlier. Then he turns around and leans against the washbasin. Then he stays still, then he gets bored. He walks in the direction of the toolbox in front of the far left cubicle. He bends down, squats. But then he stand half upright again. Something is wedged in the right-hand pocket of his trousers. Sobirin stands up and gropes around in his trousers pocket. A watch. Sobirin smiles, holding the watch carefully.

(Note for the director: Sobirin took the watch that the hotel guest had left behind when Wid and Hilmar were arguing and Sobirin had the opportunity to turn and face the mirror above the washbasin. When he turned around again after Wid asked him a question, Sobirin's hand was already in his trouser pocket, holding the watch.)

Sobirin is still holding and looking at the watch when Wid comes in. Sobirin starts.

SOBIRIN You didn't go for a smoke outside?

Wid doesn't answer after he sees what is in Sobirin's hand. He approaches Sobirin. He takes the watch that Sobirin is holding.

WID *(flatly, with certainty)* This is the guest's watch that was left here, isn't it?

Sobirin does not answer.

WID *(flatly, coldly)* Why did you take it? Why did you say...?

Wid doesn't continue. He puts the watch on Sobirin's chest and half pushes him. Sobirin silently takes back the watch. Wid goes to leave, Sobirin does not stop him.

When he gets to the door Wid turns around.

WID I was going to ask Hilmar earlier if I could work at his travel agency. I wanted to know your opinion about this because you always tell me not to be reckless and headstrong in trying to make money in an unfamiliar environment.

Sobirin remains silent.

WID But I think now that it's better if I decide for myself. Hilmar is still waiting in the lobby.

Sobirin tries to say something but Wid cuts him off.

WID Thank you, you've helped me find my first job in Bali. I did indeed sell my mobile phone to be able to eat. But I wouldn't take a watch that someone had left around.

Sobirin has accepted that he cannot stop Wid from leaving.

WID I think it's better if I join with Hilmar. I didn't come to Bali to steal. Nor to look after a hotel lobby toilet. I came to Bali to 'picnic', to see beautiful places that I'd never seen before in my life.

Wid goes out.

SOBIRIN *(not daring to move far from the place where he is standing because he has been discovered stealing, calling out but in a constricted way)* Wid! Wid!

Wid doesn't come back.

Sobirin calls out again. He rushes towards the door but doesn't dare open it. He just stands near the door. He looks again at the watch he is holding, Then he leans his bottom against the washbasin. Tired. His eyes look at the broken urinal, his left hand holds the watch which he just obtained.

The lights slowly go out.

Balinese gamelan (or some other musical form) is heard again playing loudly.

The Balinese gamelan/music slowly fades away.

The end.

JONED SURYATMOKO

Suryatmoko was born in Solo, Indonesia in 1976. His educational background is in International Relations Studies (Bachelors degree) and Media and Cultural Studies (Masters degree), both from Gadjah Mada University in Yogyakarta, Indonesia.

He has run his theatre group, Gardanalla Theatre, since 1997 and produced various performances. Known as a theatre-maker and playwright, he also works as a media consultant for community-based media programs with various international, as well as local, NGOs in Indonesia.

Currently he is the Festival Director of the Indonesian Dramatic Reading Festival (IDRF), and a Theatre Specialist for the Creative Community Program, initiated by the Kelola Foundation and the World Bank.

https://idrf.wordpress.com

BARBARA HATLEY (TRANSLATOR)

Hatley taught Indonesian Studies at Monash University, then at the University of Tasmania, and is currently a Professor Emeritus in Asian Studies at the University of Tasmania.

Her major research interests are in Indonesian performing arts, modern literature and gender studies. Barbara's publications include: *Javanese Performances on an Indonesian Stage: Contesting Culture, Embracing Change* (NUS Press, 2008), *Theatre and Performance in the Asia Pacific: Regional Modernities in the Global Era*, co-authored with Denise Varney, Peter Eckersall and Chris Hudson (Palgrave, 2013), and an edited volume on performance in post-Suharto Indonesia – *Performing Contemporary Indonesia: Celebrating Locality, Constructing Community* (Brill, 2015). She previously produced many Indonesian language plays with student groups, and her translation of one of these, *Time Bomb* (*Bom Waktu*) by Riantiarno, is published in *Time Bomb and Cockroach Opera: Two Plays* (The Lontar Foundation, 1992), republished in *Islands of the Imagination: Modern Indonesian Plays* (Manoa, Hawaii University Press, 2014).

NADIRAH

ALFIAN SA'AT

For Yasmin Ahmad

First performed at The Substation, Singapore, December 17–19 2009. Directed by Zizi Azah Abdul Majid.

Characters

NADIRAH Bte Mansor – 20

SAHIRAH Bte Abdullah – her mother, 46

MAZNAH Bte Kamsani – her best friend, 20

FAROUK Bin Haji Osman – a fellow undergraduate, 22

ROBERT Goh – a doctor, 52

Cast

NADIRAH – Siti Khalijah Zainal

SAHIRAH – Neo Swee Lin

MAZNAH – Shida Mahadi

FAROUK – Hatta Said

ROBERT – Tony Quek

Time

Now.

SCENE 1

Farouk and Nadirah are in a tutorial room at a university campus.

FAROUK Want to rehearse one more time?

NADIRAH No need.

FAROUK We still have time.

NADIRAH What time is your class later?

FAROUK It's all right. No worries if I'm a bit late. My friend's reserved a seat.

Pause.

NADIRAH OK... we rehearse again?

FAROUK Your wish.

NADIRAH Farouk, why can't you do it?

FAROUK I told you. I've got a quiz the day after.

NADIRAH It's just a quiz. How much? Ten percent?

FAROUK Five percent.

NADIRAH Just five percent. You don't need to study.

FAROUK Eh, are you the one taking Kinematics or me?

NADIRAH You're a Hafidz. How old were you when you memorized the Quran? Twelve, right?

FAROUK That's different.

NADIRAH Because you didn't understand? What you were saying?

FAROUK Who said I didn't understand?

NADIRAH You're twelve and you could understand? Did you know Arabic at that time?

FAROUK Sometimes you don't need to know... to understand.

NADIRAH How's that? Don't you need to know what it means when you say your prayers?

FAROUK But you can understand just from the sound.

NADIRAH The sound?

FAROUK The way the sound seeps and resonates in your body.

NADIRAH We can't depend on 'resonance' next week. They'd better understand what we're trying to deliver. Farouk, am I going to be the only vice-president there?

FAROUK The Hindu society is also sending their Vice Prez.

NADIRAH If we're the ones initiating this meeting, shouldn't we send our own President down?

FAROUK Nadirah, have some faith in yourself. Just follow whatever's on your Powerpoint slides.

NADIRAH Farouk... can't we say, 'no thank you'?

FAROUK What do you mean?

NADIRAH I understand your concern. The issue of evangelism on campus must be dealt with before it creates tensions. I like what you've written here: "Does having the space to practice also mean having the space to preach?"

FAROUK That's not just some catchphrase. That's the very basis of our stand.

NADIRAH So, we'll propose that evangelistic activities be suspended. For the time being. But what if... we let the people who are being preached to make their own decisions?

FAROUK Oh, so the campus becomes a battlefield. Who's got more weapons, more soldiers, ends up the winner.

NADIRAH No Farouk... don't use words like 'battlefield'. Like a market... for different ideas.

FAROUK So, you think that kind of competition is fair?

NADIRAH Why must we use that kind of language... battlefield, competition. We're not fighting for territory right?

FAROUK Nadirah, this is a question of tactics. If you want to spread your religion, nobody's stopping you. But don't resort to tricks. Don't end up bribing other people. Some make promises, if you join our religion, you'll have more friends. If you become a member, there are free gifts.

NADIRAH But if we're preaching to others, doesn't that mean we're bribing them too?

FAROUK Nadirah...

NADIRAH If you join our religion, the reward is heaven. Right?

FAROUK Be careful of the things you say. If you go too far it's blasphemy already.

NADIRAH No, this is something my friend raised. I'm just passing it on. The other day she asked why atheists can't sit in during our interfaith meetings?

FAROUK Well, it' called inter-faith. Not inter-faithless.

NADIRAH She feels that we should also listen to the opinions of those with no religion.

FAROUK Nadirah, for us sitting at that table, at least we're united by one thing. We're believers.

NADIRAH But in different gods. Sometimes if you're talking about the Buddhists, there's not even a god.

FAROUK So who does your friend want to represent? The Atheist Society? We're discussing as representatives of religions. We're not there just to present our personal views.

NADIRAH Maybe they should set up their own society.

FAROUK I'm sure there are a lot of things they can discuss. What do you think their holy book will be? *Little Red Book* or *Mein Kampf*?

NADIRAH Just because they're atheists doesn't mean that they worship Mao or Hitler. That's stereotyping.

FAROUK But it's OK if we're stereotyped? Terrorists, suicide bombers, oppressing women... But we're hoping that you can challenge those views.

NADIRAH Me, Farouk? How?

FAROUK Actually, I could make time to go for that meeting. But for the sake of our society's image, it's better if someone from the fairer sex represents us.

NADIRAH So, it's not because I'm capable?

FAROUK I've told you already. You've got a great Powerpoint presentation. Just clean up a bit of the spelling.

NADIRAH There are spelling mistakes?

FAROUK You have to change the spelling of 'god'.

NADIRAH Eh? Did I spell it wrongly?

FAROUK No, change the small 'g' to capital 'G'.

Maznah enters.

MAZNAH Oh sorry. Finished your meeting?

NADIRAH Yah.

MAZNAH Can we not go to Canteen B today? I'm sick of the food there. OK? Let's go to Subway. *(Notices Farouk looking at her)* I'm craving the... tuna sandwich.

FAROUK Ah, when is this one going to reform? Wearing like that... don't you have enough cloth at home?

MAZNAH Farouk, you talk exactly like my mother. Have you been to her Tupperware parties?

FAROUK My eyes hurt looking at you dressed like this, Maznah.

MAZNAH If it pains you so much then don't look.

FAROUK Your best friend's so pious. And then you...

MAZNAH I'm like Gandhi.

NADIRAH Gandhi?

MAZNAH I read this story once. There was one time when Gandhi met up with Queen Victoria in England. And then he was wearing his... what's that thing... that Indian men wear... that they wrap around their waist...

FAROUK Dhoti.

MAZNAH Ah, Dhoti. And then the Queen asks him, Aren't you a little underdressed?' And he answered, "But you're wearing enough for the both of us." See, me and Nadirah, we complement each other.

FAROUK Your wish then. I'm just saying. I have to go for class.

MAZNAH ... just now, you and Nadirah, just the both of you in this room?

FAROUK Why?

MAZNAH No, it's just that, if you're not related, then isn't that... sinful cohabitation?

FAROUK This is a classroom. It's not a hotel.

MAZNAH Oh, you don't know what happens in classrooms. Undergrads these days...

FAROUK Are you hinting something?

MAZNAH Farouk, I'm just saying. I'm not judging. I swear! Just saying.

FAROUK Whatever.

MAZNAH Whatever!

Farouk exits.

MAZNAH He just adores playing Big Brother doesn't he? Why is your boyfriend so preachy?

NADIRAH Excuse me. Don't start silly rumours.

MAZNAH But the both of you are so matching! I can just imagine. You pray together, and he leads in front.

NADIRAH Yeah, right. Is that your secret fantasy?

MAZNAH And then you'll have so many children! When they're still toddlers you'll be dressing them in tudungs[1] and skull-caps. So devout cute! And then you'll teach them to call you Ummi.[2] 'Ummi, can I have a doll?' 'No darling, the doll is like a little idol, right? Here, play with your pillow.' 'Ummi, can I have sweets?' 'No darling, if you eat too many sweets then you'll lose your teeth, here have some dates. The Prophet loved eating dates.'

NADIRAH How come I'll turn out like that? Which Sheikh did I marry?

MAZNAH Oh, oh! Exchange student. In my Asian Cinema class. From Turkey. His eyes are turquoise. He's like a male version of Aishwarya Rai.[3] I can introduce.

NADIRAH You are so random, you know. I don't think so.

MAZNAH Nadirah, when was the last time you went out with a guy?

NADIRAH Went out?

MAZNAH Oh yah, there's no such thing as going out. If there's mutual connection, then you have to quickly get married. If not then every time you go on a date it's the three of you.

---

1. Tudung – a type of headscarf or hijab
2. Means 'Mummy' in Arabic
3. Indian Bollywood Actress

NADIRAH What do you mean?

MAZNAH Because Satan has tagged along!

NADIRAH If it's fated then fine. We don't have to force these things.

MAZNAH Yah, you tell me this now. Later when you're 40, you'll be hanging out at Darul Arqam[4] hunting for Caucasian converts. Who knows, maybe you're a tudung party girl. Right?

NADIRAH Maybe I won't even get married.

MAZNAH It's a sin not to get married, you know!

NADIRAH What if... once bitten twice shy?

MAZNAH Who bit you? You've never been married.

NADIRAH Not me. I'm not referring to myself.

MAZNAH Oh please, Nadirah. It's not hereditary! Your mother just met the wrong man.

NADIRAH Yes, that wrong man happens to be my father.

MAZNAH Your mother's got her own life. You also have your own. Come, it's my lunch treat today. Yesterday I just got paid for tuition.

SCENE 2

Nadirah is in her living room, cutting her fingernails. Her mother, Sahirah enters, a Chinese woman who is wearing a tudung. She is carrying an NTUC[5] plastic bag.

SAHIRAH Assalaamu'alaikum. [Peace be upon you.]

NADIRAH Wa'alaikumsalaam. [Peace be upon you too.]

SAHIRAH Why are you cutting your nails at night? Later your Mummy die then you know.

NADIRAH That's the wrong superstition. That's when you 'sabung' your legs.

SAHIRAH What is sabung?

---

4. A meeting place to assist religious converts
5. Name of a supermarket chain

NADIRAH Like this.

Nadirah lies down on her front, and crooks her knees so her legs are in the air.

SAHIRAH Ah, you know if you do that your mother die, you still do. You don't love your Mummy, right?

NADIRAH But you were the one who asked me to demonstrate! Anyway I don't believe in these things.

SAHIRAH But still you shouldn't cut your nails at night. I remember your father always got angry when you do that.

NADIRAH Mummy, this is an old superstition. Last time, there was no electricity in the villages. So if you cut your nails at night you might accidentally cut your finger. Anyway if you think it's so taboo why don't you help me cut?

SAHIRAH How old are you already, Nadirah? Do you want me to feed you with my own hands as well?

NADIRAH You can do manicure for other people, but not for your own daughter.

SAHIRAH That one they pay me, Nadirah. How much you want to pay?

NADIRAH You mean you can't even do it free for your own family?

SAHIRAH OK-lah, discount.

NADIRAH Mummy, sometimes you are so Chinese you know!

SAHIRAH So rude! You talk to your Mummy like that?

NADIRAH I'm just teasing... are you angry?

SAHIRAH I can do your hair for you. Long time I never do. *(Caresses Nadirah's hair)* Your hair is getting thin, ah?

NADIRAH Mummy don't start lah.

SAHIRAH Start what?

NADIRAH You're going to say it's because of the tudung.

SAHIRAH I also wear tudung what.

NADIRAH Yah, but you're going to say I must let my hair breathe.

SAHIRAH *(removes her tudung)* I work in a hair salon. Of course I know all about hair.

NADIRAH Then you invent lah, tudung that can let hair breathe. Maybe got micropores. I'm sure it'll sell out.

SAHIRAH You don't wear your tudung at home, right?

NADIRAH Yah, so?

SAHIRAH So, you stay at home more lah. No need to go out so much.

NADIRAH Why can't I go out?

SAHIRAH You're always not at home. We haven't had dinner together for so long.

NADIRAH Mummy, you know my classes end late. And then it takes a lifetime to get from Boon Lay to Tampines.[6] If I sleep on the train my dreams macam[7] mini-series. Episode 1, Boon Lay. Episode 4, Outram Park. Episode 10... hah? Only at Bedok?

SAHIRAH And then weekend also you not at home.

NADIRAH I have community work.

SAHIRAH Yah, you and all your little orphans. You orphan your Mummy you don't care.

NADIRAH What lah, Mummy. Are you sulking?

SAHIRAH You think you get merit points by spending time with those kids, but you get more merit points spending time with me. Even the Prophet said that heaven is looking at your mother's feet.

NADIRAH It's not looking at your feet, Mummy, but at the sole of your foot.

SAHIRAH Ah, you know also. You want to smell heaven you have to smell my shoes first. *(Pause)* Maybe I should get a maid.

NADIRAH Why would you want to get a maid?

SAHIRAH At least this house not so empty. When I'm at home, all I do is watch TV.

---

6. Metro journey from west to east lasts one hour
7. Means 'are like', 'resemble'

NADIRAH Mummy, people get maids to help with the housework, not to make friends with them.

SAHIRAH Never mind. At least got someone to keep me company. Then if you are naughty also I got someone to complain to.

NADIRAH Don't you have friends at the salon?

SAHIRAH You know they change staff right?

NADIRAH You didn't tell me.

SAHIRAH You're always not at home, how can I tell you? Now they have all these new China workers. The Malaysian ones have all gone back.

NADIRAH Even Sally?

SAHIRAH Yah lah. These China workers all can work for less pay. They're very good workers lah, just that they don't understand why I cannot speak Mandarin. I told them, I am Chinese Peranakan. So they ask, oh, so is Peranakan like the Hui Muslim in China? From Henan? I said, no lah, the Peranakans in Singapore are usually not Muslim. I'm Muslim because I converted. And then I end up just confusing them even more.

NADIRAH You never told me Sally was leaving. I didn't even have the chance to say goodbye.

SAHIRAH You visit her lah when you go to K.L.[8] Oh yah, talking about K.L., you got a letter. *(Rummaging through her plastic bag)* This is bill, this is bill, ah, this is yours.

NADIRAH What letter is it?

SAHIRAH From your darling father lah.

NADIRAH Eee. What does he want?

SAHIRAH I don't know.

NADIRAH The stamp nice or not?

SAHIRAH It's a picture of a frog.

NADIRAH Oh, the frog series! I don't have that one yet. *(Takes the letter)*

SAHIRAH Aren't you going to read the letter?

---

8. Abbreviation for Kuala Lumpur, capital city of Malaysia

NADIRAH What for?

SAHIRAH Yah, in front of me you pretend only. Later in your room you'll lie down on your bed, open the letter, read many times, then hold it to your chest and start daydreaming.

NADIRAH Eee. I am never that dreamy OK? What for he want to send letter? He can email me what. Malaysia don't have internet or what?

SAHIRAH Oh, so you and your bapak[9] have been exchanging emails lah?

NADIRAH No... he doesn't even have my email. But he tried to add me on Facebook.

SAHIRAH What's that?

NADIRAH It's... aiyah, difficult lah to explain. Anyway, I rejected. *(Silence)* OK lah, OK lah, I'll read the letter in front of you.

SAHIRAH Eh, I never force you, you know.

NADIRAH Yah, but the way you look at the envelope, your eyes like X-ray. *(Opens the envelope and reads the letter)* My dearest daughter who is fondly missed... eee why he write like this? I thought only Malay compo[10] you write like this.

Nadirah continues reading, silently to herself. Sahirah observes her.

SAHIRAH What does he want?

NADIRAH He's turning fifty next week. And he's throwing a birthday party.

Nadirah examines the inside of the envelope. She extracts a plane ticket.

SAHIRAH What's that?

NADIRAH Plane ticket.

SAHIRAH He's bribing you. So Malaysian.

NADIRAH It's SIA.[11] How long is the flight there?

---

9. Malay word for 'father'
10. Short for composition (at school)
11. Abbreviation for Singapore International Airlines

SAHIRAH I think fifty minutes? You take longer to go to school.

NADIRAH Then give me Business Class for what? Want to watch what show? They show the safety video and I've arrived already. He's wasting money.

SAHIRAH That means he really wants you to go lah.

NADIRAH Why he ask me, never ask you?

SAHIRAH Because I am ex-wife. But you are not ex-daughter.

NADIRAH I'm not going if you're not coming along. It's going to be so awkward.

SAHIRAH But you got all your step-brothers there what.

NADIRAH Eee, those Bumiputra[12] brats? I just want to slap them when they start speaking in their International School accents.

SAHIRAH You should go lah. When was the last time you took an aeroplane?

NADIRAH When I was six... remember? We all went for holiday in Australia.

SAHIRAH You got good memory ah? Six years old story also can remember.

NADIRAH Mummy, not because I have good memory. But because the memory of it was good. Don't you remember?

SAHIRAH Don't know lah Nadirah. Want to remember also for what?

NADIRAH Every day we would go to the beach. And bapak taught me how to swim.

SAHIRAH Nadirah.

NADIRAH Yah Mummy?

SAHIRAH If you want to go, you go. I won't get angry. He's your father, right? And you haven't visited since you started uni.

NADIRAH You're just saying this, but later you're going to start sulking.

SAHIRAH Really. I won't feel slighted. It's just for one day right?

---

12. Means 'Malaysian of indigenous Malay origin'

NADIRAH *(looking at the ticket)* I'm going on Friday, and then I come back on Sunday.

SAHIRAH It's just three days. And it's not as if you're home on weekends. Just don't forget to come back.

NADIRAH I will go there... but just to show my face.

SAHIRAH You don't have to say that just to make me feel better.

NADIRAH Mummy, you know that they're sooo pretentious. His wife thinks she's a Datin.[13] When I was there the last time, we had tea time, Mummy. And the tea is not Boh[14] you know, it's Earl Grey. With scones and shortbread.

SAHIRAH Did she make them?

NADIRAH Of course not lah. I'm sure she asked her maid to buy them. She's got two Baby Belling[15] ovens at home, but she never use.

SAHIRAH OK, Mummy wants to pray now. You keep that ticket carefully. You know you're so careless, if...

NADIRAH ... my clit isn't stuck on my body, I would have lost it long ago.

SAHIRAH You know also.

NADIRAH I don't understand why when you say that you look like you're showing off. That's not some classic proverb you know, that's a very vulgar saying.

SAHIRAH But I like it. It sounds very wise.

NADIRAH If you still have your ablutions, they're going to be void if you talk dirty.

SAHIRAH Never mind, I can take my ablutions again.

Sahirah exits. Nadirah starts to tear the area of the envelope around the edges of the stamp.

---

13. Wife of a Datuk, a title conferred by a king or sultan on a rich or talented person
14. A brand of tea from Malaysia's Cameron Highlands
15. A type of small convection oven with hotplates and grill

SCENE 3

Robert is in Sahirah's living room, reading a newspaper.

ROBERT You need any help there?

SAHIRAH *(offstage)* No, I'm OK.

Robert's cellphone rings. He answers it.

ROBERT You tell her to come back in an hour's time, can? I'm still having lunch lah. It's not serious, right? Oh, I know, that primary school teacher. Always tells me her principal bullies her. Aiyah, she probably wants another M.C. Gastric,[16] right? I'll be back at two.

Sahirah enters carrying a plate of rice and a bowl of rendang.

ROBERT Wah, you actually have time to cook, ah?

SAHIRAH I cook in the morning, before I start work. Anyway this is simple lah.

ROBERT What's this?

SAHIRAH Rendang.[17] And I got some more, got sayur lodeh,[18]got sambal sotong.[19] You can stand a bit hot or not?

ROBERT No problem. I love chilli!

Sahirah exits and enters again with two more bowls.

ROBERT You call all this simple?

SAHIRAH Just anyhow only lah. *(Silence)* Oh! You don't eat with hand!

Sahirah exits and enters again with a fork and spoon.

ROBERT Mmmm. The meat is so tender. You still cook Nonya[20] food or not? My mother last time, her ayam buah keluak.[21] Classic.

---

16. Local parlance for a medical leave due to gastritis
17. A spicy meat dish from Indonesia
18. A soup prepared from vegetables in coconut milk, popular in Malaysia
19. Fresh squid (calamari) cooked in a classic Malay sauce with chilli
20. Means 'Peranakan' (Chinese who have adopted some Malay customs, resulting in a hybrid Sino-Malay culture)
21. Spicy chicken cooked with black nuts called buah keluak

SAHIRAH A bit lah. But more Malay food. Of course some Nonya food I cannot make anymore.

ROBERT Like what?

SAHIRAH Like babi pongteh.[22]

Robert laughs, and then starts choking. Sahirah pats his back.

SAHIRAH Oh no. Are you OK? You want some water?

ROBERT No need. I'm OK. Next time if you want to joke, warn me first.

SAHIRAH When was I joking? I was stating a fact.

ROBERT Does your daughter speak Peranakan[23] with you too?

SAHIRAH Of course. She's Malay.

ROBERT Yah, but Malay and Peranakan are not the same.

SAHIRAH Of course some words I don't use with her. If I say 'gua lu'[24] with her, she'll scold me. She'll tell me that only Minah Rock[25] talk like that.

ROBERT How old is she now?

SAHIRAH She's twenty years old.

ROBERT Have I seen her before?

SAHIRAH I don't know. I have photo. You want to see?

ROBERT Sure.

Sahirah takes out a photo album from under the table.

SAHIRAH This one Malay house lah. We keep album at living room.

Robert looks at the photos in the album.

ROBERT She's very fair ah? Look like Chinese. Why got these empty pockets?

---

22. Braised pork with fermented soya bean

23. Baba Malay, a creole language mixing the Malay language with many Hokkien words. It is mainly used by members of the older generation.

24. 'Gua' and 'lu' mean 'I' and 'you' in Baba Malay, but these pronouns are also used as street slang by working-class youngsters

25. Girls who like rock'n'roll music

SAHIRAH Oh, those were all my ex-husband photos.

ROBERT What did you do with them? You burnt them?

SAHIRAH I can't be bothered to burn. I just keep them somewhere else.

ROBERT I want to see what your ex-husband looks like.

SAHIRAH OK lah. Last time a lot of girls like him. Because he's rich. Family business. Last time his company got Singapore branch.

ROBERT Oh, then how did you meet him?

SAHIRAH I was his secretary.

ROBERT Oh. Talking about secretary, you know that woman who works at my dispensary? I think she likes me lah.

SAHIRAH Of course lah, you're a doctor.

ROBERT She always wear this strong perfume, tau.[26] And I asked my locum, do you notice or not, the perfume that she wears? And he said what perfume? Then I realized, she only wears it when I'm at the clinic.

SAHIRAH Are you interested?

ROBERT I've known her for so many years already. Anyway, I wanted to explain why I'm still wearing my ring. Because of this woman lah. If she wasn't interested in me, I would have taken it off a long time already. Of course I miss my wife. But we all have to move on.

Silence.

ROBERT *(flipping through the album)* This one your family?

SAHIRAH Yah. During Chinese New Year.

ROBERT And who are these?

SAHIRAH My two sisters.

ROBERT Hmmm. You're the prettiest ah?

SAHIRAH Really? Most people would say my younger sister.

ROBERT She's pretty also lah. But I think you have the nicer smile. So what was your name?

SAHIRAH My name?

---

26. Means 'y'know'

ROBERT During that time.

SAHIRAH Stephanie. All my sisters start with 'S'. Samantha, Stephanie and Sarah.

ROBERT And then your Muslim name?

SAHIRAH Sahirah Binte Abdullah.

ROBERT What does it mean?

SAHIRAH A lot of meanings. Sahirah in Arabic can mean pure, can mean moon, can also mean the one who's awake at night. It's supposed to be romantic lah. You know, I think like this Arab woman, in the garden, under the moonlight. Big dark eyes, long eyelashes. Not like mine lah.

ROBERT Then what about Abdullah?

SAHIRAH If you convert, then automatically your father's name is Abdullah. It means 'servant of God'.

ROBERT So did your husband choose that name for you?

SAHIRAH No, I chose myself. I remember the book he gave me. On the cover got picture of baby.

ROBERT So what's it like to change your name after... how many years?

SAHIRAH Twenty-six. You get used to it lah. After I gave birth to my daughter here, we moved to K.L. Met new people, made new friends. It was like starting a new life. I left Stephanie behind in Singapore.

ROBERT And what about your family?

SAHIRAH We kept in touch. You know the salon? It's my cousin's. After I came back to Singapore, she was the one who helped me settle down. At first she wasn't sure if I could work at the salon. You're doing other people's hair but your own hair you cover. But a lot of Malay customers started coming.

The doorbell rings.

ROBERT Who's that? Is your daughter back?

SAHIRAH No. She usually comes home in the evening.

ROBERT Maybe her school ended early today?

SAHIRAH You think so? Alamak.[27] How ah?

ROBERT How what?

SAHIRAH How do I explain what you're doing here? Alamak I feel like teenager caught red-handed like that.

ROBERT I'm a doctor.

SAHIRAH You're a man.

ROBERT House call.

SAHIRAH For what?

ROBERT You got... breathing difficulty.

SAHIRAH Hah? Later she get worried, how?

The doorbell rings again.

SAHIRAH Now I really got breathing difficulty.

ROBERT Doesn't she carry her own keys?

SAHIRAH Yah. You're right. It's probably not her. I'll go and see.

The doorbell rings. Sahirah approaches the door and peeps through the viewfinder.

ROBERT Who is it?

SAHIRAH Look like salesman.

ROBERT Ah. You can breathe properly now.

SAHIRAH I almost got a heart attack you know.

ROBERT What was he selling?

SAHIRAH I don't know lah. Eurasian man. Maybe he's selling Bible.

ROBERT Do they still do that? Selling door to door?

SAHIRAH Not really lah. Sometimes they give you flyer. Some church event, with overseas speaker. I don't understand lah. On the door we put the sticker with the Arabic words. They should know it's a Muslim house.

ROBERT Yah lah, but maybe they can't read the Arabic?

SAHIRAH No need to read. You see already, you know.

---

27. Means 'O my Goodness!' word combines Allah (God) and Emak (mother)

Silence.

ROBERT I'd really like to meet your daughter one day.

SAHIRAH Yah lah, but not like this. Just now when I heard the doorbell, I almost wanted to hide you inside the cupboard.

ROBERT Your cupboard so big ah? You can say I'm here to check up on your diet. See whether the food you make got high cholesterol or not.

SAHIRAH Where got doctor so special?

ROBERT It's not the doctor who's special. It's the patient.

SAHIRAH You keep talking, but the food you never eat.

ROBERT I haven't eaten home-cooked food in such a long time. Maybe I should have lunch here more often.

SAHIRAH Then I can try preparing some Nonya dishes. Long time I never try.

ROBERT Yah, you can experiment on me.

Sahirah is embarrassed and exits. Robert continues eating.

ROBERT Where are you going?

SAHIRAH *(off-stage)* I'm getting you a drink!

SCENE 4

Nadirah and Maznah are on campus.

MAZNAH Mehmet Özkan. That's his name. And then there are dots above the 'O'. So exotic right?

NADIRAH Maznah, what do you know about Turkey?

MAZNAH Nothing.

NADIRAH And then you're already in love with him? I give it... two months?

MAZNAH I know a bit about Turkey, OK? They do oil wrestling. I bet you he's very moisturized. And then they have this dance where they spin around and then the skirt gets raised... what's it called?

NADIRAH Belly dancing?

MAZNAH I know if it's belly dancing. That's for women. This is a dance for men. This dance is where they wear that tall hat on the head, and then they turn round and round...

NADIRAH They're called whirling dervishes. They're Sufi.

MAZNAH And then we're Sunni, right?

NADIRAH Correct.

MAZNAH Then do we clash?

NADIRAH Maz, you're always asking me, why don't you go and find out yourself?

MAZNAH What's the use of having a friend like you if I can't ask you?

NADIRAH So what am I now? Your Islam Answers Dot Com? You're subscribed to the Muslim Society mailing list. You can ask whatever you want.

MAZNAH I don't know how to ask. I don't understand.

NADIRAH What don't you understand?

MAZNAH I know that when you start, you have to say 'peace be upon you' first.

NADIRAH That's just a formality. It's not a problem if you don't follow it.

MAZNAH No, if I don't follow the rules then it's so obvious I'm so ignorant.

NADIRAH Please lah Maz, nobody cares. The most important thing is that you ask.

MAZNAH The other thing I don't get are the acronyms. If you write 'Allah', then you have to write S-W-T. What's that?

NADIRAH Subhana Wa Ta'ala. [Glorious and exalted is He.]

MAZNAH And then 'Muhammad saw'? What did he see?

NADIRAH It's not 'saw'. S-A-W. Salallahu Alaihi Wa Salam. [Peace be upon Him.]

MAZNAH And then 'P-B-U-H'?

NADIRAH Peace Be Upon Him.

MAZNAH There, you see? Some are in Arabic, some in English, how do you expect me *not* to get confused?

NADIRAH Maznah, you're just giving excuses.

MAZNAH I can ask you personally lah. Less intimidating.

NADIRAH If you prefer to ask personally why don't you come for our meetings?

MAZNAH Oh, please. I walk into a room filled with tudung girls and suddenly I feel hot. And then, 'Oh, sister Maznah, we're so glad you could join us!' It's bad enough they have to call me by my full name. And then there's this sister sister business.

NADIRAH What's wrong with calling you 'sister'?

MAZNAH I have enough problems with my own family. I don't need an extended one.

NADIRAH They are trying to be friendly.

MAZNAH Please. It's about personal space, OK? It's like when you're outside. And then this old man comes up to you. "Peace be upon you", he says. What are you going to do? You have to answer, right? "Peace be upon you too." And then he reaches into his bag and takes out – Muslim calendar, Quranic verses. And you feel cornered. You are obliged to buy. Because you answered him.

NADIRAH When he greeted you like that it's a form of blessing, Maz. Why must you get so defensive?

MAZNAH I just don't like it. I feel like a victim of cultural blackmail. I know I am Malay, and I know I am Muslim. I just don't need to be reminded all the time.

NADIRAH But why must you be so sensitive?

MAZNAH Because if I want to buy something, I'll look for it myself. You don't have to look for me. *(Pause)* So how can I find out more about Sufism? Is it like, deviant teachings?

NADIRAH It's not deviant. Sufism is like a more spiritual Islam. Why don't you read Imam Ghazali? But if from Turkey, you look for the writings of Rumi.

MAZNAH *(jotting down in her notebook)* ... Rumi. Wherefore art thou, Rumi?

NADIRAH *(reads an SMS on her handphone. She sighs)*

MAZNAH Whassup, Nadirah?

NADIRAH Another person cancelled.

MAZNAH Cancelled what?

NADIRAH The meeting on Friday. This means we have to cancel the whole thing.

MAZNAH Is this the thing you discussed with Farouk that day?

NADIRAH Yah. Now I have to tell him. *(Writes an SMS)*

MAZNAH So, since you're free on Friday, what do you say we chill out at Holland V?

NADIRAH I don't know.

MAZNAH Eh, we haven't had our bonding sessions in a long time.

NADIRAH It's not enough that you get to meet me in school?

MAZNAH How can I get enough of you, Nadirah daughter of Mansor. Anyway the scenery here is completely unappetizing! We're surrounded by Chinese bumpkins from engineering. Everyone's face like they just woke up.

NADIRAH I'll see how.

MAZNAH What do you mean, see? We are there to see! We'll wear our sunglasses, you drink your Sunrise, I'll have my cigarette, we'll pretend to talk but our eyes are checking people out.

NADIRAH Maz, maybe I need a break. Spend some time alone.

MAZNAH What's wrong?

NADIRAH We tried so hard. And then suddenly in the last minute everybody's cancelling.

MAZNAH Why is the meeting so important?

NADIRAH We had our first one before this. We got all the religious societies together and we discussed "Youths and Morality: Challenges Ahead". After the meeting, everyone had good vibes. Everyone was saying, let's do this more often.

MAZNAH And what's the topic this time?

NADIRAH "The Limits of On-Campus Evangelism". Actually at first it was "On-Campus Proselytisation". But some people were not comfortable. So we had to change it.

MAZNAH As a literature student, I should tell you that there's still a problem with the title. You put in a word like 'limits', I'm sure people will resist. They're going to think you, who are you to try and control us?

NADIRAH So what's your suggestion?

MAZNAH "On-Campus Evangelism: Let's Talk About It".

NADIRAH Maz, that sounds like your own talk show.

MAZNAH *(imitating a TV presenter)* 'The issue of evangelism on campus has raised some concern among our students. Tonight, we talk with the vice-president of the Muslim Society.'

NADIRAH It's my pleasure to be here.

MAZNAH Miss Nadirah, what are your views on evangelism on campus?

NADIRAH Based on feedback from our members, there is some perception that the evangelizing activities of some groups have been intensifying of late.

MAZNAH Would you care to elaborate?

NADIRAH Well, I think it's best if the groups were to explain this by themselves. We do not intend to put the spotlight on any particular group or individual.

MAZNAH So what is your group's position on this?

NADIRAH My president believes that campus should be a secular space. It should be a common space where religion does not intrude.

MAZNAH But... how secular is the campus, really? Because there is a designated prayer room for Muslims.

NADIRAH Yes, but that space is not in full public view.

MAZNAH So when you mean common space, do you mean visible space?

NADIRAH I think that is one working definition. We intend to refine this through our discussions.

MAZNAH Miss Nadirah, excuse me for pointing out the obvious, but it's quite visible to us that you're a Muslim.

NADIRAH Yes, so perhaps visibility is not what we mean when we say common space.

MAZNAH So what do you actually mean by common space?

NADIRAH This proposal was put forward by my President. I am just representing his views.

MAZNAH So is it possible that you might hold quite different views?

NADIRAH My president believes that not all religions have the same financial resources and numerical advantage. He thinks that those religions whose native language is English, for example, have greater influence than those which rely on other languages. To protect these minority religions, he thinks we should restrict evangelism on campus grounds.

MAZNAH You haven't answered my question yet. What are your personal views on this? *(Pause)* Off the record.

NADIRAH Off the record, I feel, it's all right if you want to spread your religion on campus. Because if you're afraid of your believers crossing over to another side, then the solution is education.

MAZNAH And if they insist on joining another religion?

NADIRAH We will advise them, but even in the Quran it is said, 'there is no compunction in religion'.

MAZNAH So what you're saying is, if other religious views are a virus, then instead of controlling the virus, you work on vaccinating those who are vulnerable? Did you notice how many 'V's' I used in that sentence?

NADIRAH I wouldn't use terms like virus...

MAZNAH It's a metaphor.

NADIRAH You have to choose your metaphors correctly.

MAZNAH Just one last question before we wrap up. If you can't even seem to agree with your own president, then how do you hope to reach an agreement with all the other religious groups?

NADIRAH I didn't say I disagreed with Farouk. In principle I agree that we should suspend evangelism on campus for the time being.

MAZNAH But you just told me something else.

NADIRAH Those are my private views.

MAZNAH So your private and public views are different?

NADIRAH Maybe.

MAZNAH Then what's the point of holding these dialogues?

NADIRAH Maz, you really like doing this, you know.

MAZNAH Doing what?

NADIRAH You have so many questions for everything. But when we ask you to participate you throw up all kinds of excuses.

MAZNAH So you're pissed off?

NADIRAH We just have to try it first. We won't know if we don't try.

MAZNAH OK-lah. I just wanted to tell you, don't let it affect you too much. You have school, you have projects, and now you have this kind of stressful CCA.[28] I don't like seeing you like this. You don't even have time to meet Mr. Mehmet Özkan. Aren't these supposed to be the best years of our life?

SCENE 5

Sahirah is in the living room. We hear the doorbell ring. Sahirah opens the door. Nadirah enters wearing a sweater and carrying a travel bag.

SAHIRAH Mummy's daughter is back! Eh, you wear this sweater, like you just come back from cold country!

NADIRAH It's not the country that's cold. It's Changi Airport.

SAHIRAH How are the K.L. people?

NADIRAH Like that lah. Auntie Zaiton's hair is getting higher and higher. Like the Prime Minister's wife.

---

28. Abbreviation for Co-Curricular Activity

SAHIRAH How was the birthday?

NADIRAH We had prayers on Saturday, and then he threw a party on Sunday. *(Approaches the table)* Any mail for me?

SAHIRAH Don't have. You expecting something?

NADIRAH Eh, you went to Night Safari?

SAHIRAH What's that?

NADIRAH This ticket. And Singapore Flyer. Wah, Mummy, I go to K.L., over here you enjoy ah. Who did you go with?

SAHIRAH With Sally lah.

NADIRAH Mummy, didn't Sally go back to Malaysia?

SAHIRAH No, she came down for a short visit.

NADIRAH Mummy. I visited her in K.L. What are you talking about?

SAHIRAH Oh! Not Sally lah, I went with some of the new girls at the salon. They wanted to go sightseeing.

NADIRAH Then why did you tell me you went with Sally?

SAHIRAH I don't know. Now that I'm old I'm getting forgetful.

NADIRAH There's something you're not telling me...

Silence.

SAHIRAH Why don't you sit down first. I'll get you a drink.

Sahirah exits. Nadirah takes a seat and removes her tudung. Sahirah enters carrying a glass of water.

NADIRAH I bought some keropok lekor.[29] You want?

SAHIRAH No, it's fine. *(Pause)* Nadirah, Mummy... has a new friend.

NADIRAH OK. Good! Now we don't need a maid!

SAHIRAH It's a male friend.

NADIRAH Mummy you have a boyfriend!

SAHIRAH Nadirah. He's not a boyfriend.

NADIRAH Then?

SAHIRAH I said he's a male friend.

29. Popular fish fritter snack, a specialty from Terengganu, East Malaysia

NADIRAH Isn't that the same thing?

SAHIRAH He's not a boy.

NADIRAH Oh no.

SAHIRAH What?

NADIRAH He's your neighbour. The one along your stretch of shops.

SAHIRAH How you know?

NADIRAH He's liked you for a long time right?

SAHIRAH I didn't know.

NADIRAH But Mummy, I think he goes to Batam[30] you know.

SAHIRAH Batam?

NADIRAH *(now confused)* Who are you talking about?

SAHIRAH *(also confused)* Who are you talking about?

NADIRAH This isn't the old man who works at the Sri Dewa barbershop? The one who likes to wear those awful net T-shirts?

SAHIRAH Oh, that one? No. You think just because we both cut hair we–

NADIRAH I don't know. At least you have something in common.

SAHIRAH No...

NADIRAH Don't keep me in suspense! Who?

SAHIRAH He's a doctor.

NADIRAH Wah, not bad ah Mummy. Not just any man. A doctor!

SAHIRAH He's the GP. In the clinic next door.

NADIRAH Which one? The fat one?

SAHIRAH He's not so fat lah. His name is Robert.

NADIRAH Mummy, are you serious?

SAHIRAH What for I want to joke?

NADIRAH How long has this been going on?

---

30. An Indonesian island where retirees are known to have affairs with younger women

SAHIRAH Why you ask me like that?

NADIRAH What's wrong?

SAHIRAH You sound like my mother.

NADIRAH Mummy, no, I'm curious.

SAHIRAH I don't know. How are your brothers?

NADIRAH They are fine, Mummy. They're always trying to switch names. If I say, this is Nazri, right? Then he'll go, you're wrong, I am Nazron. They think I don't know. You can tell them apart easily because Nazri doesn't have his front teeth. Mummy don't change topic. When did this happen?

SAHIRAH It's been a few months already.

NADIRAH And you were keeping it from me?

SAHIRAH At that time I wasn't so sure. But now I think it's serious.

NADIRAH How serious?

SAHIRAH Serious enough to tell you.

NADIRAH So when am I going to meet him?

SAHIRAH Anytime you want. He wants to meet you also.

NADIRAH How old is he ah, Mummy?

SAHIRAH He's fifty plus. He was married once, but his wife passed away. He's a really nice man.

NADIRAH Does he have children?

SAHIRAH No. But he might have one soon.

NADIRAH Mummy... you're not...

SAHIRAH What? No! Are you mad? I was referring to you!

NADIRAH Thank God. I thought you're giving me a new sibling.

SAHIRAH You think I'm what?

NADIRAH Mummy, I'm sorry.

SAHIRAH How can you think of something like that? Your Mummy is forty-six, Nadirah!

NADIRAH So Robert is ready? I shouldn't call him Robert. Mister... what's his surname?

SAHIRAH Goh.

NADIRAH Robert is 'R'... 'R' got what ah... Rahman, Rahim. No, he must choose himself. Mummy I'm so happy for you! Darul Arqam got this good marriage course. During your time did you go?

SAHIRAH Your bapak got an ustazah[31] to teach me.

NADIRAH Now everything is systematic already. Mummy you know nowadays you don't have to put 'Abdullah'. If Robert wants he can have his name changed to... Rahman Goh. I think Rizwan also nice. Or maybe choose something like yours. Start with 'S'. Salim. Sahirah and Salim. Nadirah Binte Salim. You think I must change also or not?

SAHIRAH Nadirah, maybe he doesn't want to change his name.

NADIRAH What do you mean?

SAHIRAH Robert is a Christian.

NADIRAH He's a strong Christian?

SAHIRAH He goes to church every Sunday. The one at Avenue Two.

NADIRAH You've been there?

SAHIRAH This morning I went.

Nadirah drinks from her glass.

SAHIRAH But just to see.

NADIRAH What is there to see?

SAHIRAH See him with his friends, his relatives...

NADIRAH Did you wear your tudung?

SAHIRAH No. I didn't want people to stare at me.

NADIRAH Which people?

SAHIRAH The people in the church.

NADIRAH Or the people outside? You didn't want them to see this woman, in a tudung, entering a church? Right? What time did you go?

SAHIRAH Around nine-thirty. Why?

---

31. Female religious teacher

NADIRAH I was having breakfast. We sat in the garden. We ate scones. There were six types of jam. I was thinking of you. Sunday. You start work late. You're still sleeping. Maybe next weekend I will surprise you. I go into your room. I see your legs, your veins, you stand so long in the salon, you have varicose veins. I'm carrying a tray with scones. A cup of coffee in your favourite Ikea mug. Six types of jam. I wake you up. Mummy, I made breakfast. You say, what's this? Were you dreaming last night? Or maybe you say, am I dreaming right now? I looked around me. Bapak, Auntie Zaiton, Nazri, Nazron, Yati the maid. They have this kind of breakfast every Sunday. This is family. Six types of jam. I also have family. At nine-thirty I was thinking of you. But you never think of me.

SAHIRAH I always think of you, Nadirah.

NADIRAH If you think of me, you won't go to church, Mummy. You won't take off your tudung.

SAHIRAH Nadirah, Mummy is not going to be a Christian. Mummy was just accompanying Robert.

NADIRAH On Saturday I went shopping with Sally. She helped me to pick stuff for you. *(Nadirah takes out a plastic bag)*

SAHIRAH What did you buy?

Nadirah leaves the plastic bag on the table. Sahirah opens it. She takes out a few tudung scarves.

SCENE 6

Farouk is in a tutorial room. Maznah enters.

MAZNAH Eh, where's Nadirah?

FAROUK She said she's going to be late.

MAZNAH Oh. I thought she was only seeing me.

FAROUK I thought so too. *(Silence)*

MAZNAH Had your lunch?

FAROUK I'm fasting today.

MAZNAH Payback fast?[32]

FAROUK No. Asyura Fast. *(Silence)* Never heard of it? It's an optional fast. On this day the Prophet Moses was saved by Allah from the Pharoah's army. If you fast today you can be forgiven for all the sins from last year. It's such a waste not to do it, right?

MAZNAH Yah. Never mind. Maybe next year I'll ask Nadirah to remind me.

FAROUK You have the Muslim calendar right?

MAZNAH My mother bought one.

FAROUK What's the use of buying only, you have to always refer to it. Later when you go home, take a look, it's now the month of Muharram. I'm sure it's written down, tenth Muharram. The Asyura Fast.

MAZNAH All right Farouk, later when I get home I'm going to read that calendar from front to back. Should I memorise the prayer schedules also?

FAROUK If you can, why not?

MAZNAH Why don't you do it first? You're a champion right, at memorizing?

Nadirah enters, holding a drink.

MAZNAH Nadirah! You're not fasting today?

NADIRAH It's my time of the month. How come you know it's the Asyura Fast today?

MAZNAH I've been dabbling in research. You can call me Sister Maznah.

FAROUK I was the one who told her.

MAZNAH Eh, but I'm really doing my research. Serious! That day I went to look for Rumi. His *Mathnawi*. Have you read it? Let me read this part. *(Opens her book)*

"The life of lovers is in death:
You will not win the Beloved's heart
Unless you lose your own."

---

32. A 'catch-up' fast due to being unable to fast during menstruation

Romantic right? I showed it to Mehmet yesterday. He was quite impressed.

NADIRAH You're looking for all the stuff about love.

MAZNAH You're the one who asked me to look for Rumi.

NADIRAH Look at how he spelt 'beloved'. With a capital 'B' right?

MAZNAH Yah... so?

NADIRAH If the 'beloved' is with a capital 'B', that means it's referring to Allah.

FAROUK "You will not win the Beloved's heart
Unless you lose your own."

That means you will not receive the grace of God unless you surrender your heart to Him.

MAZNAH Thank you, Ustad Farouk, for that explanation that has given us much food for thought and removed our doubts. May Allah give you a long life and grant you good things. Amen.

FAROUK Ah, there you go, making fun of me again.

MAZNAH Thank you for knocking all the poetry out of those lines.

NADIRAH Sorry, but today's agenda is me. What am I going to do now?

FAROUK Have you met up with... what's his name?

NADIRAH Robert. Not yet. I also don't know how I'm going to discuss this with him.

FAROUK What are your mother's plans with Robert?

NADIRAH They're going to get married.

FAROUK And Robert's going to convert?

NADIRAH Civil marriage.

FAROUK Civil marriage? You know, right, that Islam doesn't recognize civil marriage? If she wants to go ahead with it then it means she's committing adultery.

NADIRAH Farouk, don't talk about my mother like that.

FAROUK This is a growing problem, you know? Now if the husband or wife doesn't want to convert, never mind. Just go ahead with a civil marriage. They don't know that when they have a child, it's out of wedlock. It's illegitimate!

NADIRAH My mother is too old to have children.

FAROUK But adultery is a terrible sin, Nadirah. If they're in another country they'd be punished by stoning.

NADIRAH But we don't have those kinds of laws here.

FAROUK So your mother is turning her back on Islam?

MAZNAH Farouk, can you calm down? I think Nadirah needs our support.

FAROUK Maz, Nadirah's mother is going to become an apostate.[33] We don't have hudud[34] laws here. People say it's extreme – whipping people, cutting off their hands. Fine. But we also don't have apostasy laws. That's why her mother brought Nadirah back to Singapore. If they were still in Malaysia, do you think she'd be able to do this?

MAZNAH I don't think she was planning that, Farouk. She came back to Singapore because her family is here.

FAROUK When did she get divorced, Nadirah?

NADIRAH When I was eight years old.

FAROUK She's smart. Because under Islamic custody law, as long as the child is below nine years old, custody goes to the mother. When she's trying to keep you, she follows syariah law. Now when she wants to get married, she can just ignore syariah laws.

MAZNAH Farouk, are you saying her mother plotted this all these years?

FAROUK First it's her friend who starts to stray. And then after that it's her own family. See Nadirah, you give them so much face, and now they're all taking advantage.

MAZNAH Which friend?

FAROUK I don't have to say, Maznah.

---

33. A person who renounces his or her religious faith

34. Strict religious laws

NADIRAH Come on, this isn't about her. This is about me.

MAZNAH I don't understand why you have to punish people who want to convert. Isn't religion a personal matter?

FAROUK Look at our Malay community. We're the ones with the highest number of drug addicts. The abortions. The divorce rates. We're a minority, when it comes to all these social problems we're the majority. But there's at least one percentage that we can be proud of. You know how many Malays are Muslims? Ninety-nine point six percent. No other race has this. Look at the Chinese. Christians, Buddhists, Taoists. Same with the Indians. But we're Ninety-nine point six percent. This kind of figure shows our solidarity. We're not divided like the other races. People are amazed when they see us, every Friday, the cars lined up on the roads, everyone crowding to go and pray at the mosques.

MAZNAH We're born into the religion. Of course it's close to one hundred percent!

FAROUK But at least, as a minority, we stand as one. Look at the Chinese. Chinese educated versus the English educated. Enemies. One side is called potato, the other is called pumpkin. And why? Because they're too influenced by the West. But we have Islam to shield us from Westernisation.

MAZNAH Yah, of course. To avoid being Westernised, choose the most anti-West of all the religions.

FAROUK Islam has become part of Malay identity. Let me ask you, what have the Malays contributed to the world?

MAZNAH I think the word amok is from Malay. Orang utan also.

NADIRAH Farouk have you finished your lecture?

FAROUK Our Sister Maznah here doesn't seem to understand why the soul of the Malay race is Islam. Look at Singapore. The people who live here come from China, and India. Do you know how long their civilisations were? If you want to compare with us Malays, we have nothing. But if you look at Islamic civilization, if we look at the contributions to mathematics, medicine, philosophy...

MAZNAH Yes, Farouk, I understand. Islam has contributed so much to Malay identity. But Malay culture has contributed to Islam too. We have greater gender equality than in the Middle East. If you look at Mnang[35] culture it's the women with the power. Thank God we're not living in Saudi Arabia; the women can't even drive cars there!

FAROUK Maznah, I'm trying to explain to you why that 99.6 per cent is so important to us.

MAZNAH If it's so important why don't you set up a radio station? 99.6 FM. With DJ Farouk Osman keeping you company. The whole programme is religious songs and sermons. You know what I think? All this clinging to religion gives us the opportunity to cover up our shame. Malays don't become professionals. They don't become entrepreneurs. Malays are poor. But if you bring in religion, you can say, oh, Malays don't chase after material things. That man might look like a security guard, but his CPF[36] for the afterlife runs into the millions.

FAROUK Last time it was a hundred percent. And then it was ninety-nine point eight. Now it's ninety-nine point six. So Maz, it makes you happy to see it go down some more?

MAZNAH This is not about what I like or don't like. This is about Nadirah's mother wanting to be with someone that she likes. But the problem is someone like you is worried that some percentage will fall. To you, that would mean the Malay community is breaking up.

NADIRAH Farouk. That percentage... that's for the Malay community right? But my mother is Chinese. So what difference does it make?

FAROUK But when she embraced Islam, doesn't that mean that she became Malay?

MAZNAH Farouk, why are you taking engineering? Why didn't you take sociology? It's so hard like this, you know.

---

35. Refers to the Minangkabau people, a matrilineal ethnic group indigenous to the Minangkabau Highlands of West Sumatra, Indonesia

36. Abbreviation for Central Provident Fund, a compulsory savings scheme

FAROUK Nadirah, I feel that it's best if you let me talk to Auntie Sahirah. I think her problem is that she hasn't had the chance to understand Islam better. She's just going through all the requirements without any deep understanding. We can't blame her. She just lacks guidance.

NADIRAH You want to meet my mother?

MAZNAH What makes you think she wants to see you?

FAROUK Why don't you try and arrange? OK?

NADIRAH You won't feel weird talking to her? She's twice your age, you know?

FAROUK Nadirah, when it comes to knowledge, age shouldn't matter.

SCENE 7

Farouk and Robert are in Nadirah's living room. Farouk is wearing a Manchester United jersey.

ROBERT So you are Nadirah's...

FAROUK Schoolmate.

ROBERT You must be quite close.

FAROUK We're both in the same society.

ROBERT I haven't even met her and I get to meet you first. How long have you known her?

FAROUK Two years.

ROBERT I heard from her mother she's a very independent girl.

Pause.

FAROUK I heard you're a Christian.

ROBERT Yes. I'm quite active in my church.

FAROUK Mr. Goh.

ROBERT You can just call me Robert.

FAROUK Robert. People have this idea that Islam is a difficult religion. But actually, fundamentally...

ROBERT Fundamentally...

FAROUK Yes. At its core, there are five pillars.

ROBERT I've heard of that.

FAROUK And from those five pillars, you move upwards, you build a house, you make your prayers more perfect, you perform good deeds...

ROBERT And then one day you find yourself standing on the rooftop, close to God.

FAROUK You get the idea.

ROBERT Is that why Malays like to renovate their homes?

FAROUK Mr. Goh.

ROBERT Robert. That was a joke. I didn't mean it...

FAROUK No, I understand.

ROBERT Please go on.

FAROUK I was saying, this idea that Islam is difficult, full of rules, making a lot of demands on its followers. I just want to share this story with you. One night the Prophet went on this trip. We call it the Night Journey, Isra and Mihraj. During the Mihraj the angel Jibreel...

ROBERT That would be Gabriel?

FAROUK Yes. The angel that revealed the Quran to our Holy Prophet.

ROBERT In the Bible he is the one who informed Mary that she would bear Jesus.

FAROUK Yes. Mariam. In Islam, she is considered one of the most righteous women. There is one whole surah[37] that is named after her. Anyway, the Mihraj...

ROBERT I'm sorry, carry on...

FAROUK Jibreel lets Muhammad ride on this flying horse, known as the Buraq. The horse brings Muhammad to the highest circles of heaven, where he meets the earlier prophets like Nabi Ibrahim, Musa, Isa...

---

37. A Quranic verse

ROBERT And Isa is Jesus, right?

FAROUK Yes. The prophet Jesus. And then the Buraq takes Muhammad to see Allah in the highest heavens. Allah commands him to tell his followers to pray fifty times a day.

ROBERT Fifty times?

FAROUK Yes. So Muhammad comes down, and he tells Musa *(senses that Robert is about to interrupt)* – yes, also known as Moses, and Moses says that's impossible and that Muslims will never do it. So he asks Muhammad to ask for a reduction, and Muhammad goes back and forth, each time more afraid to face his Lord. And finally they agree on five. So if you think about it, five is nothing compared to fifty.

ROBERT Of course. Let me share a story with you. And it involves a journey too. You know, I was born into a Christian family. But I was never religious.

FAROUK I understand. You have to build on your faith, your iman.

ROBERT But my wife was a very devout Christian. She always tried to bring me along to church, but I always gave excuses. And then one day, she found out that she had cancer. When she discovered it, it was already quite advanced.

FAROUK I'm sorry to hear that.

ROBERT So there I was, telling my patients to go for their Pap' smears, and my own wife had cervical cancer. Early detection could have saved her. Irony right? Irony or tragedy?

FAROUK I think... both.

ROBERT Anyway, after she passed away I started going through her things. And that was when I found her copy of the Bible. She had underlined some passages, and written notes at the side. The handwriting she left behind suddenly made me feel closer to her. It was as if she was speaking to me beyond the grave. And I felt as if God was speaking to me as well. And then, Farouk, I knew. The way I could be reunited with her was to believe. Believe in Jesus Christ and the Resurrection. It's said in the Bible: "Whoever believes in Him should not perish but have everlasting life. For God did not send His Son into the world to condemn the world, but that the world through Him might be saved."

FAROUK So, if you want to reunite with your wife, what are you doing with Cik[38] Sahirah?

ROBERT We enjoy each other's company. She's been a great comfort to me.

FAROUK Sorry for asking this, Robert, but who do you want to be with after you die?

ROBERT I don't understand.

FAROUK Let's say your late wife is in the Christian heaven. But Cik Sahirah, if she's a good Muslim, she will be in the Muslim paradise. What I am saying is, if you believe what you believe, and if I believe what I believe, then you will have one wife in heaven and one wife in hell. Who do you want to be with?

ROBERT Can't I be with both?

FAROUK You must choose.

ROBERT But Muslims are allowed more than one wife, right?

FAROUK If you are saying that because you are interested in becoming a Muslim, then good. But I should remind you that to be able to have many wives is not a proper reason to turn to Islam. In fact Allah is all-seeing, and He sees into our hearts and He knows what our intentions are.

ROBERT I was just kidding. *(Silence. Robert drinks his coffee. Farouk also drinks from his cup)* I see you support Manchester United. So far, they're having quite a good season ah?

FAROUK Robert. Do you get what I am saying so far?

ROBERT Of course. By the way, have you been to Old Trafford? I was there once.

FAROUK You also support Man U?

ROBERT No, I'm a Liverpool fan. But I went for a trip to Anfield, Stamford Bridge, Old Trafford.[39] My soccer pilgrimage. And I tell you, when I sat behind the dug-outs my hair was

---

38. Pronounced 'Chik', equivalent to 'Madam'
39. Home grounds for Liverpool, Chelsea and Manchester United football clubs

standing up. At Old Trafford, I sat right behind this Bayi... I mean Sikh family...

FAROUK The ones always on TV?

ROBERT Yah. So which position you play, Farouk?

FAROUK Midfield. Always wanted to play striker but I can never score. You give me an open goal and I will shoot to the keeper. You still play?

ROBERT Used to a long time ago. I played in the Chinese position.

FAROUK What's that? Wing?

ROBERT No lah. I play defence. Jia Yi[40] is an unusual case. I think Malays play midfield better because you guys are more creative.

FAROUK Really? Maybe because we gentel[41] a lot. But I don't like to gentel lah. Waste time. Better to pass the ball forward.

ROBERT Must gentel a bit lah. If not who want to watch?

FAROUK Robert, I can try to teach you if you want.

ROBERT I'm too old already lah. This tummy needs an extra pair of legs just to carry it around.

FAROUK No, not about soccer.

ROBERT Eh this season Ferguson never buy any star players ah? How to win the triple like that?

FAROUK We don't need to go on a shopping spree like Chelsea or Man City. Ferguson knows we've already got quality in our young players. Anyway, we have Rooney, Berbatov, Giggs...

ROBERT Glory Man United.

FAROUK Why?

ROBERT A bit vain ah, don't you think? At least Liverpool fans we encourage each other. "You'll Never Walk Alone".

FAROUK Robert, I'm sorry, I can discuss football with you all day but...

ROBERT But what, Farouk?

40. Refers to Shi Jiayi, a China-born naturalised Singaporean football midfielder
41. Means 'fondle' in Malay, but also soccer slang for 'dribble'

FAROUK I wanted to talk with Auntie Sahirah, but she asked me to talk to you.

ROBERT And what is there to talk about?

FAROUK Your marriage. I know you think I'm young. But if you prefer to talk to someone your age...

ROBERT When I talk about soccer, age doesn't matter.

FAROUK But we're not here to talk about soccer.

ROBERT Farouk. You support Man U. I'm a die hard Liverpool supporter. You know what I'm saying?

FAROUK I know you've been trying to avoid the topic.

ROBERT Young man. You haven't been listening. At the end of the day, it's 'The Beautiful Game'. Right?

Silence.

FAROUK But don't you want to be on the winning side?

ROBERT Farouk, when you love your team, you'll stick with them no matter if they win or lose.

FAROUK And what team is Auntie Sahirah supporting?

ROBERT That's for her to decide, isn't it?

FAROUK But you won't try to influence her?

ROBERT Maybe she doesn't even like soccer. You know lah, to some people it's just some guys running around trying to chase a ball. Maybe if we go to England she'll skip all the soccer sites.

FAROUK What happened to "You'll Never Walk Alone"?[42]

ROBERT I'll probably end up singing it by myself.

Farouk drinks. Robert follows suit.

SCENE 8

Sahirah is in the living room, cleaning up the table. Nadirah enters.

SAHIRAH You can't always do this, you know.

NADIRAH What? Do what?

---

42. Liverpool supporters' adoptive song and mantra

SAHIRAH Every time he comes you lock yourself in your room.

NADIRAH I have work to do.

SAHIRAH He really wants to meet you.

NADIRAH What for?

Pause.

SAHIRAH What song were you playing just now? From outside can hear.

NADIRAH You don't recognize?

SAHIRAH A bit familiar.

Nadirah takes a seat. She flips through a magazine. She starts singing, casually.

NADIRAH A is for Allah, nothing but Allah
Ba is the beginning of Bismillah [opening phrase of the Quran]
Ta is for Taqwa, [faith], bewaring of Allah
And Tha is for Thawab a Reward
Ja is for Janna, [paradise] the Garden of Paradise
Ha is for Haj, the blessed Pilgrimage
Kha is for Khatam [ending] the Seal of the Prophethood
Given to the Prophet Muhammad
Salallahu Alaihi Wassallam [Peace be upon Him]
Allah *(Sahirah joins in)*
There's only one God
And Muhammad is his Messenger
Allah
La ilaha ilallah [There is no deity but God]

They repeat the phrase.

NADIRAH You remember.

SAHIRAH The chorus I remember. Who sang ah?

NADIRAH Yusof Islam. You were the one who taught me when I was small. We had the cassette in father's car.

SAHIRAH Yah. You never got tired of the song. What was his name before that?

NADIRAH Siapa? [Who?]

SAHIRAH Yusof Islam.

NADIRAH Cat Stevens.

SAHIRAH He's got a beard right?

NADIRAH Even before he converted he kept a beard.

SAHIRAH Where did you find the song?

NADIRAH On Youtube.

SAHIRAH Now so many things you can find on Internet.

NADIRAH Yah. Even got Quran, you know, Mummy. You can listen to other people read. And some more they got translation.

SAHIRAH That's good.

NADIRAH Mummy, I was thinking... on weekends, maybe we can go for some classes together.

SAHIRAH Weekends? What about your community work?

NADIRAH You said I wasn't spending time with you.

SAHIRAH What class is this?

NADIRAH Mummy, how about we learn Arabic?

SAHIRAH But you learnt already in school.

NADIRAH Never mind. I can go and accompany you.

SAHIRAH What for?

NADIRAH I know sometimes we pray and we don't know know what we're saying. We just recite the words but we don't think about the meaning.

SAHIRAH I see first lah. You know Robert is only free on weekends.

Pause.

NADIRAH So, are you really going to register?

SAHIRAH Next month.

NADIRAH So fast?

SAHIRAH We're not getting any younger, right?

Pause.

NADIRAH Why you don't let Farouk talk to you?

SAHIRAH Nadirah, why should I?

NADIRAH Because you won't listen to me.

SAHIRAH Listen about what?

NADIRAH Civil marriage is wrong, Mummy. Muslims don't go into civil marriage.

SAHIRAH Robert isn't a Muslim.

NADIRAH Then you?

SAHIRAH You know for more than half my life I've been Muslim.

NADIRAH But do you believe? You pray, you fast, you read religious books... but do you believe?

SAHIRAH Why you suddenly ask me like this?

NADIRAH If you never believe then why you raise me as a Muslim?

SAHIRAH Because you were born a Muslim.

NADIRAH Then what about you?

SAHIRAH I wasn't born a Muslim.

NADIRAH So that gives you the right to apostasy?

SAHIRAH Who said anything about apostasy?[43] Eh, Nadirah, you think you're talking to who? Small kid is it? I'm your mother you know!

NADIRAH If you never believe, why did you make me wear a tudung when I was small?

SAHIRAH Nadirah, enough.

NADIRAH Why send me to madrasah?[44]

SAHIRAH I said enough.

NADIRAH Why didn't you just feed me with pork?

SAHIRAH *(shouting)* Because I didn't want to lose you!

Nadirah is stunned into silence.

---

43. The act of abandoning one's faith through word or deed

44. An Islamic school for religious instruction

SAHIRAH Your father wanted Auntie Zaiton as his second wife. Did you know that? But I wouldn't give him permission. People said I wasn't a good wife. I should understand that if he marries, at least it won't be adultery. He's a man. Men have desires. And then in court your father started telling the judge I wasn't a good mother. I carried you for nine months. I gave you milk from my own body. But thc judge and your father were asking me whether I was fit to take care of you. Your father told him, I'm just a convert. Only been a Muslim for eight years. I cannot guide you. I cannot teach you. You know last time, when I picked you up from the madrasah? I always looked around. Maybe your father sent down people to spot check on me. But when they see you, wearing your tudung, they cannot say anything. You were safe. We were safe.

NADIRAH So you just let the madrasah teach me? And you don't have to learn?

SAHIRAH So easy for you to say, Nadirah. Your food, your clothes, where do you think they came from? One day, your father stopped sending money. I didn't want to go to the court again. I worked day and night so that they won't take you away.

NADIRAH Mummy, is Robert going to turn you into a Christian?

SAHIRAH You know, Robert would have wanted a Christian wedding. But he knows that's not possible. That's why this civil marriage is the best chance we have.

NADIRAH I imagine if you're on your deathbed. And then I'm not by your side. I can't help you say the proper verses. But Robert is there. He tells you to accept Jesus. Mummy, when I die I want to see you again. There's only one heaven. Don't you want to see me again?

SAHIRAH Why you talk about death, Nadirah?

NADIRAH Because this life is just preparation for what comes after, Mummy.

SAHIRAH You don't know how many times I've thought about dying.

NADIRAH Why?

SAHIRAH Because... my life is spoilt.

NADIRAH What do you mean, spoilt?

SAHIRAH You know how I met Robert? Because I always go to his clinic. Get cough syrup.I couldn't sleep at night. So tired, but cannot sleep. So many things running through my head. Sahirah. What did the book say? The one who's awake at night. Who is Sahirah? Who's Stephanie? Not a good wife. Not a good mother. Her daughter teach her. What is Malay? What is Muslim? But what can she teach her daughter? I take cough syrup. I can sleep. I can dream. Our garden in K.L. I sweep the leaves. The beach in Australia. I sweep the sand. The salon. I sweep other people's hair. Sometimes the leaves mix with the sand, mix with the hair. Robert knew something was wrong. He asked me. Are you addicted to cough syrup? I started crying in his clinic. I'm so lonely, I said. I never knew anyone could be this lonely.

NADIRAH What do you mean lonely, Mummy? I'm here.

SAHIRAH But you have your own life. I keep thinking, I was like you once. I was twenty years old also. What happened to that girl? What did I do with her life?

NADIRAH Mummy, whatever happened in our life, it's all predestined.

SAHIRAH So don't you think it's destined that I met Robert?

NADIRAH Mummy, we're also given free will to do what is right.

SAHIRAH So if bad things happen to you, it's your fate, but if it's good things, then it's not fate?

NADIRAH I'm saying don't use fate as an excuse to do bad things.

SAHIRAH Why is being with Robert a bad thing? He's not a bad person, Nadirah. He's a doctor. He's helping other people. He's helping me.

Pause.

NADIRAH Bapak emailed me this morning.

SAHIRAH You told him about Robert?

NADIRAH Yes.

SAHIRAH What did he say?

NADIRAH He said I should go up to K.L. and discuss with him.

SAHIRAH He's sending you plane tickets again?

NADIRAH Bapak said they all miss me. The twins keep asking when I'm coming again.

SAHIRAH And you miss him too.

NADIRAH He's my father, isn't he?

SAHIRAH You used to call him 'the K.L. person'. So when are you going?

NADIRAH I don't know. Maybe after my exams. I have school holidays for a month.

SAHIRAH You want to stay there for a month?

NADIRAH Why not? I have family there.

SAHIRAH Then, who am I?

NADIRAH Mummy and Nadirah is family. Mummy, Nadirah and Robert is three people.

SAHIRAH So can't three people live together?

NADIRAH There's not enough room, Mummy.

SAHIRAH How many rooms you need? It's just three of us.

NADIRAH There's not enough room for more than one god.

Nadirah exits.

SAHIRAH How do you know it's not the same god?

SCENE 9

Nadirah is in a tutorial room on campus. Maznah enters, wearing a tudung.

MAZNAH Sister Nadirah!

NADIRAH What's this?

MAZNAH What?

NADIRAH You look different.

MAZNAH I wonder why.

NADIRAH Whose is this?

MAZNAH Eh sister Nadirah, that's not nice. Which Minah[45] Tudung did you think I stole this from?

NADIRAH No, is this your mother's?

MAZNAH This isn't borrowed, OK? This is my own. But the brooch is my mother's. You should have seen her. She took out her jewellery box, and then she spread out her entire brooch collection on the bed. So many brooches, she can open a shop.

NADIRAH Was she surprised when you asked to borrow a brooch?

MAZNAH She was so happy. I have never seen her that happy ever since I finished the Arabic alphabet book.

NADIRAH So are you joining us later?

MAZNAH I'm nervous. Later you'll all start crying. Sister Maznah, you've come back to the righteous path! You look so sweet in that tudung. There's this glow on your face, like you're shooting light rays into the world.

NADIRAH Maz, you're always complaining that people are so guarded around you. But it's not because of your tank tops you know, it's because you're so sarcastic.

MAZNAH What are you discussing tonight?

NADIRAH Farouk's doing a presentation.

MAZNAH About what?

NADIRAH The ways to improve your prayers.

MAZNAH How complicated can that be?

NADIRAH No, there's still so many things we don't know. He's going to make comparisons among all the Sunni[46] schools. For example, according to the Hanafi[47] school, if husband and wife come into contact, your ablutions are still valid.

45. Means 'Malay girl'

46. A denomination of Islam

47. One of the four schools of legal jurisprudence in Sunni Islam

MAZNAH I'm sure that information will come in useful some day.

NADIRAH Some of the stuff he's researched on is also interesting. Did you know that you can carry a baby and pray at the same time?

MAZNAH Nadirah, isn't that all trivia?

NADIRAH It's not trivial.

MAZNAH I didn't say it was trivial. I said it's all a bit... micro? What happened to that interfaith meeting you're organizing?

NADIRAH We've postponed it.

MAZNAH So when do you think you'll hold it?

NADIRAH I don't know.

MAZNAH Why do you sound so blasé? I thought this was your pet project.

NADIRAH Maz, people are just not interested.

MAZNAH You don't have to make it a big thing. You just start small.

NADIRAH We should focus.

MAZNAH On what?

NADIRAH On being good Muslims.

MAZNAH But reaching out and having dialogue... isn't that all part of being good Muslims too?

NADIRAH Maz, if we can't take care of our own house, we have no right to peek into other people's houses.

MAZNAH I see. So if you're not a good housekeeper you can't be a good neighbour?

NADIRAH No. *(Pause)*

MAZNAH This is about your mother right?

NADIRAH I don't want to talk about it.

MAZNAH Have you met up with Robert?

NADIRAH No. I don't see why I should.

MAZNAH Why? You're going to be his daughter.

NADIRAH I will never be Nadirah Binte Robert. OK?

MAZNAH I don't understand. Your father can marry again, but your mother can't do the same.

NADIRAH That's different.

MAZNAH Why is it different? Robert's a human being too.

NADIRAH You don't know anything, Maz. You're not going through it, you have no idea.

MAZNAH OK. How about this. Let's say your mother falls in love with a djinn.[48]

NADIRAH What nonsense are you talking about?

MAZNAH But he's a Muslim djinn, OK? OK, which one do you prefer, your Mum marrying a non-Muslim human, or a Muslim djinn?

NADIRAH Maz, djinns are not supposed to be visible. How can you love someone if you can't see them?

MAZNAH There you go.

NADIRAH What?

MAZNAH You refuse to see Robert. How can you like him if you don't see him? People used to say, 'you can't love if you don't know.'

NADIRAH Can I ask you something?

MAZNAH Tanyalah. [Sure.]

NADIRAH What caused the change? Why this change of heart?

MAZNAH Oh no what's this? Am I supposed to make a testimony?

NADIRAH No. Farouk's been lecturing you for so long. To no effect. And then all of a sudden...

MAZNAH I've been reading.

NADIRAH Rumi?

MAZNAH I finally got my own copy. *(Takes out a book by Rumi)* My library copy was overdue for almost a month!

NADIRAH So what did you learn?

MAZNAH Let me read this.

---

48. Arabic word for a genie

"The minute I heard my first love story
I started looking for you, not knowing
How blind that was.
Lovers don't finally meet somewhere.
They're in each other all along."

NADIRAH Your 'lover' is with a capital 'L' right?

MAZNAH But only because it's at the beginning of the line. When I read it, I thought of Mehmet. He came all the way from Turkey, and I'm from Singapore, but we'd been carrying each other inside us all this while.

NADIRAH Are the both of you serious?

MAZNAH If it's not serious, then why would I put on the tudung? You know, his father is some cleric in Istanbul.

NADIRAH Maz.

MAZNAH What?

NADIRAH You have to do it for the right reasons.

MAZNAH It's not the only reason.

NADIRAH If you and Mehmet don't work out, then what are you going to do? Are you going to stop wearing your tudung?

MAZNAH Don't question my faith.

NADIRAH My mother became Muslim because she fell in love with a Muslim man. Now she's in love with someone who isn't. Is changing religion like changing your clothes?

MAZNAH How do you know Mehmet and I won't work out?

NADIRAH How did my mother know she'd be divorced one day? Don't just do it out of love. The most important thing is to love God. You must be moved to get closer to Him. There are limits to human love. But the love from God is never-ending, for eternity. Just make sure you know what it is you're falling in love with.

MAZNAH But how do you love God if you can't love another human being?

Silence.

NADIRAH Why don't you do that tonight?

MAZNAH Do what?

NADIRAH Come for the session. And do a presentation.

MAZNAH On what?

NADIRAH On what you just said. We'll do a discussion on the Beloved. Ya Habibi. Divine love and human love.

MAZNAH Are you challenging me?

NADIRAH Don't you want to show off your mother's brooch?

MAZNAH Don't play, OK? It's got pseudo-precious stones.

NADIRAH Come, OK? Seminar Room Five at HSS.[49]

MAZNAH Don't keep challenging me, I might just go. But won't Farouk get angry? He's done all his research, and suddenly I'm the one doing the presentation.

NADIRAH Don't worry. I'm the Vice President. And tonight we're having a special guest. Sister Maznah will be sharing some of her favourite passages from Rumi.

MAZNAH But I'm telling you, I'm doing the interpretation. I'm the literature student. Farouk can sit quietly in one corner.

SCENE 10

Sahirah is in the living room. She is filling a small bag with toiletries.

SAHIRAH Nadirah! What are you doing inside?

NADIRAH Wait!

SAHIRAH You've been saying 'wait' for how long already?

Nadirah enters, lugging a travel bag.

SAHIRAH Here. Facial wash, shampoo, toothbrush...

NADIRAH Thanks Mummy.

SAHIRAH How many bras and pants did you pack?

NADIRAH What lah.

SAHIRAH Don't accidentally pack mine.

NADIRAH If it's your bra it wouldn't fit me.

SAHIRAH Ah, what else is missing?

49. Abbreviation for Humanities and Social Sciences

NADIRAH Passport!

Nadirah exits. Sahirah slips the small bag into the travel bag.

Nadirah enters.

SAHIRAH What time is check-in?

NADIRAH In half an hour.

SAHIRAH See, I told you to start packing early. You ah, when you want to pass motion then you start looking for toilet.

NADIRAH Mummy, that's not another classic proverb. What else eh? Phone charger... OK.

SAHIRAH Nadirah. I want to tell you a few things.

NADIRAH Yes Mummy.

SAHIRAH You be careful, you know? Do everything properly. Listen to what people say. Don't let them later say that I never teach you.

NADIRAH I know.

SAHIRAH Don't do things as you please. You're going to another country. It's not your own house anymore.

Nadirah walks towards Sahirah and they embrace.

Robert enters.

ROBERT Everything ready?

NADIRAH Yah.

ROBERT Are you sure you don't want me to send you?

SAHIRAH She's going with Maznah. They're taking a cab.

ROBERT There's an airport surcharge, you know. I can send the both of you.

NADIRAH It's OK. Thanks.

Nadirah kisses Sahirah's hand. She also kisses Robert's hand. She exits. Sahirah takes a seat.

ROBERT How long is she going to be away?

SAHIRAH One month.

ROBERT How come of all places–

SAHIRAH Israel? Ask her school lah.

ROBERT Isn't it dangerous there?

SAHIRAH You think so? Just some places only, right? But the teachers will accompany them. So I'm not so worried.

ROBERT Yah lah, I'm sure she can take care of herself.

SAHIRAH Alamak.

ROBERT Apa? What?

SAHIRAH I don't know whether she remembered to take her compass.

ROBERT Why would she need a compass? She's going on an excursion, not trekking.

SAHIRAH No, the prayer compass.[50]

ROBERT Don't worry. There are many Muslims there.

SAHIRAH Really?

ROBERT A lot of arabs in Israel. A lot of mosques there also.

Sahirah lays her head on Robert's shoulder.

ROBERT You haven't been to church with me for a long time. Everyone's asking for you. You want to go tomorrow?

SAHIRAH Farouk's coming tomorrow.

ROBERT What does he want?

SAHIRAH I asked him for breakfast.

ROBERT You think he's interested in Nadirah?

SAHIRAH He's a nice boy. You like him?

ROBERT He reminds me of myself when I was younger.

SAHIRAH Yah lah. Soccer addict like you.

ROBERT No, he's very sharp. Very logical. We science students recognize each other.

Sahirah closes her eyes. She starts to hum the song 'A is for Allah'.

ROBERT What song is that?

Sahirah's voice gets softer.

---

50. Used to find the direction of Mecca so that Muslims can orientate their prayers correctly

ROBERT Are you sleepy? You want to go to bed?

SAHIRAH Hmm.

Sahirah's voice gets softer.

ROBERT Are you sleepy? You want to go to bed?

SAHIRAH Hmm.

Lights fade.

Cat Stevens' 'Wild World' is played.

Now that I've lost everything to you,
you say you want to start something new,
and it's breaking my heart you're leaving,
baby I'm grieving.
But if you wanna leave take good care,
hope you have a lot of nice things to wear,
but then a lot of nice things turn bad out there.
Oh baby baby it's a wild world,
it's hard to get by just upon a smile.
Oh baby baby it's a wild world.
I'll always remember you like a child, girl.

Lights down.

The end.

ALFIAN SA'AT

Sa'at is a Resident Playwright with W!LD RICE, one of Singapore's most recognised theatre companies. His published works include three collections of poetry, *One Fierce Hour*, *A History of Amnesia* and *The Invisible Manuscript*, a collection of short stories, *Corridor*, a collection of flash fiction, *Malay Sketches*, two collections of plays as well as the published play *Cooling Off Day*.

He has been nominated ten times for Best Original Script at the Life! Theatre Awards, eventually winning in 2005 for *Landmarks*, in 2010 for *Nadirah*, in 2013 for *Kakak Kau Punya Laki* (*Your Sister's Husband*) and in 2016 for *Hotel* (with Marcia Vanderstraaten).

In 2011, he was awarded the Boh-Cameronian Award in Malaysia for Best Book and Lyrics for the musical *The Secret Life of Nora*. In 2013, he won the Boh-Cameronian Award for Best Original Script for the play *Parah*.

In 2001, Sa'at won the Golden Point Award for Poetry as well as the National Arts Council Young Artist Award for Literature. He has also been nominated for the Singapore Literature Prize three times, for *Corridor* (Commendation Prize, 1999), *A History of Amnesia* (2004) and his translation of the novel *The Widower* (2016).